Nathan Littleton

Chiswick, 1764. Apthorp, 1770. Littleton, 1784

Exercises at the centennial celebration of the incorporation of the town of Littleton

Nathan Littleton

Chiswick, 1764. Apthorp, 1770. Littleton, 1784
Exercises at the centennial celebration of the incorporation of the town of Littleton

ISBN/EAN: 9783337281250

Printed in Europe, USA, Canada, Australia, Japan

Cover: Foto ©ninafisch / pixelio.de

More available books at **www.hansebooks.com**

CHISWICK, 1764.   APTHORP, 1770.   LITTLETON, 1784.

EXERCISES

AT THE

CENTENNIAL CELEBRATION

OF THE

INCORPORATION

OF THE

TOWN OF LITTLETON,

JULY 4th, 1884.

PUBLISHED BY THE TOWN,

1887.

CONCORD, N. H.:
N. H. DEMOCRATIC PRESS COMPANY.

CONTENTS.

	PAGE
INTRODUCTION,	5
INVOCATION,—Rev. George M. Curl,	11
ADDRESS OF WELCOME,—Hon. Geo. A. Bingham,	13
CENTENNIAL ADDRESS,—Rev. J. E. Rankin,	14
RELATIONS OF LITTLETON AND THE STATE,—A. S. Batchellor,	32
THE PIONEERS OF LITTLETON,—James R. Jackson,	58
RELATIONS OF LITTLETON AND BETHLEHEM,—Hon. John G. Sinclair,	72
RELATIONS OF LITTLETON AND VERMONT,—F. J. Eastman,	77
NEWSPAPERS AND NEWSPAPER MEN,—H. H. Metcalf,	102
THE PROFESSION OF THE LAW,—Edgar Aldrich,	126
THE PROFESSION OF MEDICINE,—Chas. M. Tuttle, M. D.,	133
THE CHURCH,—Rev. J. E. Robins,	187
LITTLETON ABROAD,—S. B. Page,	199
EDUCATION,—Dana P. Dame,	205
AGRICULTURE,—Rev. F. H. Lyford,	223
MANUFACTURES,—D. C. Remich,	232
MERCHANTS AND TRADE,—Wm. J. Bellows,	242
LITTLETON AND THE RAILROADS,—John M. Mitchell,	259
WOMEN OF LITTLETON,—Rev. C. W. Millen,	276
LITTLETON AND THE WAR OF THE REBELLION,—Capt. George Farr,	292

APPENDIX.

EARLY HISTORY AND GEOGRAPHY OF LITTLETON.—Adams Moore, M. D.,	299
STATISTICS OF POPULATION AND PRODUCTS,	314
INDEX,	321

INTRODUCTION.

This volume contains the several addresses delivered on the occasion of the Centennial Celebration of the incorporation of Littleton. The committee having the preparations for that event in charge, assigned to various gentlemen papers covering nearly the entire history of the town. Of these, that on the "Relations of Littleton and Vermont," originally assigned to John M. Mitchell, was prepared by F. J. Eastman, of Northfield, N. H.; that on "Education," assigned to Warren McIntire, by Dana P. Dame; that on "Merchants and Trade," assigned to C. F. Eastman, by William J. Bellows. A paper on "The Women of Littleton," assigned to Hon. Harry Bingham, was not prepared owing to a pressure of other public engagements, but an address delivered at the Congregational Church by Rev. Charles E. Millen, on the same subject, is printed herewith, as it was originally prepared for this volume. The closing paper was prepared by the late Adams Moore, M.D., and delivered as a lecture in the vestry of the Congregational Church in the winter of 1859.

The celebration of the Centennial of Littleton was suggested in the local papers in February, 1884. At the annual town meeting, held in March of that year, the subject was discussed and the following resolution adopted:

"*Resolved*, That the sum of three hundred dollars be raised and appropriated to defray the expenses of a Centennial Celebration of the corporate existence of Littleton, said sum not to be paid out unless the citizens of the town raise and pay over to the appropriate committee a like sum."

Under this resolution, the Moderator appointed the following committee: Harry Bingham, George Farr, Henry L. Thayer, Ira Parker, Cyrus Eastman, O. C. Hatch, A. S. Batchellor, Henry L. Tilton, Otis G. Hale, James R. Jackson, Frank T. Moffett, Frank Albee, Fred A. Robinson, George C. Furber and E. C. Stevens.

At the first meeting of the committee, the following organization was effected: Chairman, H. L. Tilton; Secretary, James R. Jackson; Treasurer, O. G. Hale; Corresponding Secretary, George C. Furber; Committees on Music, Ira Parker, H. L. Tilton, Oscar C. Hatch, Frank Thayer, Frank Albee; Amusements, Ira Parker, A. S. Batchellor, F. A. Robinson, E. C. Stevens, B. H. Corning; Finance, Cyrus Eastman, H. L. Tilton, O. C. Hatch, O. G. Hale, H. F. Greene; Entertainment, Cyrus Eastman, H. L. Thayer, H. L. Tilton, George Farr and William J. Bellows; Ways and Means, B. H. Corning, Ira Parker, William H. Mitchell, D. C. Remich, Frank Thayer, E. C. Stevens, F. A. Robinson, George K. Stocker, William A. Haskins, H. A. Johnson, A. S. Batchellor, M. F. Harriman, G. H. Bellows, W. F. Robins; Grounds, E. C. Stevens, Fred A. Robinson and Henry F. Greene.

Mr. Tilton refusing to serve as chairman, A. S. Batchellor was subsequently elected to fill that position.

Some difficulty was experienced in fixing upon the proper date for the celebration. The act of the Legislature dividing the town of Apthorp, and constituting those of Littleton and Dalton, was passed November 4th, 1784. But in the latter part of the preceding June, the proprietors of Apthorp, Messrs Little, Dalton, Morey, Phelps and Tracy, had practically divided and given to the two towns the names they still bear, and by which they were locally designated from that time. It was finally decided to hold the Centennial on the fourth of July, and that it should be celebrated in the spirit foretold by John Adams. "It ought," he wrote, "to be commemorated as a day of deliverance by solemn acts of devotion to God Almighty. It ought to be solemnized with pomp and parade, with shows, games, sports, guns, bells, bonfires and illuminations."

With this end in view, the executive committee adopted the following programme, the execution of which was placed under the immediate supervision of Captain George Farr, Marshal of the Day, with his assistants, William H. Mitchell and James H. Witherell :

PROGRAMME.

1. Salute, thirteen guns at daybreak. Committee: Joseph Ide, B. F. Heath and Elbridge Young.
2. Grand Spectacular and Processional Display of Antiques and Horribles. Prizes: For best display, $15; for second, $10, and for third, $5. Marshal, Charles R. Coburn; Committee, Alden Quimby, James H. Rowell and Robert H. Whittaker.
3. At 9 A. M., Civic Procession to form in front of Union Hall, in the following order:
    1st. The Saranac Cornet Band, headed by Major A. H. Bowman.
    2d. Eureka Drum Corps.
    3d. Co. F, 3d Regt., N. H. National Guard (Moore Rifles), Capt. John F. Simpson.
    4th. Marshal Sanders Post, No. 48, G. A. R., Wm. A. Crane, Senior Vice Commander.
    5th. Hose Company of the Littleton Fire Department.
    6th. Littleton Brigade Band, D. F. Chase, Leader.
    7th. Officers of the day, Invited Guests and Speakers in carriages.
    8th. Citizens' Procession.

AT THE GROVE.

1. Music, - - - - - - Saranac Band
2. Invocation, - - - - Rev. George M. Curl
3. Address of Welcome, By the President, Hon. Geo. A. Bingham
4. Music—Under direction of Prof. Frank R. Brackett, Glee Club
5. Reading of the Declaration of Independence, William H. Mitchell
6. Music, - - - - - - Brigade Band
7. Centennial Address, - - - Rev. J. E. Rankin, D. D.
8. Music, - - - - - - Glee Club

ADDRESSES.

9. Relations of Littleton and the State, - - A. S. Batchellor
10. The Pioneers of Littleton, - - - James R. Jackson
11. The Relations of Littleton and Bethlehem, Hon. John G. Sinclair

12.	Relations of Littleton and Vermont,	F. J. Eastman
13.	Newspapers and Newspaper Men,	H. H. Metcalf
14.	The Profession of the Law,	Edgar Aldrich
15.	The Profession of Medicine,	Charles M. Tuttle, M.D.
16.	The Church,	Rev. J. E. Robins
17.	Littleton Abroad,	S. B. Page
18.	Education,	Dana P. Dame, A.M.
19.	Agriculture,	Rev. F. H. Lyford
20.	Manufactures,	D. C. Remich
21.	Merchants and Trade,	William J. Bellows
22.	Women of Littleton,	Hon. Harry Bingham
23.	Littleton and the Railroads,	John M. Mitchell
24.	Littleton and the War of the Rebellion,	Captain George Farr
25.	Music,	Saranac Band

AFTERNOON SPORTS.

2 P.M. Base Ball Match for a purse of $20. Committee: C. P. Chase, L. E. Collins.

3:30 P.M. Sack Race. Prize, $2. Committee: George E. Lovejoy, Fred H. English, P. F. Ouvrand.

Greased Pig Race. Prize, the pig.
  Large pig trained for the occasion,
  Shows his teeth and growls on the least provocation.
Committee: George L. Whittaker, Frank Bowles, George W. Richardson.

Go-as-you-please-race, 30 minutes. Prize, $5, $3, $2. Committee: Geo. H. Tilton, Fred A. Goodall, Ray T. Gile.

Wrestling Match, boys in town. Prize, $5, $3, $2. Committee: H. A. Johnson, B. F. Robinson, George S. Bellows.

Jumping, Running Broad. Prize, $2. Committee: Dr. M. F. Young, G. F. Lane, H. H. Farr.

Potato Race. Prizes, $2, $1 and potatoes. Committee: H. A. Eaton, R. M. Dow, Myron H. Richardson.

EVENING.

1. Salute. Thirty-eight guns at sunset.
2. Concert, - - - - - Saranac Band
3. Grand Display of Fireworks.

The day opened auspiciously—bright and clear. It had hardly been ushered in before it was manifest that a vast concourse would be in attendance. The streets were soon thronged with men, women and children. The parade of the Antiques and Horribles attracted much attention, and was greeted on all sides with cheers and shouts of laughter.

The Civic Procession formed at the appointed hour and marched to the grove on the farm of Gabriel G. Moulton, at the westerly end of the village. This grove is formed of sugar maples, open and clear of obstructions, carpeted with nature's sheen of emerald. It occupies a commanding position, overlooking the valley of the Ammonoosuc for nearly thirty miles. To the southwest, and not more than a mile distant, is the site of the Caswell cabin, the first dwelling erected in town, while to the east the sinuous course of the river is traced to its source among the everlasting hills. The ground where the historical exercises took place formed a natural amphitheatre, which was filled with a large and attentive audience. The Marshal announced the following as the officers of the day:

President, Hon. George A. Bingham; Vice Presidents, John Farr, Cephas Brackett, Cyrus Eastman, Josiah Kilburn, Truman Stevens, Solomon Whiting, George B. Redington, William Jackson, Alden Moffett, Trueworthy L. Parker, John Merrill, Azra Eastman, David Millen, Henry D. Bishop of Littleton, Richard W. Peabody of St. Johnsbury, Horace Cushman of Dalton, Isaac Miner of Whitefield, Joseph Albee of Monroe, Charles Goodwin of Lisbon, Alba Caswell of Concord, Vt., and Edwin Abbott of Lancaster.

The exercises were necessarily lengthy, but were received with marks of approval. Some of the papers were given only in part, while others were entirely omitted, with the understanding that they would subsequently be printed.

In the afternoon a large concourse witnessed the games and other sports, and in the evening, on the same grounds, one of the largest audiences ever assembled in Littleton, gathered to listen to the concert by the Saranac band and to view the fireworks.

The concert programme was as follows:

H. B. BURNHAM, Director.

1. QUICKSTEP—"Battle of Gettysburg." Arranged by J. M. MISSUD
2. SELECTION—"The Vision." Baritone Solo, " BROOKS
3. SCHOTTISCHE—"Love at Coney Island." " LOVEJOY
4. AGNES POLKA—Eb Clarinet Solo. " T. H. ROLLINSON
5. QUICKSTEP—"Charter Oak," " J. B. CLAUS
6. SONGS OF HEAVEN WALTZES, " E. STRAUSS
7. SELECTED.

The entertainments of the day were closed with a fine display of fireworks, one of the best ever witnessed in the northern part of the state.

This volume is published under the supervision of the Committee on Town History, authority for that purpose having been granted by a vote of the town. passed at the meeting held in November, 1884. Some delay has been caused by the failure of several of the speakers to put their addresses in form for publication. It is now given to the public in the hope that it may serve to awaken an interest in the history of the town, and aid in gathering material which will enable the committee in the near future to present a more complete narrative.

GEORGE FARR,
CHARLES F. EASTMAN,
BENJAMIN W. KILBURN,
FRANCIS H. LYFORD,
RAY T. GILE,
A. S. BATCHELLOR,
JAS. R. JACKSON,
} Committee on Town History.

Littleton, N. H., Feb., 1887.

PROCEEDINGS.

The Marshal, Capt. George Farr, having called the assemblage to order, announced the names of the officers of the day, and requested them to take places upon the platform.

Hon. George A. Bingham, the president, invited the Rev. George M. Curl, pastor of the Methodist Episcopal church, to offer the invocation.

INVOCATION.

Almighty God, our Heavenly Father, Maker of all things, Judge of all men, we thank Thee for life and its blessings. We bless Thy name for the leadings of Thy providence, which has brought us together to enjoy this Centennial Anniversary. We ascribe all glory to Thy name, that, as a people, we have been prosperous, peaceable and progressive. We thank Thee for the peace which reigns throughout our community. We acknowledge Thy providence in the gift, the continuance and the triumph of our religious institutions. Our churches, schools and all branches of culture and progress arising from these are helped by them. We pray that the degree of success which we have had may continue and that right may triumph over error, till not only in this town, but the world over, men may acknowledge God as their Father, Jesus Christ as their Saviour, and the Holy Spirit, their Sanctifier, and from this be able to acknowledge the universal brotherhood of man. We rejoice that as responsible beings, we have a right to form and maintain a government for ourselves and that we may, under God, bless the world and bring glory to the cause of our Lord. Help us, O God, to use our liberty and influence for the right. That we may ever seek the culture of the good, the true and the beautiful, and strive to lift the world up to God.

We thank Thee for our prosperity in business, for the great achievements of man, the heights to which he has climbed by persistent effort and the help of God. Lord, continue to us these blessings, and help us to appreciate Thy gifts, reciprocate Thy love and work out our salvation. As a people, Gracious Father, help us to study Thy will, seek the truth and pursue it, till all forms of evil shall be swept from our land and Thou shall reign in the hearts of these people without a rival. Bless the Temperance cause here and hasten the time when Littleton shall be as free from rum as Heaven is from sin. May we remember our success is in Thee. Bless the exercises of today. May all be done decently and in order. As we see from the past how Thou hast led us, grant to continue to lead and keep us, as a people, until, without the loss of one, we may be gathered into the house of many mansions, not made with hands, "eternal in the heavens," and we will ascribe all the glory to Father, Son and Holy Spirit, world without end, AMEN.

The President said: In 1776, when the representatives of the United Colonies of America assembled in Congress, they declared that when it becomes necessary for one nation to dissolve the political bands which have bound it to another, it is but just to themselves and the opinions of mankind that they announce the causes that impel them to the separation. We propose to read at this time the Declaration of Independence that was made in Congress assembled in 1776.

The Declaration of Independence was then read by W. H. Mitchell.

ADDRESS BY THE PRESIDENT.

The President said: You have assembled on this occasion for a double purpose. One hundred years ago this town was substantially an unbroken wilderness, and we meet today to celebrate the centennial year of its incorporation. It is a great day for Littleton. The Littleton of one hundred years ago, with its unbroken forests, filled with wild beasts and traversed by red men, is changed. The forests have become cultivated fields, the wild animals have given way to civilized life, the red men have gone and the white men have come, in numbers a hundred fold greater. Yes, Littleton is one hundred years old. We nowhere see the evidences of premature decay or paralytic age; but, on the contrary, we see marked signs of thrift and hear promises of greater growth yet to come. But we do not meet today for the sole purpose of celebrating the glories of Littleton. We are a part of a great and mighty people, whose territory extends from the gulf to the lakes and from ocean to ocean, with whom we join in celebrating the birthday of our national existence. On the fourth day of July, one hundred and eight years ago, the representatives of the thirteen united colonies of America, in congress assembled, declared to the nations of the earth that they were, and of right ought to be, free and independent states, and by the grace of God and the strength of their own right arms the people have maintained the fiat from that day to this. It is also to commemorate the glorious deeds of the fathers, and signify to the civilized world that we are not unmindful of the blessings of a free government, that we celebrate this, the fourth day of July, eighteen hundred and eighty-four.

ETHICAL CHARACTER OF AMERICAN CIVILIZATION.

CENTENNIAL ADDRESS BY J. E. RANKIN, D. D.

The President said: In the last hundred years in the Town of Littleton, many men have lived and died. We have with us today a descendant of one of its early settlers who, in his day and generation, was a man of activity and influence among men.

The descendant is his great grandchild, the Rev. J. E. Rankin, D. D., of Washington, D. C., who will now deliver the Centennial Address.

ADDRESS.

MR. PRESIDENT:

Town-building is the exponent of civilization. Civilization culminates in towns. There can be no high state of civilization, without associated life; life related to other life; dependent upon other life; ministering to other life. In early times, this associated life was largely for defence; and towns were walled towns, and the walls had towers of observation, to scour the horizon for enemies. Towns, too, were built with blood, and cities were established with iniquity. "Go to," said the dwellers in the lands of Shinar, "let us build a city, and a tower whose top may reach unto heaven; and let us make us a name, lest we be scattered abroad upon the face of the whole earth." It was the instinct of civilization. Even savage life has its villages; and, as you ascend the scale of civilization, you find a people more and more bringing their best things and treasuring them up in their principal towns. It is said that Paris is France: so, too, is London, England; and Edinburgh, Scotland. We mean by this that civilization brings all her first-fruits, her literature, her arts, her monuments, her most characteristic things, and lays them at the feet of her capital city. And in the archives or the ashes of this city, the crowning proofs of her civilization will be found. Herculaneum, Pompeii, Nineveh, Troja, have yielded the secrets of their civilization.

All civilization has an ethical character; has an end for which it exists. There is a French civilization in which life is looked at as mainly for pleasure and glory; where social intercourse is full of persiflage and bonmots, and serious things, such as duty to man and duty to God, are treated with a shrug: where even a battle is like a picnic, and the guillotine is the center of a holiday. And there is an Anglo-Saxon civilization, whose watch-word is duty: is the thing which is owed to God and to man; where life is lived as under the eye of the great task-master, and between two eternities, out of whose galleries spectators are looking; and where men go to battle as from their knees, and take victory as by the interposition of God Almighty. It is said that revolutionsn ever go backward. French revolutions have usually gone backward. They have only been paroxysms, not movements. They have not had an ethical basis; only a theatrical one. They have often been movements in open defiance of ethical laws. Think of the fact, that during the reign of terror, when the French revolution had burst out into its most lurid flames, was eating up its own children, twenty-three theatres were open nightly in Paris, and sixty halls of public dancing, and the cemeteries were inscribed, "Here is an eternal sleep." Here were the ethics of that period. And think of the other fact, that when Anglo-Saxon civilization undertakes such stern business as changing civil institutions, as founding states, she makes a solemn league and covenant with God; she takes the sacrament, she brings her iron-clad yeomen into the dust in prayer, and then she hurls them upon her foes, as though God-winged; bids them take ship and cross oceans, as the Pilgrims did, bids them lift the axe against the trees, and plant towns in the wilderness, as have done their children.

The subject which I shall discuss this morning is the Ethical Character of American Civilization.

I. What is civilization? It is the movement of man from the savage state to the town state. The old-time New England town I regard the flower of highest civilization. The word civilize means to make into a civis, a citizen; to take the nomadic man, the warring man, the wild man, the barbarous man, the Arab, the man whose hand is against every man and every man's hand is against him, and make him into a man, whose hand is for every man, and every man's hand is for him; who can dwell in human society in peace; who can adorn it, and perpetuate it. This is civilization. Burke says that in Europe "civilization has depended upon two things: the spirit of a gentleman, and the spirit of religion." The gentleman is the counterfeit Christian; I mean the man who has put on Christianity's outside. Religion makes the only true gentleman. The genteel man is a product earthly; the gentleman, a product divine. One is artificial, like a paper flower, the other a creature of life. The genteel man depends upon his relation to the family (*gens* the family), from which he originates; the gentleman, upon his relations to the race, created in God's image. "You may depend upon it," says Coleridge, "religion is, in its essence, the most gentlemanly thing in the world. It will, alone, gentilize, if unmixed with cant; and I know nothing else that will, alone. Certainly, not the army, which is thought to be the grand embellisher of manners." Of course there are gentlemen in the army, but buttons and epaulettes do not make gentlemen.

De Tocquevilleth ought he had found the germ of American civil life in the town. He was right. The town makes the citizen; the civis. The town is the republic in miniature; the republic brought down to such dimensions that the wayfaring man, though a fool, need not err therein; may understand its workings; putting him to tuition as a citizen; training him to self-government, making him a little republic; beginning at once the process of civilization. The town meeting, where town officers are elected, town business is transacted, is the primary school of the republic. President Lincoln said that every Northern regiment had men in it who could administer the affairs of the nation. It was the fact. And each man was taught it in the town meeting. There a man learns that he has duties to the public; or, in other words, to his brother man in the aggregate. Here is a New England township with its 36,000 acres of unbroken wilderness; the echoes wakened by the sound of the waterfalls, the howl of the wolf, and the woodman's axe; highways to be surveyed and cast up; water privileges to be sought out and occupied; school houses and churches and colleges to be built, and all the common interests of a new settlement to be looked after. And this is all to be done by self-taxation; all to be dug out of the earth by individual hands and then laid on the common altar. Here are twelve voters with seventeen acres of arable land, thirteen acres of mowing land, nine horses and oxen, eleven cows, two three-years-olds, and two one-year-olds, scattered over these 36,000 acres; and the problem is civilization! I take the inventory of this town of Littleton in 1784, one hundred years ago. Off these seventeen acres of arable land, these twelve voters agree to raise sixteen bushels of wheat for school purposes. Wheat is the only currency which the land mints. In all these rude, unhewn log cabins there are heard the voices of children and the footsteps of the coming generations, and bread for the body must be given in exchange for bread for the mind. And these same twelve voters, knowing that they and their children have souls as well as bodies, determine that there shall be preaching for two months, the ensuing summer; and so again so many bushels of wheat,—of the meat that perisheth—shall be set apart to this sacred use: to bring to their doors the bread which comes down from Heaven. For are not these pilgrims going Canaan-ward?

Here you see, at once, something serious is going on. Here is not only a warfare against Nature's wilds, her primeval embattled trees, her rocks, her undrained marshes; but love for children, love for country, love for God: a warfare against illiteracy, vice and godlessness! And these twelve yeomen, with future generations tugging at their farmers' frocks, as they swing the axe helve, and imbed the axe deep in the hearts of these forest giants, that fall one after another with a crash before them; as they fence in their little clearings and furrow up the earth's surface with that keel that does for the land what the ship's keel does for the deep, and scatter there the precious seed-corn, which is, at once, food for body and mind and soul; as they make their thoroughfares and their bridges, are only doing for the earth what she is doing for them. They are civilizing her. She is civilizing them, for the work is reciprocal. Three generations pass across her surface. They have gone hence to be here no more forever. No, I mistake. They rest from their labors and their works do follow them. They live in their children's children. The same names, perhaps, are on the town records as a hundred years ago. The twelve voters have increased to 977. The grand list has gone up from $29.90 to $1,477,005.00. And here are churches, and school houses, and bridges, and aqueducts, and manufactories; while the hills are covered with flocks and herds, and here and there smiles out the thrifty farm house, with its great barns full of machinery, like an arsenal of peace, and its meadow land waving with green and gold. The woods are no longer trackless wilds of desolation, the habitation of bears and wolves, but they crown the summits like temples, and clap their hands with joy that man has set up his dominion over them. These one hundred years have been a movement of these twelve first settlers from the rude life of the wilderness, where earth does almost nothing for man, except to give him game and footing as he hunts it, to town life; that is, to life where earth's ministrations are at their maximum, and where what she brings forth has commercial value against whatever genius can devise, art can construct, or enterprise can bring from the four quarters of the globe. Churches, do you want them? They are here; schools, and books, and teachers, and farm utensils, and fabrics; pictures; whatever will make man noblest, truest, purest, gentlest; whatever will make woman the fit companion of a creature made in God's image, comforter, counselor, helpmeet; here it is all at your very door. And this is civilization!

II. I call your attention to the fact, that one civilization is distinguished from another by its ethical character, by the moral qualities of habit, and of life which go into it; which prevail in it. At first thought, one might doubt this. We might be tempted to classify civilization according to what occupies the outward man, as is done in some of the foreign civilizations; to call farm-life less civilized than commercial life, and commercial life less civilized than professional life, or life in different departments of the government. But if we have defined civilization right, as that state in which man recognizes and takes the obligations of the citizen, begins to unfold into civilization's highest bloom—the true gentleman—comes under the law of human brotherhood and God's fatherhood, the outward employment can have little to do with it. I know the old couplet,

"When Adam delved, and Eve span,
Who was, then, the gentleman?"

And yet the grandest characters that any civilization has ever produced, have been the delvers and the ditchers, the spinners and the weavers, who have been that civilization's pioneers. Thomas Carlyle tells us that, potentially, his father was a nobler man than he; that if he were asked to determine which had the greater original endowment, that father or Robert Burns, he should hesitate which to say. "O, when I think," writes he, after his father's death. "O, when I think that all the area in boundless space he had seen was limited to a circle of some fifty miles diameter, and all his knowledge of the boundless time was derived from his Bible, and what the oral memories of old men could give him and his own could gather; and yet, that he was such. I take shame to myself. I feel to my father, so great, though so neglected, so generous also toward me, a strange tenderness and mingled pity and reverence peculiar to the case, infinitely soft and near my heart. Was he not a sacrifice to me? Had I stood in his place, could he not have stood in mine, and more? Thou good father! well may I forever honor thy memory! I can see my dear father's life in some measure, as the sunk pillar on which mine was to rise, and be built." The grandeur of a family is often under the surface; comes from the being of men, who never speak of themselves.

The very idea of the first Plymouth colonies was that God would, perhaps, make them stepping-stones to those who should come after them. This is why they tried wintry seas and the wilderness. They felt that there was to be a civilization in this new world, for which the benighted and oppressed of other lands were waiting; for which they were on their knees pleading with the King of Kings! If future generations could step on them and find firm footing, as they crossed over to a land, such as they had dreamed of in exile, as they had seen in high vision, they were content. They heard the tramp of these future generations; they were willing it should go over them, dead. And this was the temper of a large part of early American civilization, and especially that of the East. There was a self-sacrifice, a chivalry and heroism about it which it is beautiful to see. "The glory of children are their fathers." These early settlers could expect no material return during their own generation. What had an unbroken wilderness for them? Only hard work and nameless graves. They were at least one generation distant from the common comforts of life. They stood there for their children and their children's children; nay for humanity, the world over. Today, a man goes to a distant territory in the United States. In less than a half-generation, he appears in Washington as a Member of Congress, as a Senator, as a railroad king, as a cattle king. He has got dominion over something and made a good thing out of it. He has roughed it a few years, with money furnished him by others, within a few hours reach by telegraph, within a few days reach by railway, of the great metropolitan centers of civilization. He goes into a mining speculation, or a cattle raising speculation, or a railroad speculation, and, presto! here he is back again. His ethics have been to get on, himself. I do not mean that there are no hardships in leaving the older civilization of the East. Much of the earlier settlement of the West has been in the primitive spirit of the

Pilgrims. But the struggle has been shorter and the returns more immediate. But of late, the returns themselves have become different. There is very little talk about stepping stones unless we can step on others; about planting institutions for the benefit of others, and especially of other generations, of other peoples. Men are after another kind of plant.

Take this glimpse of old-time New England civilization. The first child born in the town of Littleton, the town whose inventory in 1784 I have quoted, was born in a dense wilderness, six or eight miles from the nearest neighbor. The night previous to his birth, his mother, with her seven children, spent the anxious hours in a log barn, the father with his loaded gun at the door awaiting the attack of a party of Indians. The next day father, mother and the little brood of children took a canoe, with all they could carry away, and went down the river to a fort. At nightfall the Indians came and left their home in ashes. They had saved their lives, but lost their all. Eighteen years after the first settlement of the town, there were but nine families in it, though some of these families were almost nine times larger than the modern size of families, children then being considered a gift of God, not an encumbrance! The Caswell family, above alluded to, had fourteen children, thirteen of whom reached their four-score years. In June, 1788, Peleg Williams, in behalf of the town, thus represented the state of things in a petition to the state legislature. The territory of the town was unsurveyed and untaxed. The inhabitants had to go fifteen miles to mill, to market and to court house, over a public road of eleven miles, which was next to impassable; and they were in such a situation that they could not live there, nor could they move away, and they besought the interposition of the legislature. This was the environment of old-time civilization.

Seeing the embarassments of our situation; seeing the barbarisms that are still marring our heritage; bloodguiltiness in the South; Mormonism on the Pacific; the canker of corruption eating into the heart of everything, we flippantly talk of a stronger government. There is no stronger government, except God's government, and this in-arches us, as the skies do. American civilization is unlike all other civilization upon the face of the earth in its ethical strength. It is right in the sight of man, it is right in the sight of God. It is government by consent of the governed. It can never be overthrown, but by their consent or connivance. There have been republics before, but no republics founded upon the rights and duties of man, as such; none deriving their authority from God, as man's Creator. We have the perfect, the ideal theory of government, and if it does not work right it is because of those who are working it. The Father of the Republic went down to the bed-rock and built there. Nobody can go deeper or find anything stronger. God has put upon every creature of His, His image and superscription, and we have recognized it in our fundamental things. The great charter is greater than the Magna Charta of King John. It includes not only the clergy, and the barons, and the freemen, but all men. Our fathers found themselves men. They traced man back to the Creator, God, and then crowned him King in that Creator's name. The Magna Charta of King John read, "No freeman shall be taken, imprisoned, disseized, outlawed, or exiled, except by lawful judgment of his peers, or the law of the land." The phrase was *Nullus liber homo!* three words which Lord Chatham has pronounced "worth all the classics!" Yes, but they were worth infinitely more when one of them was left out, when they no longer read, *Nullus liber homo*, but *Nullus homo!* and thus our fathers read them in the light of God.

III. I want to call your attention to some of the tendencies of the present type of civilization; tendencies away from the old-time ethical standard. I have already characterized the old-fashioned New England civilization as the ideal civilization. Progress away from it is toward barbarism. This I have declared to be the tendency of all civilization. The civilizing process of civilization is in getting it. Alison has said that in their sources of happiness the life of the English nobleman, an Iroquois of the forest and an Arab of the desert are nearly alike. It is true that people did not know so much as they do now-a-days. Neither did our first parents, before eating of the forbidden fruit. They did not have lightning-winged Mercuries scouring around all night long, to get up for them columns of horrors committed on every continent of a lost world, with which to regale them at breakfast. They had not the modern appetite for such viands. They knew outrageous wickedness, as an enormity possible to depraved man. They read of it in the Bible and in profane history, and they probably thought about their own potential wickedness, more than you and I do about ours, and were more on their guard against it.

As contrasted with such a period, the first tendency of modern civilization, of which I will speak, is irreverence; the tendency to make light of moral laws and moral government, and the value of moral character, as compared with a brilliant intellect, or great social or material prosperity; readiness to pawn everything over the Devil's counter, for worldly success. We may flatter ourselves that it is because of greater light in science and interpretation; because of more correct views of religion and a future; because of being rid of the superstitions of the past, that an arrant blasphemer in cap and bells is welcomed and cheered on the American platform, as he voices his coarse ribaldry in the ears of our young men, whom he corrupts and leads dancing to ruin at one dollar a head—playing such fantastic tricks before high Heaven as make the angels weep. But it is not so; the change is a moral one. We do know more than our fathers; but they would pity us for the way in which we know it; as the angels pitied our first parents in Eden. The things which our fathers and our grandfathers, our mothers and our grandmothers would not listen to, because they revered God and the Word of God, we listen to because they are so very funny. We give up sacred things for the sake of a joke. It is the French habit of mind. It is the laughter of the moral idiot, like the crackling of thorns under a pot. It is the ghastly grin of a decaying civilization. Put this with the other fact, thus described by Froude, the historian: "That the ablest of then living natural philosophers was looking gravely at the courtships of moths and butterflies, to solve the problem of the origin of man, and to prove his descent from an African baboon," and we see where the two extremes meet. Superficiality and frivolity, and even blasphemy, when we should look up and uncover our heads and reverently speak about things that most concern us, and a kind of demented seriousness, as though the mind had gone into a driveling dotage, when we talk about finding the origin of life, not in God, but in the lowest forms of matter! Why, such a man as the father of Thomas Carlyle, with only his Bible, his Heavenly horizons and his fifty miles diameter of an earthly one, would outweigh a cartload of such profane talkers and jesters. Such people can build up nothing—only destroy what has been built up by others. The qualities that give nobility and grandeur to human nature and human life are serious ones. Those who have them recognize that there is a sphere of thought, where man should walk softly and have his words few. The builders of states, the men and women who take their lives in their hands and go into wildernesses and lay themselves as corner stones, as a beginning of a fabric of civilization, where their very names will soon be forgotten, are not people that talk flippantly of the idea of a God, or the government of God.

In his eloquent defence of Calvinism, Froude has said some things which you and I, the descendants of the Pilgrims, ought to remember: "When all else has failed, when patriotism has covered its face, and human courage has broken down; when intellect has yielded, as Gibbon says 'with a smile and a sigh', content to philosophize in the closet, and worship abroad with the vulgar; when emotion, and sentiment, and tender imaginative piety have become the handmaids of superstition, and have dreamed themselves into forgetfulness that there is any difference between lies and truth, the staunch form of belief, called Calvinism, in one or another of its many forms, has borne ever an inflexible front to illusion and mendacity, and has preferred rather to be ground to powder, like flint, than to bend before violence or to melt under enervating temptation. The men who believed this doctrine, such as William the Silent, Luther, Calvin, John Knox, Oliver Cromwell, Milton and Bunyan, were men whose life was as upright as their intellect was commanding, and their public aims untainted with selfishness; unalterably just, where duty required them to be stern, but with the tenderness of a woman in their hearts; frank, true, cheerful, humorous; as unlike sour fanatics as it is possible to imagine any one, and able, in some way, to sound the key-note, to which every brave and faithful heart in Europe instinctively vibrated." It has been so the world over. It is the men who link themselves with God, and act as in the sight of God, whose work has stood. They have addressed themselves to their life task as though it were a thing appointed of God, and not evolved out of baboons, protoplasm and star dust! And full of mystery, though it has often seemed to them, they have never been in a mood to treat it as though acted on the boards of low comedy. Their heavens were always begirt

"With battlements, that on their restless fronts,
Bore stars!"

The second tendency of modern civilization, in which it is unlike the original type, is the disregard of the unitary form of human civilization, the home, the family. God made man, male and female; the one, the complement and counterpart of the other; and humanity is perfect only in the home; in the home where there are children under training for the future of the Republic. We have made the word Nation emphatic, by writing it in earth's soil, with war's hieroglyphics on a thousand battlefields—nay, by dipping the historic pen in home's life-blood. The national cemeteries are rich with home's contributions; of father, brother, son, husband, lover; to the significance of the word Nation. The roses have just been laid on thousands of graves where these heroes sleep. It is time for the Nation to turn around and pay back the debt, by dignifying and protecting the home, as a sacred God-given institution! The testimony of an ex-Senator of the United States, lately given under oath, is to the effect that for $500 a year, he hired the woman, now prosecuting him for alimony as his lawful wife, to live with him contrary to laws of the land and in violation of God's commandment, "Thou shalt not commit adultery"—he, the nation's law maker in this nineteenth century. Both on the part of man and woman, there is a disposition to shirk the responsibilities of home life, the care and training of children. The early civilization of this country was in the interest of home life. This civilization tends towards few children, and French flats; tends towards adultery, concubinage, infidelity to marriage vows.

Take the State of New Hampshire for illustration, and look at the constituents of population. The last census shows the population to be 346,229, of which 46,224, or about one-eighth, are foreign-born, and this foreign-born population is buying up the farms. The farms are the home nests of the people, where the eagles or the vultures are reared. The people in the quiet and sequestered homes of a country, determine the character of its civilization. They are the people who have religious and moral and political convictions. The tendency of our original population, in their children's children, is toward city civilization, which is away from town civilization—back in the road to barbarism! There is nothing more savage, more brutal, more appalling, than the recorded life of some of our great cities. Some of them are as beautiful in their exterior as Cleopatra, and as cruel. We are corralling the children of the Indians and Africans, the lately half barbarous portions of our population, and teaching them the rudiments of our original civilization; teaching them the Bible, the spelling-book; work, the use of the hoe, the scythe, the plough; while our children are hurrying from the hills and the homes and farms, where their fathers and grandfathers lived, toiled, left them their blessing and died, to be lost in city life; where the individuality of country social life and home life are wholly unknown. And who take their places in the foundation work of building up homes, of standing by the family, of moulding the civilization? There is a passage in Isaiah, "And strangers shall stand and feed your flocks, and the sons of the alien shall be your ploughmen and vine dresser." But, read it in this manner: "And strangers shall own and feed their own flocks, where once your fathers owned and fed theirs; shall plough their fields and dress their vines where once your fathers ploughed their fields and dressed their vines." This is the Scripture that is fulfilled in our day. This is another picture. Tired of the slow but solid life of their fathers, tired of living unknown, and dying unknown, if but a more glorious life might be for the children, and their children's country, when they were dead; luxurious in their ambitions and tastes; wanting to take part in spectacular things, rather than to figure in real ones, they are willing to make the original idea of home life and family life impossible, and so year by year the unitary form of the original American civilization is disappearing from the earth and our civilization is dying through the death of the unit of its life.

What is the remedy for these tendencies away from the civilization of earlier times? There are a few moments to speak of this.

I am not quite sure that there is any remedy, only to begin over again. When a nation is losing the seriousness out of her life, and thinks of her future as manifest destiny, or something that will take care of itself, without any reference to her carriage before God, or her keeping of covenant with Him; when she is careless of the mould where the citizen is formed and fitted for citizenship; when she is changing the type of citizenship from better to worse, generation after generation; when what is typical in her citizenship hastens to lose itself in the maw of her great cities; when all her desires and ambitions materialize, and she thinks nothing of value which does not yield her cent-per-cent, I hardly know what other remedy to suggest; at any rate, what remedy to expect her to apply. Law-making will not do it. Constitutional enactments will not do it; — I believe in them. There is help in both these directions, but the tendency to appeal to them, on each and every occasion, is weakness. Tacitus says, "When the state is most corrupt, then the laws are most multiplied;" and Montesquieu, "We should never create by law what can be established by morality." That is, what can be otherwise put into life. We want something in love of country, which is like that which we have in love of Christ, in religion. Love of Christ writes God's laws in our hearts. We want the laws of patriotism written in our hearts. We want to do and dare, to live and suffer for her, because we love her, at her best. We want to impress this lesson on our children. This result can be secured, if at all, by sitting at the feet of the first New England settlers. The founders of states are great teachers. They were men and women cast in heroic mould, and their teaching is all by example, and so always sincere. It is true that builders of institutions do not get as much notice in history, as it has been mostly written, as destroyers. Their names do not flame with a meteor flame across history's page, like those of leaders of armies. The names of the rebel generals are better known than those of the men who signed the Declaration of Independence. And yet the first tried to destroy the work of the last. Such men do their patient work; write their names in their deeds; level forests; dig out stumps; smooth down Nature's wrinkles; sow her surface with harvests perennial; plant institutions, and then are borne away to sleep with their fellow-settlers, near by where they first let the light of Heaven in upon the surface of Mother Earth—their very graves leveled to the common level. In a few years you can scarcely read their names upon the tombstones. Good citizenship, patient, plodding industry, bearing arms for free institutions, bearing children to take their places—these do not seem to furnish them a very grand claim for remembrance. And yet there is no grander work than theirs.

If we study the character, the motives, and the work of those who assisted in planting free institutions, we need also to look at present national tendencies in the light of this study. Are they in harmony? These men lived for the benefit of those who should come after them. They lived for free institutions, for the right to act as freemen! It dignified their lives, it hallows their memories.

In our generation, millions have died for the benefit of those who should come after them, their spirits caught up from the battle-field, as in a chariot of fire. But scarcely twenty years have passed and how many of us are already weary of the floral service with which we have been taught to honor their graves. They died for us, but how soon has their victions as we. Why not also decorate their graves? The ethics have dropped out of our estimate. I have no vindictive feelings toward the dead, even though they lifted up parricidal hands against the nation's life. But it is a question whether we will allow what seems a pretty sentiment to take the place of the serious judgment, with which even the memory of wrong-doing should be followed. The elements which have gone into our civilization, and which dominated it, have been ethical. They have been determined upon at the bar of conscience, and not at that of expediency. Are we not now in danger of applying other standards? Is it safe to do so?

The sentiment of country is not indeed the highest sentiment. The love of humanity and the love of God are higher than this. And Americans have loved their country quite as much for the sake of humanity as for their country's sake, because they saw in her progress, in her unfolding, the hope of the world! Because they saw here a continent where the principles of human brotherhood, trampled on elsewhere, might have room and verge enough for their noblest growth; where children of all nationalities could sit down under their own father's roof-tree; because they saw here the beginning of such a civilization as might fitly usher in the day when the name of country should be lost in the kingdom of God. So that here the ethical has passed into the religious. And when we pray, " Thy kingdom come, Thy will be done on earth, as it is in heaven." we think of this continent lying between the ocean of war and the ocean of peace, the ocean from which the Pilgrims came, and from which come the children of Asia as the scene of civilization in which nations shall learn war no more; where there shall be no more garments rolled in blood; where the cross shall be above all standards, and where Time's last and noblest offspring shall tread the soil made sacred by the sacrifices of the fathers, in the stature of a Christian citizenship, at which the world shall wonder.

There is something certainly in Christianity that will save us—that will perpetuate us. God casts only those nations into hell, that forget Him. When we think of the possibility that is in this problem of self government, we may eventually fail;

dust become as other dust. The day, memorial, is largely ceasing to be a holy day, a day sacred to a holy purpose, where we light our torches even at the alter of patriotism, and becoming a holiday, a day for excursions and picnics; for going to see caverns and other natural curiosities. Then, too, we think it is invidious to make distinctions in this tribute to the dead. We say those who opposed us were just as honest in their con- that after having over-run this continent with the triumphs of our proud civilization, we may be unable to hold it because of barbarous tendencies within human nature; because of making haste to be rich; because of corrupting ambitions; because we have lost our ethical balance; because we have destroyed the original type of our civilization; because we have forgotten the motives of our fathers, and the spirit of our fathers, and have turned to living for our own times, and not for the times that come after us, we feel the need of sitting at the feet of the men and the women of one hundred years ago, as we have done today. As they lived for home, for humanity, for country, for God, let us live; let us teach our children to live. As they built themselves, foundation-stones into this structure of freedom, let us go on humbly, patiently, courageously, till our civilization shall become the joy of the whole earth!

  They stood alone, our Pilgrim sires!
   Behind, that waste of ocean:
  'Mid wintry wilds, lit Freedom's fires,
   To God paid their devotion;
  The roof which arched them was the sky,
   God's light upon their faces;
  Their prayers and praises lifted high,
   Made glad the desert places!

  They stood alone! They left behind
   The work of kings and sages;
  One perfect thought within their mind,
   The bloom of all the ages;
  One perfect thought; that man is man,
   His Father, God above him!
  No king nor priest to mar his plan,
   They worship best who love Him.

They stood alone! God in them stirred!
   The seed-corn of the nations;
Through faith in Him, the step they heard,
   Of coming generations!
They see the forest wilds give way,
   They see the desert blossom;
The harvests, with their golden ray,
   Her gold give up earth's bosom.

The prairies catch a richer bloom,
   Where e'er their sons are sowing;
And famished peoples ask for room,
   To glean their overflowing.
Before their touch, the Golden Gate,
   Obedient back is swinging;
And there Pacific's waters wait,
   A hymn of welcome singing!

They stood alone! They walk in white,
   Upon the page historic!
No fracture there, no stain to blight
   That simple structure, Doric.
They builded better than they knew!
   'Tis so of all God's builders;
His perfect plan they carried through,
   Ah! that man's thought bewilders.

Their faith was better than our sight,
   They knew the sure foundation;
The struggle forward toward the light,
   God makes them, thus a nation.
Content to be but stepping stones,
   Where the great Builder lays them:
Their simple faith He thus enthrones.
   Their work, their work shall praise them.

THE RELATIONS OF LITTLETON AND THE STATE.

ADDRESS BY A. S. BATCHELLOR.

The President said: Although it was said of Littleton, in its early days, that it was too poor to live in, and that the roads were so bad that those that did live here could not get away, yet it has proved, in the end, that Littleton has not lived to itself alone. It has sent its men abroad, and its influence has received its due weight in the councils of the State.

We will now listen to remarks from Mr. A. S. Batchellor, who has not only a place in the history of Littleton, but in that of New Hampshire, as to the relations of Littleton and the State.

ADDRESS.

MR. PRESIDENT AND TOWNSMEN:

Any one of our prosperous New Hampshire towns is a fair representative of the New England town system. These local municipalities are the schools in which many of the founders of the Republic received their political education, and they may well be regarded as the political basis of the best systems of government that have yet been developed. A consideration of the relations of one of these towns to the state with which it is organized, which would not transcend the requirements of such an occasion as this, must be limited, in a great measure, to those features of the subject which are not common to all that belong to the same system. The remarks that follow are offered with an intention to treat the subject in the restricted sense, and to touch only upon those points which may have special interest to the people of Littleton.

THE KING'S WOODS.

The first that is known of the territory upon which Chiswick, Apthorp and Littleton were successively laid, indicates that it was once the abode of the Indians of the Abenaquis nation. The tribe that dwelt in the immediate vicinity was the Cohasaukes. Their principal trails or carrying places were along the valleys of the Connecticut and Ammonoosuc rivers. Over these they passed in their fishing, hunting and marauding expeditions. These are the same routes that have been successively followed by the early hunters and trappers, the exploring expeditions of Powers and Stark, the rangers of the French and Indian wars, the pioneer settlers, the soldiers and scouts of the war of the Revolution, and the surveyors, builders and travelers of our principal highways. Few of you are too young to remember the old daily mail stages to Lancaster, alternating over the Ammonoosuc and the Connecticut river routes. The old Ammonoosuc Indian trail is now the line of the railway. Sixteen trains daily bear the burdens of civilization over its iron, and suggest the memory of the dusky Indian travelers of the ancient forest valley only by the magnitude of the contrast.

No local mementoes of Indian occupancy within our limits remain, save the names they gave the rivers: Ammonoosuc,* the Fish-Place (*Namaos Auke*), and Connecticut, the Long-Deer-Place (*Quinne-Attuck-Auke*).

As early as 1752 this region began to attract special official attention.

In 1754, our Provincial government, becoming suspicious that the French might be building a fort in the Coos country, or taking other active measures to assert jurisdiction of this region, sent Capt. Peter Powers, with John Stark as guide, at the head of a small military expedition, or scout, to explore the valley and ascertain the facts about the rumored hostile occupation. On the 29th of June, this party passed up the west part of the present Littleton. On their return, they spent

---

*Many of the best authorities on our local history and the Indian nomenclature give but one m in this word and a k at the end; but custom has made the spelling, Ammonoosuc, almost universal.

the fourth of July in marching twenty miles, "about," as Capt. Powers wrote, over the site of this village, along "the meadows" and down the Ammonoosuc valley. This was twenty-two years before the first Independence Day. These were the first official visitations, by authority of the Province government, made within the present limits of Littleton.

The Coos country continued, during the progress of the French and Indian war, to be nothing but a wilderness frontier, and received the attention of government only as a part of its domain, which was at stake in the great contest, to be held and defended.

The peace of 1760 laid open the region of the upper Connecticut, as the most promising destination of the surplus population of lower New England. Its advantages for settlement were made known by the soldiers and hunters who had traversed it. The river was a natural highway, which made it accessible by boats in summer and by sleds in winter.

In 1760 the Provincial government, preparatory to the expected movement of settlers up the valley, caused a survey of the river to be made northward from Charlestown, N. H., to the north east corner of what was afterwards granted as Newbury, and the next year a continuation of the same survey was made by Hughbastis Neel,* to the north end of the great meadows, called the Upper Coos. From these surveys a plan was made, three tiers of townships on each side of the river projected, and several of them chartered without any further actual survey on the ground. The demand for land, not only for settlement in good faith, but also for speculation, was by these means very fully met.

CHISWICK.

By the grant of Lancaster on the north, Lyman on the south, and Concord, with its gore, running steeple fashion, to an apex at the south-easterly corner of Lancaster, a tract, bounded by those townships and Connecticut river was left

---

*History of Bradford, Vt., p. 10, Dr. Moore states that this survey was made by Gen. Bailey, and cites the authority of the late John McDuffee, of Bradford, Vt., and Dr. McKeen, the historian of Bradford, seems to rely upon the same authority for his proposition.

ungranted. Through some error, Gov. Wentworth, the next year after granting Concord, now Lisbon, laid another grant called Chiswick,* upon the larger part of Concord. Discovering his mistake, he compensated the proprietors of this invalid grant by giving them, instead, the tract bounded by Lancaster, Concord, Lyman and Connecticut river. This, too, was named Chiswick. No settlement of the township, however, was effected. After the expiration of five years from the date of the charter, the proprietors admitted a forfeiture and petitioned for a new grant of the same territory.

A settlement of Lancaster had been made about the time of the grant of Chiswick. The proprietors of Lancaster, by some means, procured a new survey, which located their township further up the river, bringing the lower line more than three and one-half miles further north,† and the upper line a considerable distance to the northward. Thus a large amount of what is now Dalton was abandoned and a good slice of Stonington intervale appropriated. The proprietors of Chiswick so managed it that the land abandoned by the Lancaster parties was included in the new grant, which was to supersede Chiswick.

---

*For an ancient township map of New York, Vermont and New Hampshire, showing the location of the first Chiswick, see Governor and Council Records, Vt., vol. 8, p. 430.

†In 1780, Ebenezer Willoughby ran out the distance in a right line and made it three miles, two hundred and twenty rods. Chiswick's southeast corner was three miles and ninety-two rods S., 20 E., from the northeast corner of Lyman. The easterly side line of Chiswick was thence N., 20 E., about six miles to the southeast corner of Lancaster. This was also the North corner of Concord Gore. The north line of Chiswick ran N., 26 W., about seven miles to the river. By laying off these distances on a township map one can readily ascertain where the proper boundaries of these towns would be with reference to existing locations. If the easterly line of Chiswick is taken as six miles, its north line would be south of the present south line of Lancaster, about seven and three-fourths miles on the Bethlehem line, and about six and seven-tenths miles on a straight line down Connecticut river. The old Chiswick line cut the Bethlehem line at a point about a mile above the Scythe Factory village, and would probably cross the farms of Chester M. Goodwin, George E. Bartlett, Smith E. Jones, Luther B. Towne, and the old Rix place on the Connecticut river, now occupied by Milo C. Pollard. The migratory character of that important boundary, the southeast corner of Lancaster, made a vast deal of confusion as to the true location of Concord Gore, and as to the tracts that in early times depended upon it for boundaries.

APTHORP.

The second grant was called Apthorp and was made January 18, 1770. A settlement was effected in the spring of that year, but it is doubtful if it attracted the attention of the British colonial government, at any time in the period of its existence after the perfection of the grant, and until the dispersion of the British officials by the revolt of New Hampshire. A receiver of quit-rents was, indeed. located at Haverhill, the county seat. Possibly that department had some fiscal relations with the infant town, its settlers or proprietors. But the number of polls in Apthorp was but three, as late as 1775. Such a community would naturally be regarded as of trivial importance (even as a tax-paying institution) by a government that was trembling before the uprising of a revolution that rapidly developed force sufficient to throw off the English dominion and dismember the empire.

REPRESENTATION OF APTHORP.

The policy of the Wentworths had been to restrict representation in the Provincial assemblies. The first Provincial congress, as the revolutionary legislatures at that time were designated, met at Exeter on the 21st of July, 1774. Others followed; the second, January 25, 1775, and the third, April 21, in the same year. A fourth convened at Exeter on the 17th of May. The rolls of membership have not been preserved for all of these bodies. There is no reason to suppose, however, that any of the towns situated as far north as Apthorp were represented until the assembling of the fourth congress. In that body, Abijah Larned,* of Cockburne (now Columbia), appeared as a representative. No other town lying north of Gunthwaite (now Lisbon) was represented. This congress adopted a plan of representation for the future. According to that plan, "Apthorp, Lancaster, Northumberland, Stratford, Cockburne, Colburn. Conway. Shelburne and the towns above" were classed, with the privilege of sending one representative.

---

*For sketch of Capt. Larned, see Larned Genealogy, p. 45, by W. L. Learned. Albany, N. Y., 1882.

The president of this congress was authorized to send a precept to the selectmen of Lancaster for the purposes of an election of the representative for the class. The next congress was to meet at Exeter on the 21st day of December, 1775, and the term of office was one year. Capt. Larned was returned to that congress from the Apthorp class. The fifth congress assembled according to the proposed plan. On the 5th day of January, 1776, this congress resolved itself into a house of representatives or assembly for the Province of New Hampshire. Thus the fifth New Hampshire congress became the first New Hampshire house of representatives or assembly. This Act of January 5, moreover, was our first written state constitution and the first of any American state. Provision was made for a council, to be a separate and distinct branch of the legislature, the members of which were to be chosen by counties and not by the state at large. Grafton county had one member under the apportionment of councillors. Real estate owners were alone eligible to the office of representative.

A REBELLION WITHIN A REVOLUTION.

In its provisions concerning representation, this constitution was exceedingly distasteful to the people of Grafton county, inhabiting the Connecticut valley below Lancaster.*

---

*The grantees of these townships were for the most part from Connecticut, though a considerable number were from Massachusetts, and a few from Rhode Island. As a rule, also, the first settlers came from the locality of the grantees; so that for many years the Connecticut element in the population predominated. Under their liberal charters the settlers speedily developed a system of town government surpassing in its spirit of independence and unbridled democracy even that of its prototype, the Massachusetts and Connecticut town. Their remoteness from the seat of Provincial government at Portsmouth, the sparseness of the population and the consequent danger from the Indians, naturally led to this result, among a people already by previous training deeply imbued with the idea of local self-government. The strength of the religious sentiment and the almost universal prevalence of Congregationalism as a form of belief and of church polity, greatly intensified this sentiment and lent a powerful impulse to all its manifestations. There was scarcely a function of civil government which these fierce little republics did not essay during the first twenty years of their existence. In the very beginning of the settlements, so manifest was this spirit of republicanism, that New York used it as an argument to the home government against New Hampshire's claim to jurisdiction West of the Connecticut; representing to the Lords of Trade and Plantations that "the New England Governments are formed on Republican principles, and these principles are zealously inculcated on their youth in opposition to the principles of the Constitution of Great Britain. The government of New York, on the contrary, is established as nearly as may be, after the model of the English Constitution Can it, then, be good policy to diminish the extent of Jurisdiction in His Majesty's Province of New York, to extend the power and influence to the other " And it cannot be doubted that it was the "policy" here suggested, rather than any principle of law or equity, which made the Connecticut the boundary between the rival provinces.
Proceedings Conn. Valley Hist. Soc. 1880, p. 157.

They promptly repudiated the form of government. Here was the beginning of a civil conflict of great bitterness, and only second in importance, during the time of its continuance, to the contest for Independence.

The views of the people of this vicinity can be well ascertained from the statement which they made in explanation of their refusal to send a representative according to the precept sent for the towns of Haverhill, Bath, Lyman. Gunthwaite, Landaff and Morristown.

"At a meeting legally named, in consequence of a precept from the Assembly at Exeter, for the purpose of choosing a representative, also to give in their votes for a Counsellor for the county of *Grafton*, having refused a compliance with said precept, have chosen us, the subscribers, a committee to return the precept. together with the reasons of their non-compliance, which reasons are as follows, viz. : First, because no plan of Representation has yet been found in this state consistent with the liberties of a free people ; and it is our humble opinion, that when the Declaration of Independence took place, the Colonies were absolutely in a state of nature, and the powers of the people reverted to the people at large, and of consequence annihilated the political existence of the Assembly which then was. Secondly, because the precept directs to have a number of different towns (who have an undoubted right to act by themselves separately) unite for the purpose of choosing a Representative and Counsellor.* Thirdly, because we are limited in our choice of a Representative to a person who has a real estate of two hundred pounds, lawful money ; whereas we conceive that every elector is capable of being elected. Fourthly, because that no bill of rights has been drawn up, or form of government come into, agreeably to the minds of the people of this state, by any Assembly peculiarly chosen for the purpose, since the Colonies were declared independent of the Crown of *Great Britain*. Fifthly, because if a council is necessary. every elector ought to have a choice of each counsellor, and not to be restricted to any particular limits within this state.

---

*As a matter of fact, Col. Timothy Bedel represented at one of the sessions of the Vermont Assembly three or more of these protesting towns; but, undoubtedly, he was chosen by the different constituencies, acting individually, and not in classes.

Records of Governor and Council, Vt. Vol. 2, p. 299.

For which reasons we protest against a Counsellor being chosen in this county, as directed in the precept.

EPHRAIM WESSON, ELISHA CLEAVELAND,
JOHN YOUNG, JAMES BAILEY,
JOHN CLARK, *Committee.*

Haverhill, December 13th, 1776."

Similar protests were made by other towns in the Connecticut valley, but none was offered in the Upper Coos class.

All the protests doubtless had a common origin in a conference of representative men of the disaffected towns, held at the College Hall in Hanover, (then Dresden) in the previous July.

This dissatisfaction resulted in an open revolt of these towns from the government of New Hampshire during the period of the war. They sent representatives to conventions of the towns holding similar views, on the disputed questions, at Charlestown, Hanover, Cornish and other places. At one period they considered themselves annexed to Vermont, and were represented in her legislature. Their local concerns they managed so far as practicable in town meetings, and, as to matters whereon co-operation was required, neighboring towns associated together and acted through a representative agency called a Committee of Safety.

DIVIDED ALLEGIANCE OF APTHORP.

Apthorp must have been more or less affected by these various political movements and organizations, and its relations to them were of a peculiar character.

As a member of the Lancaster class, it was represented in the legislature of New Hampshire every year from 1775, to the adoption of a new constitution for the state in 1784.

It was also admitted to representation as an individual town in the State of Vermont, June 11, 1778. In the act of the Vermont assembly of that date it was set forth "that sixteen* towns in the north-western part of said grants have as-

---

*Dresden, the territory in which was Dartmouth College, was represented in this Vermont Assembly as a separate town, as was Hanover. Counting these as two towns, seventeen were represented.
Records of Governor and Council, Vt., Vol. 1, p. 275.

sented to a union with this state agreeably to articles mutually proposed."

Apthorp was expressly named as one of those sixteen towns, but whether it was individually represented in the Vermont Assembly, and, if so, by whom, does not appear.

This union was soon interrupted by the refusal of the Vermont Assembly to create a separate county for these and neighboring towns on this side of the river. On the 22d of February, 1781, the same union with Vermont was revived, or a similar one negotiated. Gunthwaite, Morristown (now Franconia), and Lancaster were among the towns east of the river that are said to have made returns, at this later period, according to "an Union with Vermont."*

Thus the nearest settled towns on both sides of Apthorp seem to have been in the movement at this time.†

There is abundant evidence, however, of a serious division of sentiment among the inhabitants of many of the towns, which, as political organizations, joined the union or favored separation from New Hampshire under some plan.

It may be remarked that Apthorp, in 1773, had but a total population of 14. There were but three married men in the number. In 1782, there were but nine polls reported. No larger number is given for any year of the war period. However violent, therefore, party spirit may have been in Apthorp, the factions, whether for New Hampshire, Vermont or a new state, separate from either, must have been, numerically, rather small.

There are indications that the Caswells were the New Hampshire party.

The old Captain, in times of danger, seems to have betaken himself, with his family, to the fort at Northumberland, in preference to Haverhill. His sons, as soon as their age would

---

*The towns in this part of the valley, were made part of Orange County, and they constituted a Probate District, called the Haverhill Probate District. Gen. Israel Morey of Orford, was Probate Judge, 1781-2. Slade's State Papers, Vt., 472. Records of Governor and Council, Vt., Vol. 2, p. 110.

†Justices of the Peace were appointed by Vermont authority, for Lyman and Morristown among other towns east of the river, but no record of any such appointments for Apthorp has been found.

Records of Governor and Council, Vt., Vol. 2, p. 96.

admit of it, entered the army. Col. Whipple of Dartmouth (now Jefferson) and Capt. Eames alternately represented the class in the New Hampshire House of Representatives, after Capt. Larned's second term, until 1784. So far as their conduct, as we are informed concerning it at this time, can be taken as guide for our opinion, it may be concluded that the Caswells affiliated with Eames and Whipple. These men were undoubtedly loyal to New Hampshire.

On the other hand, the classification of Apthorp with the towns north of it might have been made without reference to the preference of the inhabitants; and Capt. Caswell might have gone to Northumberland, strictly under military orders, as commander of the garrison or a scout, and not by his own choice. These things might be possible, while at the same time, as a Connecticut man, he could entertain the *New Connecticut* ideas of the rights of the towns, and, as a friend of Gen. Morey and Gen. Bailey, he could sympathize with them in their desires for the establishment of a new state, or a remodelled Vermont, which should include the Grafton towns near the river, with a seat of government in the Connecticut valley. It is not yet absolutely determined who were the other inhabitants of Apthorp at the time of nullification in the grants.

The Hopkinsons were undoubtedly here, as well as the Caswells. Though Capt. Peleg Williams came at a later date than the others mentioned, he also may have been in town early enough to aid these movements. He was from Charlestown, N. H., where the ideas of the agitators for a separation flourished to a considerable extent.

Some of our people must have co-operated with Col. Bedel of Bath, the Youngs of Gunthwaite, or other party leaders in the disaffected towns, to identify Apthorp with their schemes. The record shows very conclusively that it was effected, in a measure at least, by some means. But the annexation of this or any other town east of the river to Vermont, and the scheme of forming the state of New Connecticut from a union of the valley towns, ceased to be a practical question, after Vermont, in 1782, with the full approbation of the Continental congress, if not by some mild coercion from that quarter, finally disavowed any claim of jurisdiction beyond the west bank of the Connecticut river. So far as Apthorp's connection with the Vermont union, or a new state, was concerned, it was, at the most, hardly more than a school-girl flirtation before the age of consent.

TOWN ORGANIZATION.

The only written evidences of any municipal organization of Apthorp, that have come to light at the present day, are a paragraph in Bouton's Province and State Papers (Vol. 8, p. 868) which is as follows:—"Account Jeremiah Eames for holding town meetings in Gunthwaite and Apthorp,—paid £24," and which indicates some corporate organization and action prior to June 28, 1781, the date of the record; and a passage of Nathan Caswell's letter of June 3, 1786. He writes that " precepts have been sent to the selectmen of Apthorp." This might have been done through a mistake of the state officials, based upon a premature assumption that town officers had been chosen; but Dr. Moore suggests the probability that there were town officials who failed to preserve records of the town for want of books. It is, on the whole, a reasonable conjecture that there may have been an organization of the town before its division in 1784, which the diligence of modern investigation may hereafter conclusively determine; but the historical data available at this time does not seem to justify a positive conclusion.

APTHORP AND THE WAR.

The people of Apthorp, no doubt, did their whole duty in sustaining the cause of the colonies, and in the common defence against Canadian incursions. As has already been intimated, there were seasons when the township was abandoned and the non-combatants lodged in the forts for safety, while the fighting men ranged the futher frontiers in scouts, or fought the common enemy in the regiments of rangers, or of the line. Every house was a military out-post, and every citizen a minute man.

They forgot the controversies over the boundaries of states, and knew no parties when the work of war with a common enemy was to be performed. The pioneers of Apthorp bore far more than the common burdens of war. Savages lurked in the forest, tories intrigued in the settlements, and the armies of England hovered for seven years upon the near border, now threatening, and now invading the intervening settlements. Practically, the town remained within the scene of hostilities from the beginning to the end of the Revolution.

TAXATION IN APTHORP.

While the grants were indulging in their "futile dalliance" with secession, the New Hampshire state government was, nevertheless, prosecuting the war for independence with vigor. Taxes were laid to meet the heavy demands made upon the treasury. Of the thirty-one towns in Grafton county, assessed in 1778, Apthorp was the sixteenth in amount, and bore the proportion of £1 1s. 5 3-4d. to every £1000 of the whole tax. The proportion of Apthorp in the tax of June 27, 1780, to supply the army with beef, was 850 pounds, in a total of 73,463 pounds for the county of Grafton. The beef levy of January 27, 1781, called for an aggregate of 101,100 pounds from Grafton county and 1060 pounds from Apthorp. By the act of August 30, 1781, "for supplying the Continental army with ten thousand gallons of West India rum," Apthorp was required to raise 7 1-2 gallons. It was also provided that good New England rum might be furnished instead, in the proportion of six quarts of New England rum for one gallon West India rum. For each gallon in arrears, or undelivered, the town would forfeit one Spanish milled dollar, or other gold or silver equivalent. It is very doubtful if the town was then able to raise so much rum, even for so worthy a cause. If it be considered how slight a matter it is to raise 7 1-2 gallons of the article for any purpose at the present day, an idea may be had of the potent advances of civilization in a century of the Cohos country. In such comparisons, it may not be well to emphasize the clause of the act which required *good New England rum*, for says a modern proverbial philosopher, in eloquent apostrophe:—"Farewell, good old New England rum with some tanzy in ye. Thou hast gone! Yes, thou hast gone to that bourne from which no good spirits come back."*

It appears, from the best evidence attainable, that some, at least, of these assessments remained in arrears for many years. Capt. Caswell probably referred to rum and beef, as well as money, when, on the 3d of June, 1786, he wrote that: "The inhabitants, * * * being poor and much exposed to our enemy during said war, never paid any taxes into the treasury of said state."†

Arrearages were consequently accumulated with the customary doomage.

This condition was a source of much tribulation to the early settlers, and continued to be so for many years.

LITTLETON.

The territory of Apthorp, in 1784, so far as it had not been sold to actual settlers, was in the hands of a very few persons. They petitioned the legislature for a division of Apthorp. An act was passed, in accordance with the desires of the proprietors, on the 4th of November, 1784.

By this act, Col. Timothy Bedel was designated to call the first meeting of the new town; but before the occasion for performing this duty, he died, and, in his stead, John Young of Gunthwaite was named by a subsequent act. By his agency, the town of Littleton was organized in 1787. The other part of Apthorp took the name of Dalton.

To-day we celebrate the centennial anniversary of that event.

STATE TAXES IN LITTLETON.

The new town was harrassed by the state treasurer's demands for over-due taxes, as its predecessor, Apthorp, had

---

*Josh Billings.
†New Hampshire Town Papers, Hammond, Vol. 12, p. 425.

been. None had yet been paid for any of the years since 1776. At length, such effectual representations were made to the legislature that the relieving act of June 29, 1787, was passed. By its provisions all taxes, except the portion laid on lands, from 1776 to 1784, were abated, and those on lands were reduced one-half. The proportion of Littleton in the Apthorp arrearages was fixed at seven-twelfths. State taxes, accruing prior to the division, were to be levied in the manner first indicated, and those accruing subsequently would fall upon both real and personal estate. Distinct tax bills were to be provided for the two periods.

The extents of the treasurer were stayed until the next session of the legislature.

This act failed to give the relief sought for by the inhabitants. January 27, 1789, after more representations and petitions, and action by the town, recorded as follows in the town books:—" March ye 17th, 1788 " * * " Capt. Peleg Williams voted an agent to go to the Ginrel Court, to receive Five Dollars in Cash and twelve Bushels of wheat for his services," they procured legislation which enabled them to " assess and cause to be collected all publick taxes due therefrom, prior to the first day of January 1789, on the lands of the proprietors of said town, in one tax bill, in way and manner as taxes by law are collected of non-resident proprietors in other towns."

Another difficulty was then discovered. It was in the application of the method stated in the last clause above quoted, for Littleton was not lotted and divided as other towns had been. The legislature was informed that the unsettled part of the entire town was held in a body by the proprietary. Therefore, the inhabitants prayed for an act enabling them to assess and collect the tax due from the " town, in one tax bill, on the lands therein, not confining them to any particular rights, but to sell as much of said lands in one body as will pay the tax."

They did not obtain this request. A general law was enacted, February 22, 1794, under which, in connection with the special legislation previously obtained, they attempted to lay a tax and raise money to meet the arrears. This is the town record, of date March 10, 1795: "Voted for Mr. James Rankin, to go to General Court to settle Back Taxes."

On the petition of James Rankin, the town agent, another special act was passed, June 18, 1795, relative to these arrears of taxes, which had not yet been raised and paid to the state and county.

It provided for the reduction of the paper taxes to seven shillings specie for every twenty shillings paper. Modern politicians have not suffered this method to become a lost art. It is now termed *readjustment*. The act also provided that the extents against the town be again stayed for a limited period, and powers were given certain officials, similar to those granted by the act of February 22, 1794.

The arrearages were afterwards disposed of without any further special action by the legislature. Special acts, however, were repeatedly passed, in the few years previous to 1805, to aid the town, by way of extra taxation of proprietary and other lands, in the matter of providing highways and bridges for the accommodation of the public travel.

Otherwise, the business of municipal taxation here has generally proceeded according to the provisions of the general law.

THE STATE AND THE HIGHWAYS OF LITTLETON.

The proprietors, as the early settlers state in their petition to the legislature, promised to make good roads through the town, but had been guilty of neglect in this respect. Of course something in the nature of highways had existed, but, if ever of any considerable utility, they had, at this time, fallen into the most wretched condition. Hence the state was importuned to relieve the people by special legislation. Of the urgent necessities of the case, something may be learned from the statement of Capt. Peleg Williams, agent of the town, dated June 16, 1788. He says:—"Although it is eighteen years since the town began to settle, there is but nine families in it at this time, and there is no mills in said town, nor can we git at any under fifteen miles, the Publick Road that runs through said town is eleven miles in length, and almost Impossible to pass in the same, which road your petitioners have to travel to get to mill, to market, to courts, and almost every kind of Business, so that your petitioners have got under such poor and difficult circumstances, that we can neither live in said town, nor move out of the same, except your honors will Interpose in our behalf."

This, and like appeals, met with an efficient, but perhaps rather tardy response from the state.

The town was authorized to tax non-residents for the purpose, and a road was laid out and built by a committee, from Dalton line, passing down from North Littleton, nearly on the present route, to the vicinity of what is now the site of the old town house; thence across what is now the Elijah Fitch place, to the vicinity of the Griggs cross road, but running along the ridge of the hill, west of that road as it now is, and from thence down the Ammonoosuc valley to Gunthwaite line. A detailed plan and survey of this route is recorded in the state secretary's office at Concord.

The well known Bucknam committee were also given authority, by the act of September 26, 1786, to construct a road from the vicinity of the present White Mountain House, near Fabyan's, on the Cohos and Conway road, to Littleton and Gunthwaite.

By these measures on the part of the state, and by local co-operation, the people in a few years obtained suitable highways, whereby they could either "live in the town, or move out of the same."

Legislation followed in relation to ferries, bridges, turnpikes, canals and, later on, railways. There is not space here to particularize on these topics.

THE EARLY REPRESENTATION OF LITTLETON.

Upon the adoption of the constitution of 1784, a very large legislative class was constituted, which included all the towns north of Haverhill, and west of the mountains. The second year a division was, or had been, effected, and Littleton was associated with Bath, Landaff, Lyman, Concord and Dalton. (The compilers of the appendix to Rev. David Sutherland's historical discourse at Bath are in error on their page 98, as to the representative class.) This arrangement continued till 1793, when Lancaster, Littleton, Dartmouth and Dalton were classed. In 1800, the next change was made. Littleton, Bethlehem and Dalton being classed, and so continuing till 1808. From that year this town had the privilege of separate representation, which it has never failed to utilize. Previous to 1809, but three Littleton men had been representatives. They were James Williams, in 1794, James Rankin, in 1798, and David Goodall, who was chosen by the Littleton, Bethlehem and Dalton class, seven years in succession, beginning with the year 1800.

These were all Federalists. They served before the days of railways and complimentary railroad passes, and appear to have been almost invariably at their official posts.

It may be of interest to glance at the indications found in the legislative journals, as to their opinions and actions on public measures.

Capt. Williams was one of the majority who voted the authority to the Governor, on requisition of the President of the United States, to march the state militia into any state in the Union, but he also voted for the vigorous protest that was sent to congress, against the encroachments of the federal courts upon state rights and state court jurisdiction in the matter of *The McClary*,* a case which was famous in its day. He favored the removal of the chief justice of the state from his office, and supported John Langdon for United States Senator, against James Sheafe. He voted to ratify the amendment of the constitution of the United States, which was submitted to that legislature. The state debt was scaled down at that time, and he voted with the readjusters. The description of the condition of Littleton, and the burdens of taxation, under which it labored at this time, already given, explain the attitude of Mr. Williams on this subject.

---

*Barstow's History, N. H., p. 304.

Some of the matters that engaged the attention of Representative Rankin were perhaps of less general interest. He opposed the incorporation of a Baptist society at Northwood, and antagonized the proposed exceptions to the statute of limitations, calculated to keep alive certain stale claims. He devoted some friendly official attention to the animal kingdom, being a member of a committee to frame a deer law, and opposing the bill providing for a bounty on crows. Mr. Rankin was a rigorous Presbyterian, but believing, it may be presumed, that

> "He prayeth well, who loveth well
> Both man, and bird, and beast."

his love for the Baptists was manifested in a spirit of scriptural "chastening." He voted to sustain the President in case of war with France.

Mr. Goodall was a college graduate and a retired clergyman. He became an experienced legislator, and was often designated to act upon important committees. His repeated elections by his neighbors of the three towns attest his usefulness as a representative, and his fidelity to his constituents.

A detailed examination of the records of our later representatives in the general court might be made interesting, but it would more properly come within the domain of the town historian.

PARTY RELATIONS.

'There is very little on the town records, until the beginning of the present century, to indicate the existence of a division of the people of Littleton on state or national politics. The inhabitants were Federalists, and practically unanimous in that faith. In 1801, however, nine citizens ventured to vote for Timothy Walker, the Democratic candidate (then termed Republican), against John Taylor Gilman, who had twenty-nine votes, and, as usual, was elected in the state. In the intervening years, between this and 1805 (in which year Langdon was elected over Gilman) the Federalist majority averaged about two to one. This year Gilman, had 44, and Langdon 43. The next year, 1806, the vote stood, for Langdon 43, Gilman 40, and Jeremiah Smith 3. The next year, Langdon again obtained a majority, and in 1808, only a plurality. In the fall elections of that year, for congressmen and electors, a great advance was made in the Federal vote. It is recorded as 106 to 13, in August, and in November, as 73 to 19. The Federal candidates continued to receive similar majorities until 1820, when Samuel Bell, Democrat, received 104, the whole vote, the Federalist and Democratic candidates for councillor receiving 66 and 40 votes respectively. The Plumer electoral ticket had 29 votes, all that were cast. Governor Bell, again in 1821, obtained a unanimous endorsement—124 votes. The councillor vote at the same time was 75 to 45 in favor of the Federal candidates. In 1823, the candidates for governor, Levi Woodbury and Samuel Dinsmore, were both Democrats, and their vote here was 102 to 4 in favor of the former. At this period the Federal party appears to have become extinct, and the voters subsequently divided politically as Adams or Jackson men. The next year Governor Woodbury received a large majority over all others in this place. In the presidential election of 1824 there was no division. The Adams Republicans had the whole. In the election of 1825, the town gave Morrill (Adams candidate), 101, and Woodbury (Jackson) 2. In 1826, Morrill (A.), had 95, and Benjamin Pierce (J.) 13. Next year the figures seem to be substantially reversed, Pierce having 106, Morrill 2, Harvey 16, and two scattering. About this time the people of Littleton seem to have first seriously divided themselves as partisans of Jackson and Adams. In 1828, Bell, the Adams candidate for governor. had 107, against 70 for Pierce, who bore the Jackson standard. The Adams electoral ticket obtained 135 votes, against 83 of the Jackson party. The Adams party maintained a similar ascendancy until the presidential election of 1832, in which the Jackson ticket had 80, Clay 78, and an Anti-Masonic party, on whose ticket General David Rankin of this place appeared for elector, polled 25 votes.

It was at this period that the opposition to the Jackson Democracy assumed the party name of Whigs. That party flourished for some twenty or twenty-five years.

The next two March elections, 1833 and 1834, showed a Democratic majority. In 1835, Healey, the Whig candidate for governor, secured 96 votes, Badger, Democrat, 92, and Simeon B. Johnson, 3. The next year, Governor Hill had 95 votes, against 18 for Badger, also a Democrat, and there were five scattering. In the fall, the Democratic electors had 70 votes, a majority of 18 over the Whigs. In 1837, Governor Hill received 104 votes, all that were cast for governor. There was a party contest for town representative, in which Capt. Abbott, Whig, was elected by 13 majority.

From this time on, until 1842, there was a considerable Whig majority at every election. At the March election of that year, the Independent Democracy, of which John H. White was the gubernatorial candidate, first developed strength in town, he having 33 votes. Stevens, Whig, had 176, and Hubbard, Democrat, 131. Next year, Colby (W.) had 141, Hubbard (D.) 116, and White, 33 again. In 1844, Steele (D.) had 157, and Colby (W.), 154. In the presidential election of that year, the Democrats cast 174 votes, the Whigs 167, the Free Soil, or Liberty Party, 4, and a ticket for Edmund Carleton had one. In 1845, Steele (D.) had 160, Colby (W.), 138, and Daniel Hoit, Free Soiler, 29. At this time, Hoit had been the candidate of the Free Soil party, in five successive annual elections, but this was the first one in which he had received a vote in Littleton. The next year, 1846, and in 1847, Colby (W.) had a majority over Williams, (D.); but the balance of power laid with the Free Soil vote of 34, given each year for N. S. Berry. In 1848, he, being a general candidate for both the Whigs and the Free Soilers, had a vote here of 217, against 193 for Williams (D.). In the presidential election, the Democratic electors had 170, Whig, 155, Free Soil, 29, scattering, 3. Each year following, except 1850, until the next presidential election, the Whig ticket had a plurality over the Democrats. With the same exception, the Free Soilers held the balance of power, their vote being, in 1849, 25; in 1850, 16; in 1851, 29; and 1852 (March), 31. In 1850, the Democrats had a majority of eleven over all. The Pierce presidential ticket carried the town by a majority of 18 over all,—the Free Soil vote being 20. At the next four gubernatorial elections, the Democratic candidates had a plurality, and a majority also, except in 1855, when Baker (D.) had 206, Metcalf (American or Know Nothing), 152, Bell (W.), 73, and Fowler (F. S.), 14. The Free Soil vote for these four years averaged about 18. In 1858, Haile, the Republican candidate had 247, against 224 for Cate, Democrat. At the presidential election of 1860, the Lincoln ticket had 234, Douglas, 194, the American party, 6, Breckenridge, 5, and Pierce, 1.

At every general election from 1856 to the present time, except in 1858 (state), and 1860 (presidential), the Democratic party has had a majority in Littleton.

The first vote of the Republican party in this town was in the presidential election of 1856, when in a total poll of 480, Fremont had 238, and Buchanan 241. At the last election the total vote was 808, of which Samuel W. Hale, Republican had 394, M. V. B. Edgerly, Democrat, 412, and a Temperance ticket two.

In all the foregoing statistics of elections, reference is made to the vote for governor in this town, unless it is otherwise explicitly stated.

CONCLUSION.

During the first and larger part of the century of municipal history, which we are reviewing today, Littleton was not very near the front rank of the northern towns in political or business influence. Haverhill, Bath and Lancaster long continued to be the centres of political power, social influence and business enterprise. But of these, Lancaster alone has maintained its position. When, in 1853, the railroad found a terminus at this point, the town had never had a bank or an academy. Its first newspaper was only one year old. It had never been represented upon the benches of the inferior or superior courts of the state. It had had but one state senator, and he, as the political phrase goes, had "died a yearling." It had been represented in the executive department by one councillor for the two years of

1832 and 1833. Not one of its representatives had been so much as the candidate of either party for speaker of the house, or president of the senate. Both political parties almost invariably went elsewhere for candidates for important offices. Henry A. Bellows, who was a candidate for congress, and Nathaniel Rix, were the principal exceptions to the rule. Haverhill, Bath and Lancaster were the homes of our congressmen, governors and political leaders. In the rolls of the soldiery of the wars of 1812, and with Mexico, the name of Littleton is rarely found. Among the bold battalions that did duty at Cobleigh's Meadow, however, it cannot be said that our citizens did not accomplish eminence. Were such an assertion ventured, the melon stained swords of Gen. Rankin, Col. Moffitt, Col. Eastman, Maj. Thayer, Maj. Bellows, Maj. Brackett and Capt. Bingham, might rattle ominously in their scabbards.

There was but one church edifice; and it is intimated by the Rev. E. Irving Carpenter, in his sketch of his own, the Congregationalist church, that the people had always been rather backward in spiritual matters.*

The advent of railway communication seems to mark, approximately, the beginning of a revolution in the development of the town, and in its relations with the state at large.

An estimate of the influence that the town has acquired and exerted in the state, that would be satisfactory or approximately correct, cannot be made. Some of its elements may be pointed out and briefly considered.

The constantly increasing variety of commodities produced or consumed in our midst, the improved facilities for transportation and communication, the constant interchange of ideas through the public prints, the diversification of employments, the changes in the constituents of population, and in the habits, interests, necessities and notions of the people, have wrought a revolution in the relations of this town and the commonwealth, within the century now ended.

Each of the church organizations, each of the so-called

---

*N. H. Churches, p. 556.

secret societies, the societies for the promotion of temperance and morality, some of the principal branches of trade and labor, the learned professions, the veterans of the war, the Patrons of Husbandry, now severally constitute, in the town, organized sections of state organizations of the same activities. Delegates periodically meet in council.

The interests of the town are represented in the deliberations as to the greatest interest of the whole. The influence of the town is not lost, but is combined, and the aggregate is made effective. Local interests and energies are thus federalized. All these organizations, gathering strength from all directions, and employing it in all the avenues in which it may be effective, are rendering the relations of the municipalities and the state exceedingly complex and difficult of analysis.

Other forces in our midst are even more systematically and effectively organized upon a similar basis.

This is an age of caucus government. We have come to look, in the main, to party organizations for the men and measures that give vitality and character to the political policy of the state. The policy of the party that is in the ascendancy is not altogether, or indeed very largely, a matter of its own deliberate choice. It is governed in no slight degree by the strength and character of the opposition.

Viewing the important political movements of the past thirty years with reference to these considerations, it will be observed that this town has not been without influence in the politics and statesmanship of New Hampshire in the period in question; and that this influence has been constant and unwavering. It is for others to consider it in comparison with that of other communities. It may, however, be asserted here, with propriety and truth, that at least in a third part of the century under review the town has been actively, continuously and prominently represented in political controversy and party councils, and the history of the political parties of that period is, in no small degree, the history of men of Littleton.

More especially for twenty-five years just passed, the town has given to the service of the state, as a part of its representation, men of prominent ability. While many other constituencies have been represented hardly more than in name, here somebody has been advanced, and kept at the front, under a rule that finds availability in experience and capacity for leadership. There has been no hesitancy in ignoring that doctrine of rotation in office which would supplant experience and fitness, by the advancement of inexperienced mediocrity.

By these means the relations of the town to political movements and organizations, to measures and matters that have demanded consideration in administrative, judicial and legislative stations, have been rendered worthy of attention. As to this point, the public records of the state, the columns of the contemporary press and current history, yield evidence that is abundant and suggestive.

In the general jurisprudence of the state, influences have emanated from this place, and had an effect which is recognized by all who are familiar with the subject. From the bar of Littleton, Bellows, Rand and Bingham have gone upon the bench. The influence of these, and their brethren who have long been known and felt in the deliberations of legislatures, or in the contests of the courts, will be a part of the theme of another on this occasion.

Almost the whole body of the case law, now recognized and embodied in the sixty volumes of New Hampshire court reports, has grown up in the time of these men; and in the growth of that system of law, their brain work is interwoven for all time.

The great corporations of the state have arisen in the period over which the professional careers of the oldest and ablest of our own jurists extend. Under their official or professional scrutiny, has passed much of the most important legislation, granting powers and privileges to, or restraining those great institutions. An important portion of it has emanated directly from them, or has been moulded by their judgment, counsel and criticism, or has felt the impress of their opposition or advocacy.

In innumerable other directions the town has borne honorable relations with its state. It is impossible to follow the subject further, even within its most accessible limits.

In a vast number of business enterprises our citizens have put forth energies to the advantage of their fellows. They have made the forests and mountain scenery, the rugged farms and the mountain waterfalls, pay rich tribute to the industry and capital of the state. They have borne well their part in the public burdens of peace and of war.

While the town has thus contributed to the strength and integrity of the state, the state has protected the town in peace, prosperity and security.

As a member of a republic of towns, and as a local democracy of the old New England type, the lot of this town has been equally fortunate.

It stands, at the conclusion of a hundred years of hard and often doubtful struggle, in the fair prospect of a future which shall be no less creditable to itself, and no less useful to the state, than has been its past.

THE PIONEER SETTLERS OF LITTLETON.

ADDRESS BY JAS. R. JACKSON.

The President said: Littleton has a history, all of which has not yet been written. It has also a historian who will perfect it if he continues in well doing. It is my pleasure to introduce to you, Mr. James R. Jackson, whose subject is The Pioneer Settlers of Littleton.

ADDRESS.

Mr. President, Ladies and Gentlemen:

The Pioneer is the advance guard of civilization. In every age he has gone forth with firm and steadfast steps, bearing the banner of the approaching host, and planting it in regions never before marked by the footprints of his race.

The elemental characteristics of the pioneer have been the same since the pages of history were first emblazoned with the record of his heroic deeds. Possessing a bravery that knows no fear; a fortitude, unbending amidst the greatest calamities; a perseverance, before which every obstacle goes down, like a blade of grass in the path of the rushing torrent; self-sacrificing to the last degree, and impatient of the restraints imposed by law, his nomadic spirit has hovered about the border land which separates the today from yesterday; moving on, only as the rising tide of progress invades his rude domain.

The men and women, who laid the enduring foundations of our prosperous town, possessed these traits in a marked degree. Many of the men were fresh from fields made glorious by the conflicts of the Revolution, and bore on their persons scars, which were silent but eloquent witnesses to their valor. In the severe school, incident to the life of the soldier, they acquired a training, both mental and physical, well calculated to enable them to encounter successfully the countless difficulties of frontier life.

The territory, comprised within the limits of the town of Littleton, once constituted a portion of the hunting ground of the St. Francis tribe of Indians. Its forests furnished an abundant supply of such game as the Redman sought for mercantile purposes, and its streams were alive with trout. Two trails crossed its border, one along the bank of the Connecticut, the other following the course of the Ammonoosuc.

Up to the time of the settlement of Lancaster, in 1763, it is probable that but two parties of white men had ever passed within the limits of the town. In June, 1754, Capt. Peter Powers of Hollis, with his company, marched to the Upper Coos, by order of Gov. Wentworth, to ascertain whether the French had built a fort at that point. Again, in the autumn of 1759, the fragmentary remains of the ill-starred expedition, which, under the command of Major Rogers, had destroyed the village of St. Francis, and slaughtered more than two hundred Indian braves, came straggling, in a famished, half crazed and perishing condition, along the banks of the sparkling Connecticut, paying little heed to the wealth of golden glory that crowned the unbroken forest, through which they picked their slow and toilsome way. Not many of those, who but a few months before had gone forth full of ardor and hope, lived to return to their homes. Their remains were scattered through the pathless forest, from Lake Memphremagog to the mouth of the Ammonoosuc ; and, years afterwards, the whitening bones of some of these brave men were found where, exhausted and discouraged, they had lain down to die.

JAMES AVERY,

The leading proprietor of Chiswick, was of Norwich, Conn. He seems to have been a land speculator. He held an interest in the charters of several towns in Grafton county. There is no evidence, that I have seen, that he ever took an active part in the settlement of any of them. His method appears to have been to buy up the interest of his associate proprietors and then dispose of the whole to the best customer. In this way, he secured and sold the territory described in the charter of Chiswick, March 13th, 1769, to "Israel Morey of Orford, in the Province of New Hampshire; Moses Little of Newbury, in the County of Essex and Province of Massachusetts Bay, gentleman; and Moses Little of Newburyport, in the same County and Province, merchant, for one hundred pounds, lawful money." All that Avery ever did towards the settlement of the town was to erect, or cause to be erected, a log barn on the meadows, on the farm now owned by Noah Farr. The barn was probably situated east of the road, as it now runs, and a little north of Mr. Farr's house. In it, was placed a quantity of wild grass, gathered from the intervale. Dr. Moore says this barn was built in the summer of 1769. I think he mistook the date. Avery would not have been likely to build such a structure in Chiswick after he had disposed of his interest in the town. It is more probable that it was erected in the summer of 1768, at a time when Avery possessed a lively interest in the territory. Under the terms imposed in his charter, it was soon to expire by reason of non-settlement, and he was forced to active measures to protect his interest. He accordingly built the barn with a view of beginning a settlement the following year, unless he should sooner dispose of his title.

THE NEW PROPRIETORS.

The new proprietors were men of great force of character and large business capacity. Col. Morey, for many years, shared with Col. Hurd of Haverhill the honor of being the most prominent and influential citizen in the northern part of the Province. He was very active during the Revolutionary war in protecting this section from hostile Indians, and was frequently entrusted with the execution of important trusts by the Provincial Government. Moses Little of Newburyport was a merchant of large wealth, high character and great public spirit. Moses Little of Newbury, Mass., was a cousin of the former, and was, for more than fifty years, one of the leading citizens of Essex county. Though more than fifty years of age at the beginning of hostilities with Great Britain, he joined the army with the rank of Colonel, and led his regiment with marked gallantry from the engagement at Bunker Hill to that at Princeton, when declining health compelled him to resign his commission.

The new proprietors of Chiswick did not succeed in keeping their charter alive, but they had sufficient influence with Gov. Wentworth and his council to procure a new grant in January, 1770. In the new charter they gave the town the name of Apthorp, in honor of George Apthorp, a London merchant, who was one of the grantees.

NATHAN CASWELL.

The first pioneer was Nathan Caswell. Mr. Caswell was of English descent, and was probably born in Norwich, Conn., in 1740. He was a tailor by trade. Following the custom of the time, he was undoubtedly apprenticed when a youth, and must have served his full term of seven years, as we find him subsequently describing himself as a journeyman tailor. At the age of twenty he married Hannah Bingham (who was probably a kinswoman of the president of the day). After their marriage, they resided for a short time in Hebron, Conn., and in 1765, accompanied Col. Israel Morey to Orford, of which town they were among the first settlers. When Col. Morey became interested with the Messrs. Little in the proprietorship of Apthorp, arrangements were at once made for its settlement and Nathan Caswell induced to become the pioneer in the work. Accordingly, in April, 1770, he left his home in Orford, with his wife and four sons, Nathan, Jr., Ozias, Ezra and Andrew, aged respectively, eight, six, four and two years. The journey must have been a hazardous one. There could not have been anything more than an obscure trail from Bath to the log barn on yonder meadow. How this journey was made is not known. It is likely, however, that Mrs. Caswell and two or three of the children rode on horseback as far as Gunthwaite (now Lisbon), while Mr.

Caswell and the eldest son made their way on foot. From the fort in Gunthwaite, which was situated on high ground, just this side of the Salmon Hole, they must have completed the journey on foot.

On the eleventh of April they reached the barn. Seldom, I think, have travelers, footsore and weary, found a more inviting or luxurious couch than was the bed of wild grass to these wanderers. Their rest was brief, and their joy soon turned to fear by the discovery of traces of hostile Indians in the vicinity of their new home.

Few scenes have transpired in border life of more thrilling interest than that which took place during the first night of the settlement of Apthorp. The barn stood in the midst of a magnificent grove of stately pines; a little further up, on rising ground, the birch, oak and maple mingled their leafless branches. The solemn stillness of the night was broken only by nature's voice; no axe was struck, no fire kindled; quietly the mother arranged the bed for her young boys, and then sought repose, but it came not; anxiously she watched the restful slumber of her children, fearing they might make an outcry that would reach the ears of the enemy. The husband, gun in hand, guarded the open door. When morning dawned, another son had been added to the family of this brave couple. In honor of the town, the first white child born within its limits was given the name of Apthorp.

On the following day fresh traces of Indians were found, and Mr. Caswell concluded to seek safety within the friendly walls of the fort. A dugout was hastily prepared, and in it the family floated down the Ammonoosuc to the Salmon Hole. Returning in a few days they found their barn burnt to the ground. A log cabin was soon built, and in this rude hut they made their home during the next ten or twelve years.

When the war of Independence broke out, Capt. Caswell hastened to join the rangers, then having their headquarters at the fort in Northumberland, leaving his household to the care of young Nathan, not then fourteen years old. The rangers were organized to protect the frontier from incursions from hostile Indians. Capt. Caswell served irregularly with this force during the war, and his family frequently sought protection within the forts.

His sons, Nathan, Jr., and Ozias, before they were fifteen years of age, were regularly enlisted, one in the company of Capt. Samuel Young, the other under Capt. Luther Richardson of Col. Bedel's regiment. Both re-enlisted at the expiration of their first term of service and followed the fortunes of the regiment until the close of the war.

When peace was assured to the settlement, the lands in this vicinity began to attract attention, and a marked increase in the population was the result. To one of the new comers, Ephriam Bailey, son of Gen. Jacob Bailey of Newbury, Capt. Caswell sold his interest in the meadow farm, and located on the place now known as the Adams farm, on the Connecticut river. Here he continued to reside until 1791, when he moved to Concord, Vt., and, for several years, made his home with his son Apthorp. He frequently returned here, however, and his name is found on the tax list as late as 1803. About this time, he joined his son Nathan, Jr., at Stratford, with whom he lived a few years, when he went to Canada, and there, with his children, passed the remainder of his days.

Capt. Caswell was well educated and a man of influence in his day and generation. From the organization of the town, he held office for nearly the entire period of his residence here. He was, at different times, Moderator, Town Clerk, Highway Surveyor and Selectman, the only positions then within the gift of his fellow citizens. To Mr. and Mrs. Caswell were born fourteen children, ten of whom were natives of this town. Charlotte, born April 20th, 1778, died on the same day, and her remains lie buried on the Farr farm, a place consecrated by the first birth and the first death within the limits of Littleton. Of the surviving children, all lived to be more than eighty years of age, and each left a numerous progeny. Capt. Caswell was a man of medium height, light complexion, of active habits, and jovial disposition. He is said to have possessed a large fund of information, and to have been a delightful companion. He died at Compton,

Canada, in the spring of 1824, aged 84 years. His wife died in Brompton, and her remains are buried there, some twenty-six miles distant from those of her husband.

Of the children born in this town, time will permit but brief mention. Apthorp married before reaching his majority, and settled on a farm at West Concord, Vt., where he lived until 1795, when, with many others from this section, he went to Canada. He possessed many of his father's traits, and his roving disposition kept him poor. He died in 1858, at the advanced age of 88 years. He reared a family of six children. One of them, Erastus, to whom I am indebted for information concerning the family, died a year since, aged 82 years. He was a man of high character and much respected in the community where he passed his life. John, born in 1772, died in Canada; Jedediah lived in Lisbon, and was, I think, the grandfather of Alvah Caswell of Concord, Vt. Daniel lived for a while in Canada, and then moved to Lyndon, Vt., where he passed the last years of his life. Elizabeth married Samuel Bishop, then of Brompton, P. Q. They subsequently moved to Landaff, where the wife died. They had thirteen children, one of whom was the late Russell M. Bishop of this town. Alice, the youngest of the Captain's children, born in 1790, married Samuel Pierce of Compton, P. Q. A singular parallel runs between this daughter and her mother. Each had fourteen children, both lost one in infancy, and the others lived to rear children of their own. Of the other children, little information is attainable other than that they married, had numerous children, and lived beyond the limit prescribed by the Psalmist. Two of these, early, went west, which means, probably, that they emigrated to central or western New York.

THE HOPKINSONS.

In 1773 the Caswells were joined by the Hopkinsons, who settled on the meadows at North Littleton, and though seven or eight miles distant, were probably regarded as near neighbors. Of this family little is positively known. There is no record which reveals whence they came, or whither they went. The head of the family was Jonathan Hopkinson, and there is evidence extant which shows that he had four sons, Jonathan Jr., David, Caleb and John. At the time of their coming here, the eldest son was near his majority. The census of 1775 gives but three polls then resident in town, and they were undoubtedly Capt. Caswell, Jonathan Hopkinson and Jonathan, Jr. If this census may be taken as a guide, another son was old enough to do military duty in 1776, and the other a year later, as the number returned for service in the first named year was four, and there were five in 1777. The family probably came from Rhode Island, and settled on the farm now known as the Cleasby place. Subsequently, as the sons came of age, one settled on the Parker Cushman farm, and another on the Rix place. They abandoned their improvements on these places, near the close of the war of the Revolution, and undoubtedly went to Lancaster, and Lunenburgh, Vt., where they found the soil of a more promising character. Caleb married a daughter of Capt. Peleg Williams, and remained here to harass his pugnacious father-in-law until 1786. It would not be historically safe to assert that the Hopkinsons of Coos county are descendants of Jonathan, Sr., but the probabilities all point in that direction.

THE PIONEERS IN THE WAR OF THE REVOLUTION.

During the decade extending from 1770 to 1780, the population of our town did not at any time exceed twenty souls. In the Caswell family there were ten persons, and in that of the Hopkinsons, seven or eight at the close of this period.

The record made by these isolated pioneers, in the struggle for independence, is remarkable. When the first note of alarm reached the settlement, Capt. Caswell left his family under the care of his boys, the eldest being little more than fifteen years of age, and hastened to join the patriots assembled at Northumberland for the protection of the frontier. He remained in the service until the close of the contest, chiefly as a scout, and was frequently honored by his compatriots with positions of responsibility. The services rendered by his sons, Nathan, Jr., and Ozias, have been referred to.

They were bearing a soldier's burdens long before attaining the age required for military duty. The Hopkinsons, too, with patriotic ardor, were early in the service, doing duty for a time along the Connecticut in Coos county, and, in 1778, we find them enrolled in Capt. Richardson's company, of Col. Bedel's regiment, Jonathan, Jr., holding the position of first sergeant, while his father and brothers, David, Caleb and John, ranked as privates. They followed the varying fortunes of the army until their regiment was disbanded. Thus we find the infant settlement, with but three men subject to military service, sending to the field with them five boys, who served through the weary contest with credit. We may refer to this record with patriotic pride, and challenge the land to equal it. Others surpassed it in brilliancy of achievement, in enduring service, and in the sacrifices which enroll the names of their citizens with those who gave their lives for liberty, but what other gave so much of its living possessions to the cause for which they struggled?

PELEG WILLIAMS.

Capt. Peleg Williams became a citizen of Apthorp in 1781. He purchased the improvements of the Hopkinson who began on the Cleasby place. He was born in Rhode Island, the land of Roger Williams and the Quakers, but there was little in his character indicating that he was a descendant of the founder of that state, or belonged to his mild sect, for if there was anything he seems to have thoroughly detested it was peace. He had been a soldier in the French and Indian war, and the beginning of hostilities, in 1775, found him a resident of Charlestown. He enlisted and joined the army at Winter Hill, and in November, of the following year, was commissioned first lieutenant in Stark's regiment; but in 1780, we find him commanding a company in the first regiment, commanded by Col. Cilley. Failing health compelled him to leave the service soon after. When he left his native state, his wife, son and daughter remained behind. He was accompanied to Apthorp by Sarah Wheeler, a tall, raw-boned, muscular female, who claimed to be his wife. She was certainly the one thing he seems to have feared. After the captain's death, in the spring of 1821, she succeeded in securing a widow's pension. Capt. Williams at once took an active part in the affairs of the township, and was for twenty years its leading citizen. He was one of the first selectmen of the town, its first treasurer, and its agent to secure an abatement of taxes assessed against the town by the state.

Soon after his arrival, the wife and children, whom he had abandoned years before in Rhode Island, came to town. The son, Providence, settled near the Gilman Wheeler place, and the daughter married Caleb Hopkinson. There was no love lost between the families of wife number one and that of wife number two. The Captain and his son-in-law were in a chronic state of warfare. They destroyed each others crops, burned buildings, and poisoned cattle. One of the results of this condition of affairs was to lodge the Captain in the jail at Haverhill. He did not remain long, and soon after his release went to Charlestown, where he resided two or three years. During his absence, Providence and his mother emigrated to Canada, and Hopkinson also left town.

Sarah Wheeler, during these troublesome times, remained in possession of the property. Her daughter Peggy married a Frenchman by the name of Duclarette, and the fighting character of the family was well sustained by the old lady and her son-in-law. She lived to be nearly a century old, and when ninety-four, was so vigorous that she made a journey to Canada and return, on foot.

Capt. Williams was of slight build and light complexion, domineering in manner, a brave soldier and strict disciplinarian. He seems never to have learned to govern himself, and could not easily brook the commands of his superiors or the restraints of law, a condition of temperament which probably led to his leaving the army before the close of the war. His education was above the average of the time, and he had a wide experience in public affairs. He possessed great force of character, a vigorous intellect, and a will that might break but would never bend.

ROBERT CHARLTON.

With Capt. Williams, there came to Apthorp a young man, about twenty-five years of age, whose character was in marked contrast to his own. Robert Charlton was a lover of peace and order, a respecter of law, a refined and scholarly gentleman, a sincere and devout Christian. He was born in England, and, when a mere youth found his way to Nova Scotia, whence he drifted to Rhode Island. Here he formed the acquaintance of Capt. Williams, and each admiring in the other those traits of character wanting in his own, a firm and lasting friendship was formed. Together they went to Charlestown, but when the war broke out, Mr. Charlton, while sympathizing with the Colonies, was restrained by a sense of his loyalty to the mother country from taking part in the conflict. In 1779 he was for a time a teacher in Haverhill, and also pursued that profession to some extent after he became a resident of this town. He was a surveyor, and a considerable portion of the west part of the town was surveyed and lotted by him. He was our first town clerk, and held the position for twelve years. His penmanship was of the old fashioned copper plate style, as legible as print; in beauty and minuteness, his records have not been equaled by any of his successors. He frequently served as moderator and as a member of the board of selectmen, and was treasurer in 1797. When the first church, the Congregational, was organized, he was chosen one of its deacons, and served in that capacity to the time of his death. Mr. Charlton first located upon what is now known as the Howard place, at West Littleton. He married Keziah Powers of Bath, and was the grandfather of the late John M. Charlton, Esq. He died, November 22, 1843, having been a citizen of our town more than sixty-two years, during which time he was honored and respected by all who knew him.

THOMAS MINER.

Thomas Miner was born in Groton, Conn., January 14, 1735. He came to Littleton in 1786, and made the first clearing on the farm now owned by Curtis L. Albee, Esq. Before coming here, he had lived in Woodstock and Lunenburgh, Vt., and at Haverhill, N. H. Both he and his son Isaac were Revolutionary soldiers. Mr. Miner was prominent in the affairs of the town, and was moderator of the first meeting at which that officer was elected by the votes of the people. John Young, who served in that capacity when the town was organized in 1787, was authorized to preside by act of the General Court. Capt. Miner (they seem to have all held that title in those early days) was a deeply religious man, and was active in establishing public worship. The first meetings were generally held at his house. When a minister was secured, his time was divided between the north and west parts of the town, alternately at the house of Capt. Miner and James Williams. Mr. Miner married Desire, daughter of Avery Dennison of Groton, Conn. She was a cousin of the principal grantee of Chiswick. They reared a large family. Isaac settled on the Moffett place; a daughter married Sargent Currier, the first constable of the town, and lived for a time at the north end, and subsequently on the Steere place. William lived in Lyman, and there the old captain went, in 1806, to pass his remaining days. He died in May, 1810. Many of his descendants reside in this and neighboring towns.

JAMES RANKIN.

One of the pioneers, and the first to leave an enduring impress on the business prosperity of the town, was James Rankin, who emigrated from Scotland. He first settled in Thornton, but came here in 1791. He purchased of Moses Little the mills on what is still known as the Rankin Brook, together with seven hundred acres of land, situated in that vicinity, which he divided equally among his six sons and a daughter, who was the wife of Nathaniel Webster. Mr. Rankin possessed the characteristics of his race. He was sturdy, mentally and physically, frugal, industrious and honest. He was repeatedly honored by his townsmen with positions of trust. He was treasurer of the town as early as 1794, agent to the General Court, moderator six times, and chairman of the board of selectmen in '95. One who knew him well describes Mr. Rankin as a "strict Presbyterian, gifted in prayer, and who often officiated at funerals and public religious meetings." His son-in-law, Webster, is said by the same authority to have been "a good reader, who frequently read a sermon." I might dwell at length upon the character and achievements of this noble man, but I should anticipate those who are to follow me. He died in 1802, and his remains lie buried in the cemetery near his mill, in a grave unmarked and almost unknown.

JAMES WILLIAMS.

After the close of the war, the population increased rapidly, and, in 1790, a postoffice was established. James Williams was made postmaster, and the office was at his house, at the north end, on the farm still called the Williams place. Mr. Williams came here from Cheshire county in 1789. We find him a member of the board of selectmen in 1792, and from that date to the time of his death his name appears more frequently in the records than that of any other citizen. He held nearly all the offices within the gift of his townspeople and was their adviser in business matters. He was a man of capacity, sound judgment and unquestioned honor. He reared a large family of children, all of whom were born in town. The sons engaged in business elsewhere, and all acquired very considerable fortunes.

CONCLUSION.

I had proposed to speak of the Rev. David Goodall and the mad pranks of his boys, Solomon, Ira and David, as they constitute a part of the unwritten history of our town; of Luke Hitchcock; of John Chase; of the Nurses, John and Jonas; of Jonathan Eastman; Joseph W. Morse; Ephriam Bailey; the Leonards; David Lindsey, our first justice of the peace; of Pingree; the Palmers; Albee; the Farrs and others, who are entitled to the honor of position among the pioneers, but the time allotted will not permit me to do so.

The pioneers found our town a wilderness. The first decade saw but little change in the surface. The few resolute men, who had cast their lot within our borders, had to contend with all the hardships and privations incident to border life, while the war soon threw across their pathway a savage and relentless foe that harassed them for seven long years, and often compelled them to abandon, for a time, their primitive homes. When peace at length came to the weary country their numbers rapidly increased, and the town was soon dotted with clearings.

The proprietors neglected the interests of the settlers, and, it has been charged, violated the contracts with them. For more than ten years they had no roads, mills, shops or stores. As late as 1798, the nearest blacksmith was at Bethlehem. For years they carried their wheat and corn, often on their backs, to Haverhill, and afterward to Bath, where the nearest mills were successively located. Their roads, if they may be called such, were little better than paths through the wilderness, and in winter, were often impassable for weeks, owing to the great depth of snow. In 1786, Thomas Miner, with some of the women of his household, went to Lyman on an ox sled. While they were absent the snow fell to such a depth that he could not get his team home until the following spring, and he had to draw the hay, by which they were kept alive, on a handsled. Tea and coffee were luxuries seldom or never indulged in ; the mothers and daughter spun the yarn from the roll, wove the cloth (and good honest cloth it was), cut and made the clothes for the family. They attended divine service at some hospitable house, or barn, and in winter sat through a two hours sermon without a fire, often when the temperature was several degrees below zero. They had but one mail a week until after 1810. The postman carried this on horseback, and was due here on Saturday morning. Once a storm caused a delay, and Mr. Prescott, the postman, did not succeed in reaching town until Sunday morning. He delivered his newspapers as he rode along, and tossed into the door of one of our prominent citizens a paper. It was the only one received, and furnished news for the neighborhood, but the good wife could not touch it after it had been contaminated by a Sunday delivery, so lifting it with the tongs, she dropped ti into the capacious fireplace, and the outside world, for that week, was a blank to the people of West Littleton. The woman who did this was the wife of James Rankin, the Scotch Presbyterian.

From these small beginnings of a century ago have we grown! Our progress has been sometimes slow, but never obscure or doubtful, and, today, in population, in business, in enterprise and in promise for the future, we are in advance of all other towns in northern New Hampshire. Verily " the stone that the builders rejected has become the head of the corner."

THE RELATIONS OF LITTLETON AND BETHLEHEM.

ADDRESS BY HON. JOHN G. SINCLAIR.

The President said: A little fun now and then never harms the best of men; and I have yet to learn that it is disagreeable to women. We have present, one whose bubbling wit, and eloquent appeals, can electrify as lightning from the clouds above.

We have all known him in days past. He has lived in Bethlehem; he has lived in Littleton. He was known then as "The Barnstead Boy." He is the Hon. John G. Sinclair of Florida, whose subject is The Relations of Littleton and Bethlehem.

ADDRESS.

MR. PRESIDENT AND LADIES AND GENTLEMEN:

I am extremely afraid that the war will not come up to the manifesto of my friend here who has given me this introduction. In our National House of Representatives, once, when a member was making a long, labored and uninteresting speech, and when a large part of the members had fallen asleep, and the others were giving but little or no attention, the man who was speaking became offended, and asserted that he cared not for the attention of that House of Representatives, for he was speaking to posterity. At once John Randolph came to his feet, and in his shrill tenor voice exclaimed, "Mr. Speaker, if the gentleman continues his remarks to much greater length, he may have his audience before him." [Laughter.] And when I read this programme, and see the long list of honored names which have been assigned as speakers here, today, and consider that if from the abundance of our hearts our mouths shall speak, we may be in danger of finding ourselves in the same dilemma. I propose to be brief. For what, my friends, could we do with posterity, when the woods are so full of the present generation?

I have been assigned to speak of the relations of Littleton and Bethlehem. The connection of these towns has been so close, and their commercial, political and social relations so intimate, that I find myself situated some like Artemas Ward, who, having closely and minutely examined the Siamese twins, and ascertained that the tie by which they were bound was pure flesh, and that the blood from one circulated through this tie to the veins of the other, drew himself up with a profound air and exclaimed, "They are brothers, I think." [Laughter.] As it was hard for him at that time to determine where Chang ended and Eng begun, so it is hard for me today to determine, having been a resident of both of these towns, where Littleton ends and Bethlehem begins. My friend Batchellor has told you that these two towns were from 1800 to 1808 classed for the choice of representatives. And in view of certain recent political events here in the town of Littleton, I understand that there are a large number of its inhabitants, including my old friend, Dinnis Murphy, who propose to petition the legislature, at its next session, to class the two towns again. [Laughter.] Littleton has furnished Bethlehem largely, in years gone by, with dry goods, groceries, law and physic. And Bethlehem in return has given to Littleton—let me see—what? Lumber, wood, potatoes, squash, pumpkins and members of the state legislature. [Renewed laughter.] Burnham, Barrett, Hale, Sinclair, Sinclair, Jr., and last, but not least, a gentleman, who, in addition to legal and legislative service, although a *Batchellor* now and always, has managed to give the town of Littleton a bouncing Democratic boy. [Laughter and applause.] Speaking of Democratic representatives furnished by the town of Bethlehem, a sly twinkle in the eye of my Republican friends, and the somewhat elongated visages of my Democratic friends, would seem to indicate that it would be well for them to send out for more, as in view of that severe frost which recently struck the

Democracy here, the market is about bare. But let us rejoice, my Democratic friends, that the great leader of the Democracy of Littleton, when that frost struck here, was with me in Florida, safely below damaging frost line, and I advise my Republican friends here to keep an eye to the windward, or the "old Harry" may be to pay with them yet. [Laughter and cheers.] We have in Florida a land agent, who a while ago sold a stranger, unseen, forty acres of land, which he represented to be first-class high pine. The gentleman, soon after going down that way, asked the agent if he would show it to him. He proceeded to do so. And when they had reached it, instead of the gigantic high pine which the gentleman had expected to see, he found the land covered with gnarly black-jack oak. Turning to the agent, he said, "How is this? you represented this land to be first quality high pine, I find it nothing but scrub." "Yes," said the agent, "but did you ever see any such good scrub before?" So when I come back here and find the Democratic kettle bottom up, and am told that the Republicans have got control of the whole sap-works, I exclaim, "Yes, but did you ever see such good Republicans any where else?" [Loud applause.]

But to be serious, my friends, I rejoice to be with you here today. Since I struck the state of New Hampshire, I have seen nowhere such evidences of thrift as I see here in the old towns of Littleton and Bethlehem. You have erected magnificent edifices. You have dotted your hills, since I left you, with neat and comfortable cottages. You have seized upon the water which comes leaping from yonder hills and compelled it to turn the wheels of a business which sends its manufactured goods to every state and territory of this Union. You have added to the ties which connect Littleton and Bethlehem. You have laid the rails over which the engine now takes the goods from your stores, and transports them to Bethlehem heights, and returns to you their products. And, as my friend Jackson was speaking of the pioneers of this town, I thought what would have been the emotions of those pioneers if there had burst upon their view an engine coursing up the valley of the Ammonoosuc! What would they have thought in their day? They might well have believed they had seen him whose food was fire, and the breath of whose nostrils was smoke. And if they had been told that a whisper breathed upon Lloyd Hills would be distinctly heard, in the future, at Apthorp, what would have been their answer? And yet all this has been realized.

And while these things have been accomplished by the indomitable energy of your business men here, I mark, today, that death has been busy. Many a manly form has been laid low. Many a warm heart has ceased to beat, since I left. I miss here, today, one whose manly form was wont to grace such assemblies as this. One of whom it may well be said:

> "That never King did subject hold,
> In speech more free, in war more bold,
> More tender and more true."

One whom the people of Bethlehem, with the people of Littleton alike, delighted to honor, one whose empty sleeve attested that he had sealed his devotion to his country with his blood.

And, sir, when that fated bullet sped, boys from Littleton, and boys from Bethlehem, exposed with him their breasts to the iron hail and leaden rain which swept across that bloody field of Williamsburg; and on many another hard fought field, the sons of Bethlehem and the sons of Littleton, shoulder to shoulder, side by side, mingled their blood and offered up their lives. And now, sir, on Decoration Day, the veterans of Littleton do not deem their duty to have been discharged until they have strewn flowers upon, and erected the stars and stripes above the graves of the honored dead of Bethlehem. Can ties like these be broken? Never.

Although you have not the golden wheat fields of the West, nor the white cotton fields of the South, nor the mines of the Pacific states, yet you have in yonder mountains a source of wealth; and standing here you can exclaim—

> "It is a bold and bare land,
> A rough and rude and rare land,
> A loyal, true and fair land,
> This mountain land of ours."

and proudly add, it produces men.

May God grant that the friendly relations, which have so long existed between Littleton and Bethlehem, may continue to exist until the last shock of time shall have leveled yonder mountains to their bases.

[Enthusiastic and repeated applause.]

THE RELATIONS OF LITTLETON AND VERMONT.

ADDRESS BY FRANK J. EASTMAN.

The President said: The gentleman who was to respond to the next subject, The Relations of Littleton and Vermont, is necessarily absent. It is understood that Mr. Frank J. Eastman, a native of Vermont, a former resident of Littleton, will supply the place, and his paper will appear in the report of these proceedings.

ADDRESS.

MR. PRESIDENT:

The Colonial maps of New England essentially fail to describe the present boundaries of Vermont. Gloucester, Charlotte and Cumberland counties comprised the general divisions of her territory. Waterford had borne the names of Dunmore and Littleton before adopting its present style. Concord was known as Kersboro, and the state itself is laid down on some maps as New Connecticut. On the east shore, the present Littleton has at different times been called Chiswick, then Apthorp; and Lisbon once responded to the unmusical cognomen of Gunthwaite. It is to be noticed that the same stream sported a pair of Littletons, one on each of its banks. The Vermont Littleton was chartered, November 7th, 1780, and continued to bear that title till 1797.

The New Hampshire Littleton was changed from Apthorp in 1784. Thus the two Littletons for 13 years had a cotemporary existence, separated by an imaginary line at the point of low water.

Since then, a century of years have been added to the past, and generations have lived and died within the borders of the present Littleton. What instrumentalities have had the power to work the mighty changes visible on every side? Civilization, with all it implies, has usurped the province of the wilderness.

What share of the vast accomplishment goes to the credit of Vermont in its contribution of men and women, its capital and enterprise, is the purpose of this paper to indicate. A delineation of character sufficiently true to be recognized, a brief epitome of individual achievements in any respect influencing the standing, or that may have been tributary to its fame as a town, will be attempted.

The completion of one hundred years in the life of an individual, or in the corporate existence of a town, suggests a proper observance of the epoch and the planting of a memorial milestone, which shall commemorate the event. It is eminently proper to snatch from forgetfulness the unwritten annals of the past and present at such times, and leave as heirlooms for the posterity of coming centuries the records of the era, whether humble or exalted.

The hardships of the pioneer comprised the discipline which originated his love of liberty and independence. Divest the present of those surroundings, which their toil and endurance made possible, and a skeleton only of what are now deemed necessities would remain. The thousand uses of steam, of electricity, of labor saving devices, have, to a large extent been the development of the last fifty years. Existence, with the tough forefather, for himself and family, was the stake played for while subjugating the wilderness.

There is an element beyond the culture and discipline derived from successive stages of the early settler's life which shapes the character of succeeding generations. It consists in the leaven of high resolve and determined will, which alone could have severed the ties anchored in social and religious privileges, as well as in the material advantages incident to older settlements.

Situated as Littleton is on the borders of Vermont, posessing a thoroughfare from its boundaries, east and west, over which the thrift of a large section of that state was transported every recurring winter in long lines of pod teams to Portland and Portsmouth, its fame as a stopping place, its boundless resources of pine and water-power, became themes of conversation in many a Vermont farm-house.

The wares of Franconia, its potash kettles and "hollow ware," and cooking stoves, from the days of Capt. Putnam, and even before, were legal tender with the older school of merchants like Major Curtis, the two Bracketts, and, subsequently, the Redingtons, in exchange for the pork, beef and dairies of northern Vermont. Many happy memories can be invoked which cluster around the old diving flue stove of half a century ago. Every well-to-do farmer and mechanic had this one luxury, which would hold its maple chunk and keep comfortable the kitchen in the coldest night of winter. The grandfathers and grandmothers of the present are witnesses that it would save half the wood, and bake brown bread and beans as well as a brick oven.

The rived pine shingles of Bethlehem, which found a ready market with Capt. Abbott or the Bracketts, and the shaved clapboards and sap clear boards, were greatly appreciated by those farmers who occupied the rolling hard-wood hills of Caledonia county. In 1840, said one, just as he was leaving town with two good sized loads of No. 1 shaved shingles, "Fifty years ago my father left me the farm, and the barns were covered with Littleton pine shingles. I want to leave them as good for Francis."*

Staging and mail routes naturally followed the track of this, developing commerce and communication between Littleton, St. Johnsbury, Danville and Montpelier, and the prosperity, of which all this gave promise, became an accomplished fact.

We recall Hale, Stephen, whose quaint sayings, coupled with rare powers of song, entertained his passengers, and made the trip to Vermont short and pleasant over rough

---

*Frank Drew, North Danville, Vt.

roads and rugged hills. His name recalls the ballads of the "Good Old Days of Adam and Eve." as well as "Susannah's Pig," which he rendered in a style peculiar to himself. King (Ben) and Hidden were two genial knights of the whip—safe, honest and reliable.

Col. L. A. Russell became a noted contractor, and divided receipts with the crack stage-men of the period. He hailed from Cabot, as did Quinton Cook, an enterprising harness maker, who later moved to St. Johnsbury.

Littleton, as a stage center, held a prominent place for years. The superior quality and style of the staging outfit in coaches, horses and harness, were always a topic of conversation with travelers, who came from all the states and many countries abroad.

The early hotel reputations, dating back to the day of the elder Gibb, and his son, Joseph L., the fame of whose coffee and steak had been ferried across the Atlantic, induced long miles of travel to enjoy them. The inimitable good nature of Stephen C. Gibb, under all circumstances, coupled with his capacity to adapt himself to all classes and conditions, enabled him to scale his prices of entertainment to the ability of his patrons to liquidate. Mr. Gibb was a judge and lover of horses, and had owned and sold many. His choice ran to the Morgan breeds, which he had very successfully bred in Vermont. There is no doubt that his example in this respect tended to improve the standard of excellence in his vicinity. He was one of the pioneers in hotel keeping at the Franconia mountains, when a one story house supplied all the accommodation needed for visitors. His son, J. L., subsequently, was interested in the more pretentious hotels at the White Mountains.

H. L. Thayer was three years old when he went from New Hampshire to Vermont, and when he returned, was an active, level-headed young man. He operated a store in the block now owned by Truman Stevens for a while. In 1849, he built the hotel now occupied by himself and son, gentleman Frank. For more than three decades (assisted by his accomplished wife), as proprietor or senior partner, he has dispensed the hospitality of his inn in an admirable manner. It is one of the most extensively known resorts in New England. Its reputation has been established on its merits. Its appurtenances have been well ordered in the way of its stables, livery and coaches. Scrupulous cleanliness, a grace next to godliness, has prevailed from basement to observatory, in every detail of hotel life. The rooms are large, airy, richly furnished, and no apologies are ever required for any of the thousand little outs that go to make up untidiness. The best the market can supply, prepared for the table by competent cooks, has, at all times, tempted the epicure and dyspeptic alike. The establishment has long been sought by the habitual tourist as a refuge of rest and comfort. In all the long struggle of years of ceaseless toil, through hard times and bad fortune, the veteran landlord has been cheered by a devoted helpmeet. Without woman's tact and strong sense, the reputation and prosperity adhering to this well-known house might have been altogether different. It has been, emphatically, a long pull, a strong pull and a pull altogether, in the life of this branch of the Thayer family. From the age of three years till manhood the training and education of H. L. Thayer was in Vermont. It was here he found his better half, and the twain was, and is, an investiture from that honored old state.

Richard Taft, a distinguished hotel proprietor, was born in Barre, Vt., March 14, 1812, and died at Littleton, N. H., February 14th, 1881. At the age of nine, he removed to Alstead, N. H., where he remained on a farm till 1830, when he was employed in a hotel at North Chelmsford, Mass. In two years he became a partner. He was afterwards landlord of the Washington House, Nashua, N. H., and then of a hotel in Tyngsborough, Mass. From 1844 to 1849 he was the lessee and landlord of the Washington House in Lowell, Mass. Since June 30, 1849, his life has been closely associated with the history of the Franconia mountain country. At that time he opened the Flume House. Travel had then hardly begun. Bristol was the nearest point that could be reached by rail, and there were only a few small hotels in the whole region.

The Lafayette House, at Franconia Notch, had been opened but a short time by the elder Gibb and his son. The price of board was only $1.50 per day, and the whole receipts of the first season were only $1,800.

Says Mr. William C. Prime, in the New York Journal of Commerce: "Mr. Taft was a man of exceedingly quiet demeanor, but of great ability, foresight, and cautious energy. New Hampshire owes to him a debt which it will never be able to repay for the results accomplished by his example, advice, and personal labor in the mountain country. He was, withal, a man on whom everyone relied—a man of the most unswerving probity of character. To use an expression which was constantly applied to him, 'Mr. Taft was never known to go back on his word.' He commanded the respect and confidence of all men. For many years past, though enfeebled by constant illness, he has continued to lead in all the improvements of the White Mountain hotels."

He was always keenly alive to the wonderful beauties of Franconia Notch, and never for a moment wavered in his faith in their attractions. It was one of the compensations of his last illness that he was again permitted to behold its glories and to inhale its pure and vivifying air.

Business at the Flume House increased from year to year, and in the fall of 1852, with his associates, he began the building of the Profile House, which was completed and opened to the public in July, the following year, since which time he has been one of the principal managers and the largest owner in both hotels. The Profile House has been greatly enlarged from its original dimensions, and is now one of the largest mountain houses in the country. The wonderful success which has attended it, the public generally know. Probably no man in the United States has ever really enjoyed hotel-keeping any better than Mr. Taft, and, very likely, few as well. His modesty of deportment was extreme, and only a few of the multitude who visited the Profile House ever saw him to know him. His chosen field of action was the interior of the house, away from the busy bustle of the front office, and where, as general manager, and especially as steward, he displayed those conspicuous abilities which have made him a prince among landlords. The hotel firm for four years, beginning in 1865, was Taft, Tyler & Greenleaf, but for the past twelve years has been Taft & Greenleaf. Mr. Taft was one of the proprietors of the Profile and Franconia Notch Railroad, and at his death was the president of the company. He was recognized by all as a man of great worth and sterling integrity, kind and just in all his intercourse with his fellow men, generous and benevolent to a fault. His memory will live long in the hearts of his friends and associates. Being an invalid for many years, he became a great student. He was familiar with the poets, and was well read in history, and in the arts and sciences. For the past nine months he was confined to the house. Deceased leaves a wife and one daughter, Mrs. Charles F. Eastman of Littleton, two sisters, and a brother, Denison Taft, of Montpelier, Vt. He left a legacy of $1000 to the New Hampshire Orphans' Home at Franklin, the income only to be used.

The above sketch paints in truthful colors a man who was a model in all the relations of life, and is taken from the Granite Monthly, March, 1881.

Charles Hartshorn was a native of Lunenburgh, Vt., and born Oct. 1, 1817. He was associated with Joseph L. Gibb and James L. Hadley in the Crawford House in early times, and is now a proprietor of the Waumbek House in Jefferson, but still holds his domicile in Littleton. He has business ability of a high order, and has proved successful in acquiring a good property.

William A. Richardson, recently landlord of the Union House, was also a Vermonter, born in Concord. His native ability, enterprise and tact rendered him a valuable citizen. That he was appreciated here is evidenced by the fact that he was selected to represent the town in the legislature, and in other important trusts.

In commercial pursuits, Vermont by contributions from its citizenship, has largely added to the growth of the town. Colby & Eastman may be aptly deemed the connecting link between old and modern Littleton. At the beginning of their mercantile life they made a departure from the conservative practice of the sterling old school of merchants in an almost indiscriminate credit. It was the rush and vim of charging, trusting, taking anything for pay that had a merchantable value. There were more birds in the bush than in the hand. The wise ones shook their heads or predicted disaster, and the hard times of '37 came near proving them true prophets.

Another innovation was marking merchandise at one price, and that a cash rate, thus allowing the purchaser's credit equality with his neighbor's money. Large sales and small profits was the rallying cry, and Dalton, Lisbon, Bethlehem, Landaff and a part of Vermont sent patrons, who, in their turn, advertised the wonderful prices at which many staple goods could be obtained.

Eastman, Mattocks & Co. were successors to Colby & Eastman; then Eastman, Tilton & Co., F. Tilton & Co., C. & F. J. Eastman & Co., Eastman, Tilton & Co. again, and finally C. & C. F. Eastman. With the exception of Mr. Colby, the partners, for the period of nearly fifty years, were natives of Vermont or of their descent. During this term the various companies, or the individuals composing them, were developing other industries:—Manufacturing lumber, making starch, running grist mills and various outside interests.

Col. Eastman, one of the pioneers, remained solid in the venture through all the changes and vicissitudes of the long continued business. Success being the measure of merit, he must have possessed large ability as a merchant. After fifty years of manhood's busy life, he is still vigorous and engaged in active pursuits. He has been associated with, and largely interested in, the two banking institutions of Littleton. His children are of Vermont stock on both sides. The mother, now deceased, was a daughter of the late Joseph Tilton, and sister to Frank and Henry L. C. F. Eastman, the last admitted partner of the reputable old house, is a native of Littleton. He is a young man of excellent business qualifications, and holds a strong place in the esteem of his fellow townsmen. At this writing, he is building what will be the most complete residence in northern New Hampshire, within a stone's throw of the site of the old yellow store where his father, forty-eight years before, embarked in a mercantile venture with small means, as a competitor for patronage with wealthy and well established rivals. In the struggles of the intervening period, if he could have looked down the flight of time and realized the pleasant surroundings of the new Littleton of 1884, it might have gladdened his heart. As it is, he can in all truth and sincerity say: "I have contributed my mite to the growth and standing of the town of my adoption."

Mr. Eben Eastman became interested in the concern about the time Mr. Mattocks was made a partner. Mr. Eastman, soon after his settlement in Littleton, threw the weight of his influence and devoted his time, to a great extent, in securing the construction of the White Mts. Railroad. He was one of the original board of directors, and W. J. Bellows was first clerk of the corporation. The obstacles that were overcome from the beginning to the completion of this railway are known to few living witnesses. For years after it was put in running order, the engagements and liabilities of the original projectors were a source of continual harassment, and not until long after the decease of Mr. Eastman was his estate relieved of the obligation he assumed in building the road. He had rare business capacity, combining good judgment with executive ability of high order. This was the estimate of the late E. J. M. Hale, by whom he was highly valued. Mr. Eastman was a member of the constitutional convention in 1850, with the late M. L. Gould for colleague.

Later, Mr. Frank Tilton was admitted to an interest, under the style of Eastman, Tilton & Co. From the start, he was an untiring worker, and while building a fortune for himself in legitimate trade, by fair and honest deal, established a reputation as an honorable man in all the relations of life. He was methodical in his habits, exact in his business operations and the soul of integrity. For years the writer held confidential relations with Mr. Tilton, and cannot recall, during all the time, a dishonest suggestion, an impure thought, or a profane word as emanating from him.

Subsequently, F. J. Eastman, brother to the two Eastmans heretofore mentioned, purchased an interest, and during the life of the new firm the depot store was built. Still later, Henry L. Tilton, a younger brother of Frank, secured a co-partnership, and the company operated two stores for a time successfully. In the course of events the plant became the property of Col. Eastman and his son, Charles F., who, until within two years, bought and sold largely in heavy goods.

For more than two score years the Eastmans and Tiltons transacted a large and leading business, with remunerative results. Of the eight different members of the firms, three have deceased. Henry Mattocks, a most estimable man, and father of Gen. C. P. Mattocks of Maine, died at Danville, Vt. Hon. Ethan Colby, most favorably known, still lives at Colebrook; Colonel Cyrus and Charles F. Eastman and Henry L. Tilton at Littleton, and F. J. Eastman at Northfield, N. H. Mr. Tilton is in the prime of a well ordered life and feels at home only when absorbed in the whirl of business. His diversified operations are on a large scale. He is bold yet cautious in his transactions, regarding safety and security, when obtainable, major considerations, "by all means." There is hardly a field of business involving trade, commerce or investment, in the town of his adoption and its vicinity, but in some form has felt the inspiration of his agency and influence. He has been one of the largest, if not the largest, contributor to the building interests of the town; is prominently identified with the glove manufactory, and one of the main spokes in the admirably managed banking institutions of Littleton. He is a gentleman of fine presence and of cordial address, yet one is always impressed that this exterior covers a young cyclone of buying, selling and making gain, ready to burst into action.

The two stores built for the uses of the firms are still doing a profitable business, but owned by younger men. The location of each was happily chosen, and the rapid advance of the town in the last twenty years still leaves them central and desirable sites.

There may be others who gave character to, and participated in merchandising in, the town whom we have omitted.

We note Daniel E. Thayer as an upright merchant of good repute, brother of Henry L., who was himself engaged in trade for a while, both, sons of that honest old Democrat, Daniel Thayer of blessed memory. Fred English, now in active life, is Vermont born, and son of John W. English, a sterling Vermont farmer, whose fine wool Windsor county sheep have done much to improve that industry in the vicinity.

A lively Vermonter in trade at Littleton is George K. Stocker, of the clothing firm of Lane & Stocker, in Tilton's new block.

James Carroll, long in the employ of the Eastmans and Tiltons, was a native of Barnet. For twenty-five years he has been doing a prosperous trade in San Francisco. The same affability and good nature adheres to him on the Pacific coast that made him a general favorite here. It is affirmed that he can call more people by name than any other man in the city.

Among the mechanics attracted by varied influences from the west side of the Connecticut was Abial Eastman, eldest brother of the Eastmans heretofore mentioned, now living at Northampton, Mass., at the age of eighty-four. He has been an upright man all his days in every position of life, as citizen, father, husband and son.

Hiram B. Smith was another noble work of God, void of offense, and a continual sufferer. At all times he bore a cheerful temper, which seemed above humanity. Charles C. Smith, his eldest son, was born in Vermont, and moved here when a child. He inherits many of the sterling qualities of his father, has been prominently engaged in the manufacture of tin-ware, and an extensive dealer in stoves.

Alonzo Weeks is another gift from the same state, whose qualities as a man are vouched for by the repeated bestowment of office, the most important, financially, in the gift of his fellow townsmen. Integrity covers him like a mantle.

The Hazeltines, father and son (Enoch and Frederick), were staid and reliable men and contributions to the general prosperity. Ariel Holmes, sometimes scythe maker, and sometimes lumberman, but always a Republican, has perpetrated more good than hurt. We rank him as one of the agencies that have benefitted Littleton, and he, too, is an extract from Vermont.

Truman Stevens is another contribution from the Green Mountains. Sixty years since, he left Barnet and opened his shop on the main thoroughfare of what could have been hardly named a village. His strong common sense anticipated the advantages of improved water power, which, at last, assumed form. Through his efforts, effectually aided by G. B. Redington and a few others, a dam was built, a building erected, machinery obtained, and for a short period of time a woolen factory was run under an agent, Capt. Peter Paddleford. Later, its management was assumed by John Herrin, a native of the county of Antrim, Ireland, but for many years a citizen of Vermont. Afterward, it passed into the hands of the late E. J. M. Hale, who increased the production materially. For labor, $2000 to $2500 were disbursed monthly, and large sums for wool expended in all the adjacent country. It has now become the neuclus, around which are clustered the various departments of the Saranac Glove Co., whose weekly pay roll calls for $3000 to satisfy labor alone.

Mr. Stevens might not have forecast present results, yet the full measure of his anticipations were realized. He never stood in the way of any man's honorable success. It was foreign to his nature to advance his own interests at another's expense. He never felt delight in hearing the foibles of others rehearsed. On such occasions he would demand a truce from even his most intimate friends. Invariable reliance could be placed on his representations in matters of trade; and his accounts had the consent of being exact as the multiplication table. Through all the ups and downs of sixty years of active life, he has lived without the taint of dishonor. He has told the truth, and three score of years of truth telling leaves him as stalwart a specimen of manhood at eighty-one as the state can produce.

One of the early editors in the newspaper enterprises of Littleton was H. W. Rowell of Waterford, Vt. His leaders were candid, incisive, and largely copied by the press of the state.

W. H. Stevens, who managed the woolen mill most successfully for Jordan, Marsh & Co., was from Windsor.

John Smillie, baker and confectioner, whose ancestors came from the "land of cakes," hails from Barnet, as did H. H. Kinnerson, a successful high-school teacher.

Prof. John J. Ladd first saw light in Newbury.

Anderson Miller, of Hall & Miller, is another level-headed Yankee of Scotch descent, born in Ryegate.

H. M. Parker, although living in a 99 per cent. atmosphere, has an intrinsic value beyond 100 cents on the dollar.

George C. Furber, who so naturally catches on to Littleton go-ahead-it-iveness, was a native of Woodstock.

The Cates, Ben and Calvin, who for years carried on the most extensive lumbering operations, had their birth-place in Cabot.

J. S. Frye, a noted cattle dealer, originated in Concord.

The two Gates, Ezra and Curtis, were born in Lyndon, and favorably known as excellent millers and honest tollmen.

Oscar C. Hatch was from Newbury. His predecessor in the bank, W. B. Dennison, was from Irasburg. The stockholders of Littleton National Bank have been very fortunate in their choice of cashiers. Under their administration, good dividends have been realized. Its undivided profits, two years since, had accumulated to more than $40,000. The confidence of the public is seen in the average amount of deposits, which exceeds the capital stock of the bank.

John E. Chamberlain, one of the contractors in building the White Mts. Railroad, and long its Superintendent, was a resident of Newbury. In this school, H. E. Chamberlin, Esq., present superintendent of the Concord road, and son of John E., received his first lessons. He was the station agent at Littleton from 1857 to 1864. He has managed the large trusts confided to his care with fidelity and skill, retaining the undivided confidence of the stockholders, as well as the directors, of this healthy corporation. He was a charter member of Burns Lodge, F. & A. M., and its second Master.

Norman G. Smith, born in Brunswick, Vt., for many years a resident of Coos, where he was deputy sheriff, newspaper manager, and otherwise actively engaged as a useful and respected citizen, came to Littleton fifteen or twenty years ago. He has always been known as a man of sound principle and sturdy convictions. As superintendent of highways, he has achieved success, which has kept him in that important office more years than have been allowed any other man in the village district.

Wm. Arthur Haskins, born at Bradford, Vt., has been for many years a connecting medium between Littleton and Cheney & Co.'s express. He was the first express messenger making his home here, and subsequently local agent. He resigned some two years ago, on account of impaired health. He was standing moderator for many years, and was retained in that office even after his party had been "left." He is a good musician and leader of one of our bands. In Freemasonry, he was for a long time one of the "pillars of the temple." For the ten years ending in 1881 he had been continuously Master of Burns Lodge, F. & A. M., and during substantially all of the same period, Commander of the St. Gerard Commandery of Knights Templar. While Omega Council was located at Littleton, he divided with C. H. Green the government of that body. Upon the occasion of his declining a further re-election as Master of the Lodge, in 1881, he was presented with a valuable Past Master's jewel, by his brethren, in token of their appreciation of his services.

Robert Nelson, who was the first station agent at Littleton, for the White Mts. Railroad, was a native of Ryegate, Vt.

Among the Littleton soldiers of the war of the rebellion, might be named Wm. W. Weller, born at Montpelier, Vt., who shared with Major Farr the honor of being the first to enlist from our town in '61. It was by mutual understanding that Farr's name was first recorded.

Capt. Marshall Sanders, who commanded a company in the 13th regiment, was a native of Bakersfield, Vt., born April 10, 1833. He was a Past Master of Burns Lodge. F. & A. M., and a man very much respected. He died April 4, 1866, at Littleton, from the effects of exposure in the service, and gave his name to the Grand Army Post at Littleton. He was a machinist.

Albert H. Quimby, of the firm of Quimby & Weller, carriage manufacturers, was a native of Barnet, Vt., born December 13, 1831, died September 4, 1866. He was a good artizan and a good citizen. He served in the war as a first-class musician in the Fifth regiment band.

The ancestors of Joseph Williams originated in the tropics, but Joe himself hailed from Burlington on the lake. Solitary and alone, he improvised the first saloon dedicated exclusively to the tonsorial art in Littleton. Barber shops have ever proved signals of progress, as well as of luxurious taste. They are buds and blossoms of increasing population and prosperity. Williams was a good type of his race, credulous, confiding, honest. He was accused, when party strife ran high, of voting at two or three elections before reaching his majority. If he did, he obeyed the first principle of the well-known injunction, " vote early and often."

The list of theologians attracted to Littleton from Vermont is quite formidable, and a large proportion of the number strong in intellectual force. The two Worcesters, Evarts G. and Isaac R., were clear headed and highly educated divines, who would have graced any pulpit. The pastorate of the former was short (about seven months), he being removed by death. The latter, Isaac R., succeeded him, and continued in charge of the church some five years, when he was succeeded by the Rev. E. I Carpenter, who administered to the spiritual needs of society for fifteen years longer. The three clergymen named were men, who, by their daily walks, illustrated their profession. They represented in their culture the highest type of workers in this branch of Zion. Their precepts and example have had a salutary influence, the effect of which still survives. The results of their labors were parts of the chain of agencies which have resulted in a flourishing church, surrounded by all the appurtenances which modern progress in religious organization demands. For many years this order of worshippers (Congregationalist), of which the Rev. Drury Fairbanks was the first pastor, had the only church edifice in the limits of the village. In 1850, the first Methodist church was erected. We call to mind among those who have worthily held charge as preachers and pastors as native Vermonters, Reverends H. L. Kelsey, L. P. Cushman, George S. Barnes, N. M. D. Granger, and, not least, that earnest, unselfish, old apostle, Rev. John Currier, born in Walden, Vt., in 1805. All of this list were devoted men, who ably seconded the material prosperity of the church, inaugurated under the ministry of the Rev. Sullivan Holman thirty-four years ago. Their influence yet lives in a prosperous society, which, in its early existence, was fostered by their care. In both these churches, the supply of pastors from Vermont must be recognized as commanding in those sterling qualities of character brought with them. Their memories are, and long will be, cherished for their singleness of purpose, the purity and uprightness of their lives. Some of them remain, and are filling honorable positions in the duties of their calling, working with earnestness of purpose, though divided by thousands of miles. Their labor in the aggregate will live after them, worthy of all praise.

In the department of law, the relations of Vermont to Littleton not alone concern the fame and reputation of the town. Among the illustrious examples that state has furnished, who have exalted their profession in honorable and distinguished service, are those whose renown has not been prescribed by state lines. The late Chief Justice Bellows was a native of Walpole, N. H., but most of his early years a resident of Rockingham, Vt. He commenced the practice of law in Littleton, in 1828, and rapidly rose to distinction. His affability and good faith to his clientage, the careful preparation of his suits, established for him a great legal repute, and gained a full measure of professional business. As a land lawyer he had no superior. When, from conflicting titles, confused metes and bounds, or from any cause, contestants sought his counsel, he would investigate with patient care and unequalled skill the intricacies involved and give honest advice. He would never encourage litigation as a means of offence, but would prosecute or defend what he believed to be the just rights of his clients with unyielding stubbornness of purpose against all obstacles. His frankness and urbanity in the trial of causes attracted juries, made personal friends of his following, and seldom gave provocation to his opponents. His removal to Concord, was made necessary by his increasing business. The subsequent elevation of Mr. Bellows to the office of chief justice of the state was a promotion richly earned. As an advocate, he demonstrated those qualities the coming attorney may well emulate. By the bar he was accorded fearlessness in discharge of his duty, honesty in his analysis of testimony, and ability of high order in the trial of his cases. On the bench he held an even balance. The breath of suspicion never soiled the uprightness of his decisions. He lived an honorable and useful life. His memory will be cherished by the state of his adoption.

William J. Bellows, brother of the late Henry A., was born in Rockingham, and when a young man emigrated to Littleton, where he studied law with his brother, and was admitted to the bar and became his partner. On the dissolution of the firm, he pursued his profession by himself, and later in company with John Farr, Esq. He has been active and successful in whatever pursuit he enlisted. As an editor, he manifested decided controversial ability, which has been poured out unsparingly upon the head of his friendly biographer. Mr. Bellows possesses a fine literary taste, is an easy and fluent speaker. We have somehow a lingering impression that he has a poetic nature, and at times has cultivated the muse. He is a genuine admirer of Scott, and revels with equal delight in the rhythmic measure of the Lady of the Lake, or the masterly romance of Ivanhoe. With his two sons he has built up a profitable commerce, the firm ranking high in both character and credit. As a lawyer, he was a safe adviser, having many traits in common with his brother, and perhaps more versatility of talent. If he had followed his profession, we doubt if he would have attained his eminence. Few have. Yet he has acted his part well, and Vermont has scored another point to her credit in the transfer of Wm. J. Bellows to the east bank of the Connecticut river.

Among the more recent acquisitions to the legal fraternity of Littleton, who bid fair to maintain the reputation of the town for able attorneys, we will mention the two brothers Mitchell. W. H. was a native of Wheelock, and John, though born in New Hampshire, lived in Vermont until he went to Littleton to study law. D. C. Remich is from Caledonia county, Vt. The fact that they are all associated with the Binghams is an ample voucher as to their legal value.

James R. Jackson, town historian, with his brothers, Andrew and William Jr., and sisters, Mary (Mrs. H. H. Metcalf) and Julia, were natives of Barnet, Vt. Mrs. Jackson, their mother, was born in Danville. James R. studied law with H. & G. A. Bingham, and has the reputation of being well read. He is a good public speaker, and wields a facile and pungent pen. The town history of Littleton engages his attention almost exclusively. He brings excellent capacity and adaptability to the task, in industry and painstaking, patient research. Outside its genealogical character, a feature as romantic as the rule of three, its literary merit will be conceded.

Albert S. Batchellor, of Bingham, Mitchells & Batchellor, comes from Revolutionary ancestry on his mother's side, who was a native of Vermont, and one of a brilliant bevy of girls, five of whom, first or last, resided in Littleton, viz.: Mrs. Batchellor, now Mrs. Bronson, Mrs. A. L. Robinson, Mrs. James J. Barrett, Mrs. Ariel Holmes, and the first Mrs. E. O. Kenney, nearly all of whom raised families which have inherited good names and intellectual qualities from their parents. Batchellor is recognized as one of the rising lawyers of the state. There is an ease and abandon in his style of speaking which puts him and his audience at once in favorable accord. With an excellent voice, of good compass, his subject well studied, he challenges the attention of his auditors. His propositions, whether of law or politics, are concisely and fairly stated. His manner captivates the attention and prepares the way for a favorable consideration of his argument. His good nature is a powerful adjunct in his behalf. There is nothing in his methods as an advocate which begets dissent, or throws doubt and distrust on his honesty and sincerity. He has repeatedly represented Littleton in the legislature, and was once the candidate of his party for speaker.

A fitting notice will be found in the remarks of several speakers on this occasion of the two Binghams, two more Vermonters, whose extensive practice in all the courts of the state has established their fame as successful lawyers. Both are in their intellectual prime and, fortified with more than thirty years of painstaking attention to their profession, they justly rank among the foremost lawyers of the state.

There have been few attractions for the yeomanry of Vermont to leave their fertile and easily tilled farms for the stubborn and stony hills of Littleton. It has been otherwise with those devoted to the learned professions. In the realm of medicine, her contributions for half a century past have monopolized the practice of the healing art. Graduating from the schools of Vermont and Hanover, Littleton became the Mecca for a formidable list of enterprising practitioners, who built up reputations for skill in the varied channels of their professions second to none in the state. The mention of their names would, in the minds of many competent to decide, establish this declaration.

Among them, and contemporary with the latter days of Ainsworth, at a time when Burns was in the height of his popularity, when the scholarly Moore was in the full tide of successful practice, C. M. Tuttle, just past his majority, without previous notice, came to town forty-four years ago, and announced his purpose of plying his profession in Littleton. It was looked upon as an act of temerity, if not of foolhardiness, even by conservative citizens. He was not welcomed with hospitable hands at any point, and his medical brethren were cold and distant. At once he became a target for the irony of one of his principal competitors, and the object of silent disregard on the part of another. Nevertheless, in that unassuming young man reposed the elements of character which have since carried him to the front rank of the profession in New Hampshire. He acquired more than a common school education while living in the family of a physician, who had rare qualities in treating disease, and he was at the same time under the tuition of an accomplished surgeon. The early purpose of his life (the study of medicine) was gratified amid the most favorable surroundings. During his student term he became well versed in theoretical knowledge of disease, and had more than an usual familiarity with its treatment. In the study of anatomy under the accomplished Nelson, by actual demonstration for long continued periods, he obtained that critical knowledge and minutiæ in the organism of man as an animal, which has often asserted itself in his surgery, or in his testimony as an expert before the courts. Besides these favoring conditions, he was endowed by nature with a bouyant spirit, which saw no dark lining and entertained no idea but success. He earned his way from the start. Dentistry, in connection with his limited practice, became a valuable aid, not only from the money it secured, but as an auxiliary to new acquaintance, favor and patronage.

It is unnecessary to recite the progressive steps of the subject of this sketch to eminence in his avocation and comparative wealth. They are part and parcel of Littleton's growth and prosperity. His townsmen are witnesses that an indomitable will, planted in a far from rugged frame, has enabled him to perform a prodigious amount of professional work for more than a generation.

Dr. Tuttle, through life thus far, has been a close and well read student. The current medical literature of the day is found on his table with no uncut leaves. The newest remedies are investigated and their worth determined with critical skill. In the sick room with his patient he is superb. His presence encourages the sufferer, and the mind, thus fortified, acts like a robust tonic. His resources in extremities seem exhaustless, and apparently at times he wins from the bony archer. A kind and sympathetic nature is masked behind a brusque exterior in his daily work. We have known him, after a hard day's work in inclement weather, to answer a call at midnight, demanding hours of travel over drifting roads, when there was no expectation of pecuniary reward. Said an educated and well known citizen of Littleton, "many a time has he passed a $5 note into my hand in my need, and I had no claim on his benevolence."

When testifying as an expert he had no superior. The ingenuity of lawyers cannot break the force of his evidence. He is master of the case on trial. The anatomy of the parts, the ailment under consideration, as the case may be, are made intelligible to the jury. Technical and abstruse terms are defined understandingly, and the shifts to confuse and baffle witnesses are disposed of, as cobwebs are brushed away, by this man of wonderful memory.

For more than two score years, he has been a prominent figure in the history of the town as a physician, as well as a man of business. In the latter capacity he was far from hard and extortionate. His record is written as honest in deal, faithful to his obligations, and true to his friends. Such has proved the gift of Vermont in the person of Charles Martin Tuttle.

Dr. Ralph Bugbee, a native of Waterford, has for a long period enjoyed a successful practice in Littleton and surrounding towns. He possesses an inborn capacity and aptitude for surgery, and has an accurate eye for anatomical proportion. He stands well in the treatment of acute diseases, and excels in those that are chronic. His thoroughness and persistence have resulted in phenomenal recoveries. He is an adept in nursing and staying the trip on the down hill side of life. The aches and outs of natural decay, whether heralded by broken veins or the ulcers of old age, obtain soothing relief from the store-house of his resources, whether existing in the imagination or in materiality as malignant as the sores of Lazarus. With these endowments his professional engagements could have been only very extensive.

His affable address and gentlemanly bearing have always stood him in good stead. He is an excellent financier, and invests his funds as skillfully as he mends a shattered limb. For twenty-five years, at least, Dr. Bugbee has patiently worked at his profession, and when he shall have made his last prescription, his tombstone can well bear the inscription—" Here lies a man who has been useful to mankind."

Dr. Sanger is another scion of old Vermont. His outfit came checked from Troy, nearly thirty years since. The first five years of his medical experience established a character for his system of pharmacy from an adverse standpoint, and a place for himself as a surgeon and physician worthy of all commendation. He has become an authority for the Homœopathic school of believers in northern New Hampshire. His personal qualities have attached to himself a large and reputable body of adherents. He is cool and sagacious in his battle with human infirmity, and persistent in his belief that " like cures like." Under this inspiration, he now enjoys a lucrative business, as he has from the early days of his medical career.

The Doctor is brilliant in the social circle. His ready wit and apt repartee are ward and brand in society life. He is the soul of good nature, and a general favorite with the fair sex.

In closing these brief and fragmentary notices of the three leading physicians of Littleton, who have, for a long period of years, faithfully and conscientiously, according to their best light and knowledge, healed the sick and assuaged the sufferings of its people, we must not be unmindful that others deserve a mention as within the scope of this paper. We can recall several medical gentlemen who were either natives, or had for a time pursued their calling in Vermont, who are now, or have been, a part of busy Littleton in the last forty years.

John L. Harriman of Peacham, a good dentist and M. D., A. B. Wilson of Newbury, Brown of Burke, Worcester of Peacham, were all well read and successful practitioners. Dr. H. L. Watson practiced many years in Vermont (before his settlement in Littleton), where he became distinguished, and, in fact, eminent. He was prominent in the politics of that state, his personal popularity carrying him to the senate, where his casting vote elected the last Democratic Governor Vermont ever had. His professional advice is esteemed as of the highest value, and he justly ranks among the leading physicians of New Hampshire.

It cannot be said that native Vermonters have been forgotten in the dispensation of office, either in legislative or judicial positions. The jurisprudence of the state has had representatives in the persons of Hon. Henry A. Bellows and Hon. George A. Bingham. Col. Cyrus Eastman has been one of the governor's advisors, and of four members of the state senate taken from Littleton, the two Binghams have been prominent members of that body.

Henry L. Tilton was honored by an election as presidential elector. As representatives to the legislature, the list is full, commencing with David Goodall, Jr., in 1811, and in succession Henry A. Bellows, Horace L. Goss, Horace Buck, Nathan Kinne, Harry Bingham, eighteen years, F. J. Eastman, John C. Goodenough, G. A. Bingham, W. A. Richardson, and H. F. Greene closing the list as present member for 1883 to 1885.

There were other causes besides those existing in the large colonization of enterprising Vermonters which affected the relations that have existed between Vermont and Littleton. Among them may be designated the lack of educational advantages beyond common schools. The seminary at Newbury, Vt., for various reasons besides its intrinsic excellence, attracted a strong drift of pupils from Littleton and towns near by. A large proportion of the sons and daughters, who went from home, pursued at this institution their academic course. The annual catalogues show a large scholarship from Littleton. In the days of its glory, this seminary stood without a rival. A few, who were not inclined to favor a denominational school, might have patronized Thetford or Peacham, yet the point is preserved that Vermont, in the past, by her superior educational facilities, has conferred a valuable obligation, in that the sons and daughters of Littleton have utilized them.

The early Masons obtained their degrees in the "Morning Dawn," at Upper Waterford. It was here that Drs. Burns and Moore, the Bracketts, William, Sewell and Aaron, H. B. Smith and Otis Batchelder, were initiated into the mystic rites of Free and Accepted Masonry. Nathaniel Rix, Esq., was Master, once of the governor's council, and a resident of North Littleton.

The religious privileges in the early times were maintained by a union of worshippers on both sides of the river. A ride of ten miles to Waterford and return was a duty, and never neglected without good cause. In those days, there was comparatively little of entertainment to call the people together, except of a religious character. Here, friendships were cemented, troubles soothed, sorrows assuaged, and spiritual aid and comfort vouchsafed, which smoothed the rough places in the journey of life. Who can reveal the outcome of these inter-town gatherings? We will not speculate. These occasions afforded opportunities for inculcating religious lessons, and the use of cupid's quiet devices.

Col. Timothy Edson and Sylvanus Balch, two worthy citizens of Littleton, now gone to their rest, married sisters, daughters of Judge Weatherbee of Concord, Vt. They were God fearing people. Since then, many a noble daughter of Vermont has cast her lot in Littleton with her chosen mate. In whatever position she may have been placed, as a rule, she has kept to the line of her duty, under all circumstances.

In addition to those already named, who were better halves of some of Littleton's live men, and who have nobly performed the duties of helpmates, we are reminded of Mrs. Col. Moffett, mother of a residing physician, Dr. Moffett, now in active practice; Mrs. Alpha Goodall, Mrs. Abijah Allen, the late Mrs. E. Eastman and Mrs. C. M. Tuttle, all of whom have honored the position which Providence has assigned them as wives or mothers, Mrs. Alonzo Weeks, Mrs. F. J. Eastman, and, notably, Mrs. Truman Stevens, whose intelligence and social gifts were the charm of village life. Mrs. Daniel E. Thayer was a native of Danville, and, undoubtedly, there are many others whose names we cannot recall.

It is apparent, then, that the rise of Littleton to its present importance is attributable, in no small degree, to drafts on Vermont, for its successful men of business, and for many of those who have distinguished themselves in the learned professions. We accept the fact that others have been attracted to its borders from contiguous towns, or more distant points, who possessed kindred qualities of character, and who have with common purpose, largely aided in achieving the present. The Bracketts and Redingtons, the Kilburns and Farrs, the Parkers and Barretts, would have commanded success anywhere.

Some writer, in his notes of travel, has sagely stated that large streams usually run through large villages. Causes and effects are liable to be transposed, if superficially examined, or when their relations are obscure.

The present site of the beautiful village of Littleton, embracing valley, plain, slope and hill top, in its thick studded evidences of cosy comfort and competence, is, in its entirety, a prospect of unsurpassed loveliness. There was a time when the unnamed Ammonoosuc, in rippling cascade and laughing waterfall, or in impetuous torrents, ran unnoticed towards the sea,—when the wolf and bear from the haunts and coverts of primeval forest quenched their thirst from its cooling waters undisturbed. Here nature once held her gloomy court with forbidding rocks and grim sterility as her sentinels. How changed! The wilderness has been made to blossom like the rose. Fertility and productiveness have followed barrenness and unfruitfulness. The untamed river is made subservient to the uses of man. The bleak, inhospitable hills have become a haven of rest.

This wonderful transformation has called for persistent and intelligent labor. It has been provided from the sources indicated, and the result is a monument to the memory of every man and woman, who, in any way, has contributed to the accomplishment. May the Littleton of an hundred years hence attain the same increase in all the elements of progress which the last century has made manifest in 1884.

NEWSPAPERS AND NEWSPAPER MEN.

ADDRESS BY HENRY H. METCALF.

The President said: Among the enterprises which have a place in the history of the town, is that of the newspaper. It was commenced as early perhaps as in most of the towns that were not prominent in early history. We have with us, one who participated in our early newspaper struggles. Mr. H. H. Metcalf, who will speak to you on the subject of Newspapers and Newspaper Men.

ADDRESS.

Mr. President, Ladies and Gentlemen:

The newspaper history of Littleton covers less than one-third of the hundred years which have elapsed since the incorporation of the town. The church had been an organized institution in the community for more than half a century before the newspaper made its appearance. The minister had taught the way of life, spiritual, as he understood it, the doctor had prescribed for the physical well being of the people, and the lawyer had dwelt in their midst, as the conservator of justice and good order, for nearly fifty years before a printing press had been set up in town. But it is safe to say that none of the representatives of these several professions had grown rich or famous. They had lived and died in comparative obscurity, from the lack of that newspaper criticism and commendation which brings men into public notice, stimulates their ambition, and strengthens all their powers and faculties.

Thirty-two years ago the present month, under date of July 24, 1852, there was printed in "Smith's Building," as it was then termed, the first number of the first newspaper published in town. The founder, editor and proprietor of the paper, Francis A. Eastman, was a Littleton boy, but nineteen years of age when he entered upon the work. He was a son of the late Stephen Ambrose Eastman, who, in his day, was a school teacher, wood engraver and preacher, but who died while Francis was a child, leaving him to a mother's care. The late Chief Justice Henry A. Bellows, then a resident of Littleton, had taken an interest in young Eastman, and, while still a mere boy, succeeded in inducing George S. Towle editor of the *Granite State Whig*, at Lebanon, to take him as an apprentice in the printing business. There he remained for some two years, the *Whig* office in the meantime having been destroyed by a great fire, and the paper re-established by Towle and Cragin, with the aid of enterprising citizens. For some reasons not recalled, but in no way discreditable to him or his employers, he was released from his indentures before the close of the usual term of service, returning home to Littleton, where he resided with his widowed mother, and attended the village school. But, after a time, some interested friend, hearing that A. G. Chadwick of the *Caledonian*, at St. Johnsbury, Vt., was in want of an advanced hand in his office, recommended young Eastman. He obtained the situation and commenced work. He soon manifested such interest and proficiency that he was allowed to be "out of his time," as the phrase is, and took the standing of a journeyman printer.

It was not long after, that prominent citizens of this town, conspicuous among whom was the late Ebenezer Eastman, urged young Eastman to fit up, here, a printing office, and establish a newspaper. The spirit of enterprise had then fairly begun to stir the community. The White Mountains Railroad was in process of construction, and great expectations of business prosperity were, naturally, indulged. A plan for a new county, with Littleton as the shire town and business centre, was devised, and, although never carried out, it was cherished for years in the minds of public spirited citizens. Indeed, the idea of the ultimate erection of a spacious court house, upon some commanding location in the village, was not abandoned by Littleton lawyers and citizens generally until the supreme court of the state, in the plenitude of its wisdom, had practically abandoned the time-honored and blood-bought institution of trial by jury, and adopted the custom of dispensing justice in lawyers' back offices, and other out-of-the-way places, in accordance with its own peculiar standards of propriety. Political ambition also began to fire the hearts of leading citizens, and for political advancement, as well as business growth and expansion, newspaper influence was recognized as essential.

Himself ambitious and enthusiastic, the young man was readily influenced by the offers of assistance and support, literary and financial, which the advocates of the enterprise extended, and he entered ardently into the work. He wrote and issued a taking prospectus, and canvassed this, and the neighboring towns, on foot, for subscribers. The money for the enterprise was furnished by the young editor's mother, Mrs. Lavinia H. Eastman. It was a small office, scantily equipped. The investment was $450, with which sum a second-hand Tufts press was purchased from the *American* office at Manchester,* and some partially worn fonts of type from the *Statesman* office at Concord, together with the cases, stands and furniture absolutely necessary to the work.

The paper was Democratic in politics, and was christened the *Ammonoosuc Reporter*, a name selected by Col. Cyrus Eastman, who, together with John G. Sinclair of Bethlehem, and Harry Bingham, undertook to furnish such assistance as might be necessary in conducting the paper. How extensive was the assistance which these gentlemen rendered, I am unable to say; but it is safe to assume that none of their contributions ever equalled in extent the graphic account of the "Great Republican Bear Fight," as he termed it, between

---

*This first press ever used in town, is now used in the *Sentinel* office at Colebrook, and has been ever since that paper started, having been exchanged by Mr. Bass, into whose possession it passed, with J. S. Peavey, for a smaller one, when Mr. Peavey started the Sentinel.

George G. Fogg on the one hand, and Chandler, Rollins and Ordway, on the other, which was contributed many years later by Mr. Bingham, to the columns of the *White Mountain Republic*; for the size of the paper would hardly admit of the publication of so extended an effort, in a single issue at least. It was a small sheet—22 by 32 inches—four pages, and six columns to the page; and although it would now be regarded as far from a model in typographical appearance, it was really a handsome paper for the times, and very well gotten out, considering the facilities at command. The subscription price was $1.25 per annum, in advance.

It was a great day for young Eastman when the first number was issued, and a great day for the town's people, generally, who had so long been groping in the intellectual darkness, common to all communities where newspapers are not published. Doubtless even the brethren of the Whig party rejoiced that light had broken at last, even though not tinted to their complete satisfaction.

I have been, thus far, unable to find a copy of this first number of the *Reporter*. Number eight, which bears date of September 11, 1852, is the earliest issue to be found, so far as I know.* At all events, it is the first number appearing in the files at the town clerk's office, where, under a recent wise provision of the citizens, files of all papers, heretofore and now published in the town, have been, and are to be, deposited and kept, properly bound and arranged for reference,

---

*Since the delivery of this address, a copy of the first number of the *Reporter* has been found by Mr. A. S. Batchellor, the same being in the possession of Miss Mattie Eastman of Littleton. It, naturally, presents less variety than subsequent numbers, and is made up largely of miscellaneous and political selections, without much regard to order of arrangement. It contains but two columns of advertisements, and, although foreign news occupies over a column, not a single item of local intelligence appears, except that embodied in a solitary marriage notice—that of John Farr, Esq., to Mrs. Elizabeth M. Bowman, which occurred on the 18th of May preceding, Rev. E. I. Carpenter officiating. In his salutatory remarks, Editor Eastman said: "The publication of this paper is commenced, not to encroach upon any other in the state, nor with other than kindly feelings towards all, but simply because the interests of this section of the state seem to demand it,—not merely for the advantage of a particular party or interest, but more especially as a universal business medium. * * In politics we are Democratic; waiving personal preferences and prejudices to the popular will, and for the public security; demanding of our public agents a strict construction of, and prompt obedience to, the constitution of thirty-one sovereign states; against appropriating the public funds to sectional and private purposes, whether appealed to by specious pretexts of internal improvements, or the more frank and honest avowals of speculators; in favor of a tariff that bears equally upon all branches of industry, and against a tariff for the *protection* of monopoly and aristocracy."

for the accommodation of all who may desire to consult them. And right here let me suggest, in passing, that if there be any person present who has in his possession, or knows of the existence of, any complete file, or any of the early numbers of the *Ammonoosuc Reporter*, he will make himself a public benefactor, so far as this community is concerned, by depositing the same with the town clerk, or giving information of their whereabouts, which may result in their being secured for public use.

Following the general style of the journalism of that day, the *Reporter* was not a local paper, in the sense in which the term is now understood. Very little space was devoted to the record of events, or the discussion of questions and topics of local interest. Local journalism is a thing of recent date. Twenty-five years ago, in fact, there was not a newspaper in the state presenting any such feature as a regular department of home intelligence and New Hampshire news.

In this first accessible number of the *Reporter*, I find a story, copied from Harper's Magazine, occupying the entire first page, and a portion of the second. This was after the style of the time. Newspapers then afforded very little variety compared with those of the present day. The paper, as has been said, was Democratic. It was started in the midst of a presidential campaign, and bore at the head of its editorial column the names of Franklin Pierce for President, and William R. King for Vice President; and the first article in the column, in this number, happens to be an account of the formation of a Granite Club, a Democratic campaign organization, by the students of Dartmouth college; and it appears that one of the vice presidents of the club was a Littleton boy, J. M. Bickford, now, as I understand, a lawyer in Texas; and it may also be added, that one Daniel Hall of Barrington was corresponding secretary.

The news department of the paper was devoted largely to California, the Mormons, the fisheries and foreign affairs. There were occasional scattered items of state news, but the only reference I find in the reading columns of this number, to any matter approaching local interest, is a communication from an indignant citizen of the town of Lisbon, signing himself "Truth," recounting the fact that Bela Young, postmaster at that place, had just been turned out of office, and one James Allen put in his place, notwithstanding said Young had done gallant service for his country in the war of 1812, under Weeks and McNeil, and been wounded at Lundy's Lane, while Allen had no such record to boast, and had actually opposed the government in the then recent war with Mexico. So that, as it appears, then, as now, services for the country in war did not insure a man continuance in office when party interests would be better subserved by the substitution of some other person.

Turning to the advertising columns of the paper, we find them devoted, almost entirely, to local business. This was before the palmy days of patent medicine advertising, though Dr. J. C. Ayer of Lowell had thus early availed himself of the opportunity to use the *Reporter* as a means for acquainting the people of the White Mountain region with the virtue of his preparations. Fry W. Gile and William Bailey occupied, each, a fair amount of space in advertising dry goods, and E. S. Woolson & Son made a greater display in calling attention to their stock of cloths and clothing. J. Kilburn & Son advertised as iron founders and machinists, Alonzo Weeks and Charles C. Wilder as boot and shoe dealers, and custom manufacturers; H. & G. A. Bingham, C. W. Rand and William J. Bellows as attorneys-at-law, and C. M. Tuttle as physician and surgeon. An advertisement of the "White Mountain House and Stage House," by H. L. Thayer, also appeared, in which it was announced that the house had recently been built and furnished in modern style, and that the proprietor believed himself able to gratify all the wants of his patrons—a belief which the experience of thirty-two subsequent years certainly seems to have justified.

Mr. Eastman continued the publication of the *Reporter* for two years, during which time, young though he was, he gained considerable reputation in political circles, and the measure of his ambition increased accordingly. He had attended the great mass demonstration at Hillsborough, in honor of Gen. Pierce, in August, 1852, and was one of the secretaries of the meeting. Upon the election of Governor Baker, in 1854, he was appointed one of his aids, being one of the youngest, if not the youngest man in the state who ever held such position. He aspired to a wider and more active field of labor, and announced his determination, in the summer of 1854, to close out his business and go West. On the 5th of August, 1854, he published a notice in his paper, stating his purpose to discontinue its publication at the end of two weeks, and depart for Kansas, then the great objective point for Western emigrants. As it happened, however, he did not pursue exactly that course. He sold the paper to Van N. Bass, a printer, who had worked in the office from the start, who associated with himself another printer named Lorenzo D. Churchill, and continued the publication in the same location; while he, Eastman, accepted a position upon the *New Hampshire Patriot* at Concord, at the solicitation of William Butterfield, then editor and proprietor. He continued his engagement in the *Patriot* editorial rooms for a few months, when he resigned and became editor of the *Vermont Patriot*, at Montpelier. But his thoughts were, continually turning westward, and, in 1857, he went to Milwaukee, Wisconsin, and became editor of the *Daily News* of that city. His work on that paper attracted considerable attention, and, in 1859, at the instance of the late Stephen A. Douglas, he was established as associate editor of the *Chicago Times*. Two years later he was one of the projectors of the *Morning Post*, which, though established as a Democratic paper, sustaining the war, was the germ of the present *Inter-Ocean*. Soon after the war broke out, like many others, for reasons satisfactory to himself, he joined the Republican party and was very promptly called into the public service. He was collector of the Northern District of Chicago; was two years a member of the lower branch of the Illinois legislature, and four years a state senator. He was also a commissioner of the penitentiary, under the state government, and was one of the builders of the great prison at Joliet. He also served for one term as a member of the Chicago school board. The first appointment made by President Grant was that of Francis A. Eastman, to be postmaster of Chicago, which office he held for the full term of four years. Losing a large amount of property through the great Chicago fire, and suffering other losses subsequently, Col. Eastman returned to journalism, and is now editor of the *Daily Press*, a successful and influential independent Republican paper, now on its third volume, in Utica, N. Y.*

Col. Eastman was married, in 1861, to Gertrude, only child of E. S. Barrett, a prominent merchant of Chicago, by whom he has two children, living, Barrett and Margaret, the former now a student at Racine college, Wisconsin, and the latter, a miss of three years.

Messrs. Bass and Churchill continued the *Reporter*, and did job printing (which had also been a part of the business during Col. Eastman's proprietorship). In January, following, 1855, the name of the paper was changed to the *White Mountain Banner*, and an elaborate heading secured. The former style and general make up was retained. In March, 1855, Churchill left, having disposed of his interest to Bass, who continued the publication alone until 1859. Churchill was a printer from Northfield, Vermont. Where he went, or whether he is living or dead at the present time, I am unable to say. Mr. Bass is of the impression that he went West; but is able to give no definite information concerning him. June 4, 1859, Mr. Bass announced the discontinuance of the *Banner*, finding its publication unremunerative, and transferred the subscription list to the *New Hampshire Patriot* at Concord. He continued to work as a job printer, and for several seasons, or until 1863, did the printing at the Crawford House. In 1863, he removed to Plymouth, where he has since resided, having been engaged most of the time in the job printing and stationery business. In January, 1878, he commenced the publication of the *Grafton County Democrat*, which he continued till 1883, when he disposed of the same. He is now in charge of the central telephone office at Plymouth.

---

*In 1886, Col. Eastman severed his connection with the *Press*, and is now associated in the publication of a paper in Los Angelos, Cal.

Mr. Bass is a native of the town of Bath, born July 14, 1829. He learned the printer's trade in the office of the *Spirit of the Age*, at Woodstock, Vermont. He afterwards bought the *White River Advertiser*, at White River Junction, and published the same until it was burned out. Subsequently, before coming to Littleton to work in the *Reporter* office, he was engaged for some months upon the *St. Clair Observer*, at St. Clair City, Michigan. He was married, March 27, 1857, to Susan T. Lindsey of Newbury, Vermont, with whom he is still living. They have no children.

During all this time, while a Democratic paper was published, the opposite party had not rested content with the situation. It was felt by the more ardent spirits among them that a newspaper of their own persuasion was a prime necessity. And, when, in 1855, the Whig organization had been abandoned, for the "Know Nothing," or American party, by which the state was carried at the March election in that year, a project for the establishment of a new paper was fully developed. Funds to the amount of some six hundred dollars were subscribed by Messrs. Redington, Bellows and others, to set the enterprise afloat, and an editor and publisher was found to assume the direction and responsibility of the work, in the person of a young man named Henry W. Rowell, a native of Waterford, Vermont, a son of Dr. R. F. Rowell of that town, born in 1834, who had served an apprenticeship to the printer's trade in the *Journal* office at Windsor, had been a contributor to the *Boston Commonwealth*, and Garrison's *Liberator*; had become assistant editor of the Springfield, Vermont, *Free Soil Telegraph*, at nineteen years of age, and was subsequently employed as editor of the *Aurora of the Valley*, at Newbury, which position he resigned to come to Littleton and commence the publication of the new paper, the first issue of which appeared June 6, 1855.

This paper was named *The People's Journal*. It was a somewhat larger sheet than the *Reporter* and *Banner*, being 24 x 36 inches. It had the same number of columns, six to the page, but set in wider measure. Typographically, it was well executed and made a very neat appearance. The office was established, as the imprint informs us, "one door west of the brick store," in what was then known as the Odd Fellows building, subsequently rendered famous by the occupancy of Joe Williams, the barber. The subscription price of the paper was the same as that of the *Reporter*, $1.25 in advance.

Political excitement was running high through the country generally, about this time, the slavery question being prominent, and the *Journal* set out to make itself felt. It devoted considerable space to editorial matter of a stirring nature, and also opened its columns extensively to correspondence upon political and other topics. It appears, also, from the files, that young aspirants for literary distinction were permitted to immortalize their effusions in the *Journal* to a very liberal extent. Original poetry was quite a prominent feature, and, doubtless, more than one staid matron of the present day has, now stored away in her scrap-book, clippings from the *Journal* presenting the romantic thoughts of her school days, woven into verse, and whose appearance in print gave her a keener thrill of pleasure than she had ever before experienced.

Mr. Rowell continued the publication of the *Journal* until November 2, 1860, when he published his valedictory, having disposed of the paper to William Davis. Meanwhile he, also, had become fired with political ambition to some extent, and had received consideration at the hands of his party, having been nominated and elected treasurer of Grafton county in 1858, and re-elected in 1859. In the latter year he was appointed a member of the military staff of Governor Ichabod Goodwin, and re-appointed in 1860, holding the position at the outbreak of the war of the rebellion, the following spring, when he was assigned to active duty in recruiting and preparing troops for the field, and for a time had command of the military rendezvous at Portsmouth. In 1862, Col. Rowell received an appointment in the Interior Department at Washington, and was soon promoted to Chief of the Agricultural Division of the Census Bureau, from which position he retired in 1867, and removed to Rockford, Illinois, where he was for several years connected with the press of that city.

and held various official positions—city clerk, secretary of the board of education, etc. In 1878 he was nominated as the Prohibition candidate for Congress in the fourth Illinois district, but declined. In 1879 he removed to Decatur, in the central part of the state, and established the *Daily Herald*. In 1881 he was elected clerk of the General Assembly of the Illinois legislature, in which office he served for one session, when he resigned to accept the position of disbursing clerk of the United States House of Representatives at Washington, which he held during the forty-seventh Congress, and until the re-organization effected by the Democratic party upon securing control of that body. He prides himself upon the fact that, while his accounts during the period of his services as disbursing clerk aggregated millions of dollars, upon final settlement every paper was found correct, every expenditure properly made and every dollar accounted for. He remains an earnest Republican, and expects to take the stump for the Republican ticket in the coming campaign, having been extensively engaged in that line in years past, winning a reputation as an effective campaign speaker. Col. Rowell was united in marriage, in October, 1855, with Miss A. B. Taylor of Springfield, Vermont. Their home is at Brightwood, a pleasant suburban village, just out of Washington.

In his salutatory, in taking charge of the paper, upon Rowell's retirement, Mr. Davis alluded to the fact that it had hitherto been devoted almost entirely to the dissemination of Republican principles, so that the amount of local intelligence which subscribers derived from its columns had been meagre. This defect he proposed to remedy, and also declared his intention, while advocating the former political sentiments of the paper, to treat the Democratic party with proper and due respect; a politic determination, undoubtedly, since that party was gaining strength, and evidently about coming into ascendency in town, while the *Journal* was then the only paper here published.

William Davis continued as publisher of the *People's Journal* about a year. Meantime the war came on. Times were hard, especially for newspapers. Paper stock went up in the market at an enormous rate; patronage lessened, and Davis, becoming discouraged, or patriotic, as the case may be, gave up the paper and enlisted in the Union army. The *Journal*, June 28, 1861, passed into the hands of William J. Bellows, Esq., whose name had appeared as senior editor from the 10th of May previous, the office having been removed to Tilton's block. Davis became a private soldier in company H, Third New Hampshire Regiment, and served faithfully through the war, or until severely wounded in the assault upon Fort Wagner, August 26, 1863, and incapacitated for farther active duty. He was promoted to the rank of Second Lieutenant, January 5, 1864. The place of Mr. Davis' nativity* I have not been able to ascertain; but an obituary notice, published in the *Sanilac Jeffersonian* at Lexington, Michigan, where he died, January 31, 1874, states that he was a native of New Hampshire; that his parents both died when he was a child, and he was taken and reared by a minister of the English church at Sherbrooke, Canada. When he returned to this country cannot be definitely determined, but Phineas R. Goold informs me that he became an apprentice at the printer's trade in the *Republican* office at Haverhill about the same time that he did—in 1857—and served with him there the usual time. At the close of the war he came back to New Hampshire, but soon went to Michigan, and after a time secured a position as foreman in the *Jeffersonian* office at Lexington. He afterward went to Missouri; but, being disappointed in his expectations there, returned to Michigan, and was, for a time, foreman of the *Saginaw Courier* office; but, finally, some two years previous to his death, resumed work in the *Jeffersonian* office at Lexington, which he continued as long as failing health permitted, and up to within two months of his decease. He left a widow, formerly Miss Sarah Morris of Lexington, and a little son about two years of age. The widow, afterwards married I. C. Wheeler, a lawyer of Lexington.

Mr. Bellows continued the paper here, having reduced

---

*The Muster Rolls of the Third Regiment gave his native place as Gibraltar, Spain.

the size somewhat in May, 1862, until January, 1863, when an arrangement was made for printing it at Lebanon in connection with the *Free Press*. Practically, the establishment was sold to Mr. L. W. Rowell, an employe of Mr. Cheney, of the *Free Press*, who came to Littleton and conducted the job printing business, acting also as agent for the *Journal*, which retained the Littleton imprint, and carried the names of William J. Bellows and E. H. Cheney as editors, with E. H. Cheney as publisher, to whom the subscription list was, in fact, sold. The subscription price was at this time increased to $1.50 per annum. This arrangement continued till June 4, 1864, when the *Journal* was discontinued, its list being consolidated with that of the *Free Press*.

Of Mr. Bellows' career, I am not expected to speak. He is yet with you and able to speak for himself. Moreover, he belongs, more properly, either to the legal fraternity, or to mercantile circles, than to the ranks of journalism, his journalistic experience being but an incident in his career, a most creditable one, however, it is proper to remark.

Mr. Rowell continued the job printing business, but the town was without a newspaper until the 10th of November of the following year, 1865, when he issued the first number of a small, independent local journal, styled the *Littleton Gazette*. The *Gazette* was a five column paper, printed on a sheet 19 x 24 inches, but in January, 1867, was enlarged to six columns to the page. The office was located in what is now Parker's building, where the *Republic* office is now located. The subscription price of the paper was $1.25 per annum. September 20, 1867, the *Gazette* was discontinued, Mr. Rowell having sold his printing establishment, and the business connected therewith, to Chester E. Carey.

Mr. Rowell is a native of the town of Gorham, born April 17, 1840. He learned the printer's trade in the *Republican* office at Lancaster, and was for six years engaged on the *Free Press* at Lebanon, as foreman, and in other capacities, before coming to Littleton. After selling out here, he conducted the publishing and job printing department of the *Express* at Newport, Vermont, a few months; subsequently worked on the *Free Press* at Lebanon, and, in 1869, removed to St. Johnsbury, Vermont, where he was connected with the *Times* until 1871, when he purchased the job office of that paper, and has since conducted the same, issuing, also, a monthly paper known as the *Advertiser*. He married, in 1863, Miss Fannie T. Estabrook of Lebanon. They have two daughters, nineteen and thirteen years of age respectively.

Having purchased the material and "good-will" of the *Gazette* office, for the sum of $900, and made considerable additions in type and other material, Chester E. Carey commenced the publication of the *White Mountain Republic*, the first number being issued October 4, 1867. The office was located in Union block, which had recently been built. It was a seven column paper, 23 x 35 inches, and the subscription price was fixed at $2.00 per annum—rather a high price for a paper of the size, perhaps, but as the Democracy of Littleton and all northern New Hampshire, in fact, had been without a paper of their own kind for quite a number of years, it was thought they might well afford to pay liberally for the support of such an institution at last, and the *Republic* was a Democratic paper, of the unadulterated order, as I am able to vouch. H. H. Metcalf edited the paper for the first six months. Indeed it was at his suggestion that Carey undertook the enterprise, and largely through his personal effort that the subscription list was worked up and the paper thoroughly established, the labor involved including not less than four hundred miles of travel, on foot, through this county and southern Coos. It may not be out of place to remark, in this connection, that while the enterprise was very generally and very heartily encouraged in the neighboring towns, as well as here, none manifested deeper interest, or gave more substantial assistance, than the late Dr. John W. Barney, then of Lancaster, and the late Hon. Eleazer B. Parker of Franconia, than whom two truer, nobler hearted men never lived in northern New Hampshire.

In March, 1868, Metcalf resigned as editor, and Mr. Carey, the proprietor, took full charge of the paper and conducted it until September, 1871. In the meantime, he had removed the office, first to Smith's block, in April, 1868, where he remained till February, 1871, and then to a building at the lower end of the village, which he had purchased and fitted up as a printing office and dwelling, combined. September 15, 1871, he sold the paper and printing establishment, to which he had added a Guernsey power press, previously used in the *Caledonian* office at St. Johnsbury, to H. H. Metcalf, who took possession and again removed the location to Union Block. Carey left town, and has since been employed in various printing offices in this and other states. He is a native of the town of Lempster, born March 11, 1839. He learned the printer's trade in the office of the *Argus and Spectator* at Newport, and the *Argus* at Bellows Falls, Vermont, of which Hiram Atkins was the proprietor, and with whom he went to Montpelier, Vermont, and was foreman in the office of the *Argus and Patriot* during the war. Subsequently, before coming to this town, he was foreman of the *Union* office at Lyndon, Vermont, in the employ of C. M. Chase. January 19, 1867, he married Emily L. Prouty of Newport, Vermont, who died some years since. May 30, of the present year, he married Julia A. Macdonald of Boston, Mass., and is at present stopping in the town of Washington, in this state.

The *Republic* continued in Metcalf's* hands, having

---

*Henry H. Metcalf is a native of the town of Newport, born April 7, 1841. He was reared on a farm, receiving a common school and academic education. He read law, graduating from the Ann Arbor, Michigan, Law School, in the class of 1865, pursued his studies in the office of Hon. Edmund Burke of Newport, and was admitted to the bar of Sullivan County, at the September term, 1866. He continued in Mr. Burke's office till the following year, when he determined to engage in journalism, and united with C. E. Carey—a boyhood acquaintance—in the establishment of the *White Mountain Republic*. In May, 1868, he went to Concord and engaged with C. C. Pearson & Co., as political and news editor of *The People*, then about to be started by that firm, which position he filled till the spring of 1872, when he returned to Littleton to take charge of the *Republic*, which he had purchased of Mr. Carey in the previous autumn. In May, 1874, he removed to Dover and established the *State Press*, which he edited and published till the fall of 1878, when he disposed of that paper to the Press Publishing Co. In 1877 he had established the *Granite Monthly* Magazine, devoted to New Hampshire history and biography, and in the spring of 1879, he removed to Concord, and continued that publication until November following, when he disposed of the same to John N. McClintock, and removed to Manchester to take the position of managing editor of the Daily and Weekly *Union*, of that city, under the proprietorship of Stilson Hutchins, which position he occupied for two years. In June, 1882, Mr. Metcalf accepted the editorship of *The People and New Hampshire Patriot*, at Concord, and returned to that city, where he has since resided, continuing to fill the position named. He has written much, outside his regular editorial work, and was for three years, from January, 1882, New Hampshire correspondent of the *Boston Post*. He was Secretary of the Democratic State Committee in 1869 and 1870, and a member of the New been enlarged to eight columns to the page, and improved with a dress of new type in April, 1872, until the spring of 1874, when he sold the establishment to George C. Furber, the present proprietor, who took possession May 7, and has since continuously published it, Dennis O. Wallace having been associated with him, as a partner in the business, from January 1, 1880, until October 4, 1883. In January, 1880, the office was removed to the present location in Parker's block. Since then, important improvements and additions have been made in the mechanical department; and the office is now thoroughly equipped with new presses, steam power, and all the appliances for first-class work.

Mr. Furber is among you to speak for himself from week to week; but I may say that he is a native of Woodstock, Vermont, born April 27, 1847, but resided in Canaan, in this county, from infancy till eighteen years of age, when his family removed to Allegan, Michigan. There he remained until

---

Hampshire delegation in the National Democratic Convention at St. Louis, in 1876, which nominated Tilden and Hendricks for President and Vice President. He was united in marriage in Littleton, December 18, 1869, with Mary Jane, daughter of William Jackson, by whom he has three children—Harry Bingham, born in Concord, January 25, 1871; Edmund Burke, born in Littleton, July 3, 1872, and Laura Prucia, in Littleton, February 4, 1874.

It will be noted that Mr. Metcalf's opportunities for acquaintance with men and affairs in all sections of the state have been extensive. It is doubtful if any man, now connected with the press of the state, has so intimate a knowledge of the material and personal interests of the important localities and centres as he possesses. He never manifested the slightest inclination to compromise with corrupt and unpatriotic purposes of men, or the evil tendencies of the times. He acts upon the belief that it is the highest duty of the press to maintain the integrity of the people, and wage open and unceasing war upon all forms of corruption in the body politic, without fear or favor.

His best work has been done on papers of which he has had independent control. It is not intended that his work ever lacks the full measure of industry and fidelity, but every well informed person knows that when the proprietors of newspapers have schemes, the subordinates have more freedom of expression in some directions than they do in others.

He made the *Republic* of Littleton one of the best papers that has yet appeared in the northern part of the state. He devotes much attention to the record of New Hampshire men abroad, in what Mr. Greeley termed that "outer New Hampshire." The career of a successful son of New Hampshire seldom escapes his notice.

The *Granite Monthly*, which was established by him as a magazine of state history and progress, has reached the conclusion of the eighth volume. So long as it was conducted in accordance with the plans of its founder, it was invaluable to the student of local and state history and literature.

Mr. Metcalf's religious belief is liberal, as his democracy is orthodox. He has an active interest in educational affairs, and at Littleton was a useful member of the board of education. He maintains a close scrutiny upon the educational institutions that are under state patronage, and what he regards as useless or pernicious methods, received no dalliance at his hands. His principles are firmly fixed and his presentation of opinion and argument pointed and fearless. With his industry, integrity, blameless private life, broad acquaintance and long experience in his business, early legal training, and thorough mastery of the details of his profession, he fills an important and influential place in the journalism of his party and his state.—[A. S. B.

he came to Littleton to purchase the *Republic*, having been for several years a joint proprietor of the *Allegan County Democrat*, in which establishment he learned the printing business, after purchasing his interest. In June, 1876, he was united in marriage with Miss Hattie D. Meserve of Jackson, formerly a teacher in the Littleton high school, by whom he has one child, a son, now four years of age.

On the twenty-fifth of December, 1875, to meet "a long felt want" on the part of the Republican portion of the population, James S. Peavey commenced the publication of the *Littleton Argus*, a Republican paper, of the same size as the *Republic* at the start. Its publication office was in Tilton's Block, and the terms of subscription $1.50 per annum, in advance. With the beginning of the second volume the paper was slightly reduced in size. About the middle of the second year, the name was changed to the *Ammonoosuc Valley Argus*, and with No. 41 of the same volume the original size was restored. With the beginning of the third volume, January, 1878, it was again reduced in size to six columns to the page, and the name of the *Littleton Argus* once more applied. May 3, 1878, having purchased the subscription list and good will of the *Coos Republican*, at Lancaster, whose office had been burned, Mr. Peavey removed his paper and printing establishment to that town, and merged the *Argus* in the *Republican*, which he continued to publish till January, 1881, when he sold out to an association.

Mr. Peavey is a native of the town of Gilmanton, born August 4, 1843, but removed in childhood to Rumney, which was his home until twenty years of age. He commenced learning the printer's trade in the office of the *People's Journal*, in this town, in 1861, and was, afterwards, for a time, in the *Republican* office at Haverhill; but removed with his parents to Bethlehem, about 1864. There he was engaged in farm labor, until shortly after the *Republic* was started, when he entered Carey's employ, on that paper. Later he worked in the *People* office at Concord, in the *Patriot* office, and on the *Laconia Democrat*. In 1870, he formed a partnership with E. Couillard in the publication of the *Wolfe-*

borough Democrat; but, in November of that year, started the *Northern Sentinel* at Colebrook, which he published until April, 1872, when he sold out to Albert Barker and came to Littleton, where he was engaged for a time in the *Republic* office, and, afterward, for some three years before starting the *Argus*, did the printing at Kilburn's stereoscopic view manufactory. Upon selling the *Republican*, at Lancaster, he bought a farm in that town and has since been engaged in agriculture. He married, in 1869, Miss Mary L. Clark of Chichester, by whom he has had five children, but three of whom are now living.

The *Republic* remained the only paper in town, from the removal of the *Argus* establishment to Lancaster, until January 1, 1881, when the *Littleton Journal* was established, as a local Republican paper, by B. F. Robinson and Phineas R. Goold. It was located in the postoffice building, where Mr. Goold had already established a job printing business, and where it still remains. It was started as a seven column paper, but was enlarged to eight columns to the page at the beginning of the second year. The subscription price is $1.25 per annum, in advance, the same, it should be said, as that of the *Republic* for several years past. The paper is now on its fourth volume, with a well equipped office, and in the enjoyment of a liberal patronage.*

Mr. Robinson is a native of the town of Gilford, born January 14, 1853. He removed with his family to Manchester in early life, where he attended school and prepared for college, graduating at Dartmouth in the class of 1877. In September of the same year he came to Littleton as principal of the high school, which position he held for two years, previous to entering upon journalism. In January, 1880, he married Addie, daughter of the late Edward Kilburn.

Phineas R. Goold is one of the best known men in Littleton, today, among townspeople at least. A son of the late Marquis L. Goold, he was born in Littleton, March 21, 1842. He learned the printer's trade in youth, in the office of the

---

*The *Journal* was sold May 1, 1887, to John D. Bridge, formerly publisher of the *Colebrook News*.

old Haverhill *Republican*; subsequently worked for E. H. Cheney at Lebanon, and in the office of the *People's Journal* in this town; was one year in the employ of Carleton & Harvey at Newport, and, subsequently, for a time, in a printing office in Lynn, Massachusetts, but has resided in this town constantly since 1864, most of the time in the service of "Uncle Sam," as clerk in the postoffice, or postmaster, having held the latter position for the last twelve years. January 10, 1869, he married Selvia Danforth of this town.

The scope of my subject—"Newspapers and Newspaper Men"—naturally warrants reference to natives or former residents of the town who have engaged in journalism elsewhere. How many such there are, or may have been, aside from those referred to, in connection with papers here, I know not. My opportunities for investigation have afforded me information of only one other son of Littleton who has attained celebrity or success in the journalistic world. I refer to Moses A. Dow* of Boston, founder and proprietor of the *Waverly Magazine*.

Moses Arnold Dow was born in this town, on the place now occupied by George W. Fuller, at North Littleton, May 20, 1810, and is now, therefore, 74 years of age. When he was three years old his parents removed to Franconia, where they continued to reside, and where he remained until fourteen, when he went to Haverhill to learn the printer's trade with Sylvester W. Goss, of the *New Hampshire Intelligencer*, remaining until seventeen. Subsequently, he worked for a time for Moses G. Atwood, who had started a newspaper at Haverhill. In August, 1829, he went to Boston, where he worked till the following spring, when he came back to Haverhill and remained a year, working at his trade, and attending the academy three months of the time. He then went to Boston again, but in 1832 went to Limington, Maine, and started a paper called the *Maine Recorder*. The enterprise did not prove successful, and, at the end of three months, he gave it up and returned to Boston, where he worked two or three years as a journeyman, and then went back to Maine

---

*Moses A. Dow, died at his home in Charlestown, Mass., June 22, 1886.

and started the *National Republican* at Saco, with a partner, Daniel P. Marble. At the end of three weeks he gave up his interest to his partner, borrowed $10, and returned to Boston. Before he was thirty years old he had established nine different periodicals, all of which were failures. He worked in various offices in Boston, and was for a time a compositor on the *Traveller*. Meantime he had planned the *Waverly Magazine* enterprise, which he started in 1850, entirely without capital. It was pronounced a visionary scheme, and for the first four months ran him in debt at the rate of $40 per month. But he had faith in ultimate success, and persevered. His employes shared his faith, and worked for small pay, confident of better days to come. Soon the situation began to improve; the paper gained patrons, and he found himself making money. The circulation steadily increased, till, during the war, it ran up to 50,000 weekly; and during the war period, and for five years after, the profits amounted to $150,000 per annum. A large share of his profits he invested in building the Waverly Hotel, in Charlestown, now Boston, which cost $500,000, but proved an unprofitable investment, having been built in the inflation period. He is now the owner of unincumbered real estate to the value of half a million dollars, and of the *Waverly Magazine*, which he continues to conduct, at a handsome profit. He is one of the few men, born in this state, who have made fortunes in journalism. Mr. Dow's mother, Abagail Arnold, from whom he takes his middle name, was a daughter of the Hon. Jonathan Arnold, a member of Congress from Rhode Island. A half sister of his mother (daughter of Jonathan Arnold by a second wife) married Noah Davis of Haverhill, and they were the parents of Judge Noah Davis of New York; while Governor Arnold of Rhode Island was a half brother.

Mr. Dow married Elizabeth T. Houghton of Boston, by whom he has two children—Mary, wife of Rev. G. R. W. Scott of Fitchburg, Mass., and Emma, wife of Hon. Leonard F. Cutter of Boston. He retains a strong attachment for his birthplace, and the citizens of Littleton have a continual reminder of his regard in the fine clock on the tower of the schoolhouse, placed there through his liberality, a few years since.

Another distinguished native of Littleton, who, although gaining distinction mainly as a clergyman, was somewhat engaged in newspaper work, was Rev. Nelson Ebenezer Cobleigh, D.D., L.L. D., born November 24, 1814. He graduated from Wesleyan University, Middletown, Conn., in the class of 1843; joined the New England Conference the following year, and preached in various cities and towns of Massachusetts till 1853, when he was transferred to the Southern Illinois Conference, and became professor of ancient languages in McKendree College, Lebanon, Illinois. Subsequently he held a similar professorship in Lawrence University at Appleton, Wisconsin, for three years; but returned to Lebanon, and became president of McKendree College, in 1858, retaining that position till 1863, when he removed to Boston, and assumed the editorship of *Zion's Herald*, the leading Methodist denominational organ, the duties of which position he discharged vigorously and faithfully for three years. In 1867, he became president of the East Tennessee Wesleyan University at Athens, Tennessee, holding the position till 1872, when he removed to Atlanta, Georgia, and became editor of the *Methodist Advocate*, then established in that city, continuing his editorial labor until his death, February 1, 1874. Dr. Cobleigh was a strong and incisive writer, as well as an able preacher, and many of the productions of his pen, aside from his editorial work, have been published.

Rev. Enoch Merrill Pingree, a brilliant and devoted young clergyman of the Universalist denomination, who died in Louisville, Kentucky, ere he had completed his thirty-second year, was born in the north part of the town, May 9, 1817, being the oldest child of Major Joseph and Polly (Savage) Pingree. He was educated at Newbury (Vt.) Seminary; went West at twenty years of age, and commenced teaching in Ohio, but soon entered the Universalist ministry, to the doctrines of which faith he became attached in early youth. He preached ten years in Ohio, Kentucky, and other sections of the West and South, residing most of the time in

Cincinnati and Louisville. In youth he contributed frequently to the columns of the Vermont *Universalist Watchman*, and the Boston *Trumpet*, denominational organs, and for the last few years of his life was a regular contributor to the *Star in the West*, a Universalist paper, published in Cincinnati.

George E. Pingree, a younger brother of Enoch Merrill Pingree, born in this town, but residing in youth with an uncle, Jehiel Savage, in Lisbon, served in the Union army, in the late war, enlisting under the first call for volunteers, and re-enlisting in the Second New Hampshire Regiment. He was severely wounded in the right arm at the first battle of Bull Run, and honorably discharged; but returned to the service as a captain in the Eleventh Regiment, New Hampshire Vols., and fought through the war, subsequently entering the regular army and continuing in the service till 1869. He was the war correspondent of the *People's Journal*, writing at length and most entertainingly over the signature of "Volunteer." He subsequently engaged in journalism at Moline, Illinois, where he was Moline correspondent of the Rock Island and Moline *Union*, and afterwards local editor of the *Moline Review*. At last accounts he was employed by a St. Louis publishing house in the compilation of county histories.

Mrs. E. M. Walton, a daughter of Peter Bonney, the first representative from Littleton in the General Court, who has devoted her life mainly to teaching, in which she is still engaged, as a member of the faculty of the Litska Institute, at San Francisco, California, has had considerable experience as a newspaper writer and correspondent. She went to San Francisco in 1850, from New Orleans, where she had then resided ten years, in the capacity of California correspondent of the New Orleans *Picayune*; but soon changed to the *True Delta*, for which she continued to write on lucrative terms, as long as the general demand for California news was maintained, in the meantime making a trip to the Sandwich Islands, and publishing in pamphlet form her observations upon the condition of affairs in that quarter, which publication created a decided sensation. She has since written more or less for

California papers, and yet retains a lively interest in journalism.

Mr. Frye W. Giles, a native of this town, and one of the founders of Topeka, Kansas, has for many years used newspaper columns not infrequently, and with effect. He enjoys the rare distinction of being the historian of the town and city whose first cabin he helped erect, and in whose ownership he was a sharer. That structure is the frontispiece of his history of Topeka.

Dennison Rowell, a brother of Henry W. Rowell, who resided here and worked for the latter on the *People's Journal*, was for a time a newspaper publisher in Iowa, and has been otherwise engaged in the printing business.

Rev. Charles W. Millen, a native of this town, and a prominent Methodist clergyman, now located in Brooklyn, was, for a year or two, editor of the *Prohibition Herald*, a temperance paper, published some years ago at Concord, and then at Tilton. It may be proper to add, also, that Frank J. Eastman of Tilton, long a resident of this town, in time past, has for several years wielded a fruitful pen as Tilton correspondent of the *Laconia Democrat*, and done more work in that capacity than many of the local editors have accomplished. But, when it comes to the "solid work" of the newspaper office, Miss Mary A. Smith, a Littleton girl, for many years past an employe in the *Mirror* office at Manchester, who commenced setting type in the *Banner* office in this town, some thirty years ago, and has since steadily pursued the avocation, is fairly entitled to the leading position.

Let me add, in concluding these remarks, that you, people of Littleton, have now established in your midst two weekly papers, respectively favoring the two great political parties, but mainly devoted to local interests and the news of the town and this section of the state, of which you have good reason to be proud. I know whereof I speak, for it has been for the last fifteen years a part of my business to scan with considerable closeness the columns of the fifty to one hundred different papers issued in the state; and I do not hesitate to say, that the two papers published in this town compare most favorably, in general typographical appearance, in matter and makeup, with any other papers of their class in New Hampshire. I can say truly, too, that there is no other town in the state, of the same size and population, which maintains two papers at all to be compared with yours. These journals may not rank as great organs of political opinion—that is not the function of the local paper of the present day—but as disseminators of home intelligence, as stimulants to local industry, as conservators of the public peace and prosperity, and material, mental and moral well being of your community, their value cannot be overestimated. To its newspapers, as much as to any other single agent, the town owes its growth and progress in every essential direction. They are the principal medium through which people abroad are informed of the attractions and advantages which the town has to offer, either for business or pleasure. You may have fine churches and excellent schools, eloquent preachers, able lawyers, skillful physicians, spacious hotels, well filled stores in every line of trade; but it is to your newspapers that all outside your borders look for information concerning all these matters. If they speak not for you, you remain comparatively unknown.

This is, emphatically, a reading public. There are regularly taken and read in the town of Littleton, by its own people, more than two hundred copies of the various daily papers, and not less than 750 copies of weekly papers, each week, with numerous monthly magazines and other periodicals, aside from the patronage accorded your own local papers.* This is an excellent showing for the intelligence of the community. But whatever you may do in the way of patronage for outside publications, you must remember that your first duty in this line is to support the home papers. The stronger their local support, the better the showing which they make for the town itself to the world at large.

---

*Careful investigation, made in December, 1885, showed that there were then 173 copies of daily papers, 2047 weeklies, and 345 monthly, bi-monthly and quarterly publications taken at the postoffice and news stands in Littleton, making a total of 2565.

THE PROFESSION OF THE LAW.

ADDRESS BY HON. EDGAR ALDRICH.

The President said: The next subject is "The Profession of the Law." From quite an early time in the history of the town, it has either been blessed or cursed by a greater or less number of the legal profession. I will say, however, that Littleton, in the position it now occupies as a town in the state, has not been impeded in obtaining it by its citizens of the legal profession. You will listen to Mr. Edgar Aldrich, formerly of Colebrook, now of this town, whose standing in the profession, and former residence, will enable him to impartially discuss the subject.

ADDRESS.

Mr. President, Ladies and Gentlemen:

Perhaps the leading characteristic in human nature is the desire to acquire rights in property. You observe it well marked in early youth, and yet more marked as the mind strengthens and matures; and almost co-extensive with the desire to possess, is the disposition to defend possessions acquired. Human rights, and property rights, are necessarily complicated, and hence early in the history of mankind disputes arose, and as men become more numerous, and rights more complicated, it naturally followed that a few from the many should put themselves in training with respect to the law of rights, so that they might better aid the many in the legal controversies which must necessarily arise in the development of material wealth, and of civilization and government; and such have long since been classed as members of "the profession of law." This is not the time, or place, to speak of the noble profession of the law; nor of the benefits which community and state derive from a just and courageous discharge of the duties of the calling. Nor is it the place to analyze the character, or measure the success of those who are gone, but rather to call the roll of such members of the profession as have been associated with the development of this marvelously thrifty and prosperous town during the one hundred years of its existence.

Littleton's first practicing lawyer was Joseph Emerson Dow, who located at North Littleton in 1807. North Littleton was then the most important locality in town. Yet, it failed, as it would seem, to make the sojourn of its first lawyer profitable, for, in 1811, he removed his office to Franconia.

It has been said that he kept his office in his hat, and that his business corresponded with the size of his hat. Mr. Dow was born in Haverhill, N. H., in 1777. His parents were Gen. Moses Dow (who was elected to Congress, but declined to take his seat) and Phebe (Emerson) Dow. He was educated at Dartmouth and graduated in the class of 1799. He lived in Franconia until 1829, when he removed to Thornton. He afterwards returned to Franconia, where he died. He was the father of Moses A. Dow, who presented the clock to the town. His Littleton residence is still well preserved, and is occupied by George W. Fuller.

Elisha Hinds came about 1811, and remained until about 1834, most of the time in practice. He was one of the original corporators of the Glynville Library (Littleton's first public library) in 1813. He was the first postmaster at this village, and his office was where O. G. Hale, Esq., now resides, and was then the only house on that side of the river. He was born at Shrewsbury, Mass., and died at Brooklyn, N. Y., about 1854.

Hon. Henry A. Bellows came next, about 1828, and practiced law with success. He remained 22 years, and then removed to Concord. He was a member of the legislature from Littleton, and also from Concord, after he went there. He was appointed associate justice of the Supreme Court, September 23, 1859, and held the office until October 1, 1869, at which time he was appointed Chief Justice, which office he held at the time of his death, March 11, 1873. I remember Judge Bellows; he was a pure man, and an able and upright judge, and died honored by the profession, and beloved by all who knew him.

Edmund Carleton was born in Haverhill, N. H., October 29, 1797; graduated from Dartmouth College in 1822; read law with Hon. Joseph Bell, afterwards spent a few years in Virginia, teaching, and at the same time pursuing the study of law. He came to Littleton about 1830, and settled in the practice. Mr. Carleton was considered a good counselor, and often sought to reconcile differences without resort to legal controversy. As a lawyer he was ordinarily successful, but he engaged in business enterprises outside the profession which resulted disastrously, and finally withdrew him from the practice. He was a public spirited man, and was interested in the development of the town and the cause of education. He was one of the early Abolitionists of this vicinity. He died in Littleton, March 18, 1882.

Next came Hon. Calvin Ainsworth, a native of this town. He was admitted to the bar in 1835, entered upon the practice at Littleton in 1837, and remained until 1843, when he removed to Concord, where he was engaged in the practice of his profession for 12 years, at the end of which time he went to Madison, Wis., where he died, July 7, 1873. During his life he held various positions of honor and trust. It is said that he was a good lawyer, of amiable disposition, and that his gentle manners led him along through life, with little to disturb "the noiseless tenor of his way."

Hon. William Burns was here from 1844 to 1846, when he removed to Lancaster, where he now resides in honorable retirement. He was a gifted and eloquent advocate, but ill health long ago compelled him to withdraw from the practice of a profession which he adorned.

William J. Bellows, now residing in Littleton, retired

from the practice, read law with his brother, the late Chief Justice, with whom he formed a partnership in 1845, which continued until the latter moved to Concord, in 1850; after this, he was alone in the practice for about four years—then in partnership with John Farr until about 1860, at which time he retired from the law to engage in other business enterprises which have proved profitable and successful.

Mr. Bellows was an honorable and accomplished practitioner, and ill health alone prevented him from standing among the leaders at the bar.

Hon. Charles W. Rand came in 1847, and was engaged in the practice until his death, August, 1874. He was a sound, active and excellent lawyer; held various offices of trust, and among others, solicitor of Grafton county and United States District Attorney for the district of New Hampshire, which latter office he held at the time of his death.

John Farr was admitted to the bar in 1854, and was in practice until 1872, at which time he retired. Previous to his admission to the bar he had engaged in other business. He is now one of the oldest citizens, and has been useful and honorable in all the walks of life, and is now recognized by all as one of the fathers of the town of which he is also a loyal son.

Hon. Edward D. Rand was for two years Associate Justice of the Circuit Court of New Hampshire. He was engaged in practice at Littleton with his brother, Charles W. Rand, from 1857 to 1861, when he moved to the neighboring town of Lisbon, where he now resides, rich in scholarly culture and poetic refinement—vigorous, eloquent and powerful in advocacy, and at peace with all that is good in man and nature.

John A. Winslow, a son of Admiral Winslow, of Kearsarge fame, was here from about 1863 to 1866.

David S. Whitcher was admitted to the bar in 1877, and was engaged in practice at Littleton from that time until a few months before his death, which occurred March 14, 1881. It is said that he was a man of ability, and that in all his practice he was the soul of professional honor.

John M. Mitchell was admitted in 1872, formed a partnership with Hon. Harry Bingham, and was engaged in practice at this place until 1881, when he removed to Concord, where he is now engaged in a successful practice. In 1878, Mr. Mitchell was elected Solicitor of Grafton County, and served a term of two years.

John L. Foster, now in practice at Lisbon, was here three years, from 1873 or 1874 to 1876 or 1877. He was at one time Littleton's Police Judge.

Charles W. Bolles was admitted to the bar in 1877, and was in practice in this town for two years; and is now in practice in New York City.

Edgar M. Warner was here about one year, 1881 or 1882, and is now engaged in practice at Central Village, Connecticut.

Hon. Evarts W. Farr was born in this town, October 10, 1840. He was admitted to the bar in 1867, and continued in the practice until his death. His life was eminently successful and honorable,—honorable on the field of battle, honorable at the bar, honorable in the executive council of his state, honorable in the National Congress. He died November 30, 1880, and his name is tenderly cherished by all.

Very few lawyers have been natives of this town.

Ira Goodall, who enjoyed a very successful practice for a long term of years at Bath, was a son of Rev. David Goodall. He was born at Halifax, Vermont, August 1, 1788; but spent his youth in the place, and was educated in its schools. He became a man of large means, and was prominent in the early railroad enterprises, being at one time president of the White Mountains Railroad. He was a partner of Hon. A. S. Woods for some twenty years prior to the elevation of the latter to the bench. Mr. Goodall had a large family, and among his descendants are several lawyers. He died at Beloit, Wisconsin, March 3, 1868.

Benjamin West Bonney was an eminent son of Littleton, who became well known as a lawyer in New York. He was a son of Peter Bonney, and a graduate of Dartmouth College, 1824. As a Judge of the Supreme Court in New York, he earned an enviable reputation. In 1858, Dartmouth conferred upon him the degree of L. L. D., and he was one of the board of trustees of that institution from 1865 to 1868. At the age of sixty-five, which he reached in 1868, he was stricken down at the height of his career. He was successful in business, esteemed in all the walks of life—an able and honorable man.

Of a later period is Mr. Clinton Rowell, who, though born in Waterford, is of genuine Littleton stock, bred on her farms, educated in her schools and trained by her lawyers. He is in successful practice of the law in St. Louis, and we count him as one of our worthy representatives in " Littleton Abroad."

Our genial brother Page, who was " to the manor born," is here to speak for himself. In return for the kindly things he has said of his native town, she wishes him as full approval, in all his causes, as he wins today in speaking for *Littleton Abroad*.

Thus they have come, and gone. All doing some good, and none doing much harm, I trust. The view we are taking today is retrospective, rather than present, or prospective; it is therefore not the time to speak of the present active members of the profession,* but by common consent I may be pardoned for speaking of the two older members of the profession, who are now in active practice (Hons. Harry and Geo. A. Bingham), who admittedly stand at the head of the bar of the state. They are both remarkable men—one a Roman, and the other a Greek; both strong and masterly in all undertakings—scrupulously faithful to every trust, and

---

The present bar of Littleton consists of the gentlemen to whom reference has been made in this address, and a younger generation of lawyers who are now fairly entered upon the race for professional prestige.

Albert S. Batchellor, a native of Bethlehem, born in 1850, studied law with the Binghams, was admitted to practice in 1875.

Elbert C. Stevens, a native of Piermont, born in 1847; received an academic education; studied law with N. B. Felton and G. W. Chapman of Haverhill; was admitted to the bar in 1871; came to Littleton in 1873.

Wm. H. Mitchell was born at Wheelock, Vt., in 1856; received an academic education; studied law with the Binghams; was admitted to practice in 1880.

Daniel C. Remich was born in Hardwick, Vt., in 1852; received an academic education, studied law with Edgar Aldrich at Colebrook; graduated in the law department of Michigan University in 1878; was admitted to the bar at Lancaster in 1879, he practiced at Colebrook till 1882, and since, at Littleton.

Edgar Aldrich, a native of Pittsburg, N. H., was born in 1848; received an academic education; studied law with Ira A. Ramsey, at Colebrook, and graduated in law at Ann Arbor, in 1868; was in practice at Colebrook till 1881, when the firm of Bingham & Aldrich was formed at Littleton, in 1886.

closely identified with the history and prosperity of their adopted town.

Hon. Harry Bingham was admitted to the bar in 1846, and opened an office in this town, where he has since resided, holding an advanced position at the bar, and in the politics of his state, representing his town 18 years in the House of Representatives, two years in the State Senate, and in one constitutional convention.

Hon. George A. Bingham was admitted to the bar in Vermont, December, 1848, having pursued the study of the law in the office of Hon. Thomas Bartlett of Lyndon, in that state, with whom he formed a partnership, which continued four years. He came to Littleton in 1852 and entered into partnership with his brother Harry, and has since resided in town with the exception of a short business residence at Bath. He is equally strong at the bar, has twice represented his town in both branches of the legislature, and was for four years an Associate Justice of the Supreme Court of the state; and like his brother has been the candidate of his party for congressional honors.

And thus, as we view the past, we see that Littleton lawyers have borne an honorable part in the responsibility of town, county, state, and National government, and have stamped their impress upon the law, political policy, and literature of the day.

Littleton has conferred honor upon the profession; and members of the profession have in turn reflected honor upon their town.

THE PROFESSION OF MEDICINE.

ADDRESS BY DR. CHARLES M. TUTTLE.

The President said: The next subject is "The Profession of Medicine." I think the doctors have lived in Littleton longer than the lawyers, and the oldest physician I know in town is Dr. Charles M. Tuttle, to whom this subject is assigned. If he is present he will please come forward. He does not appear. He has undoubtedly, now as often before, "had a call," (laughter) and his paper will appear in the proceedings.

ADDRESS.

Mr. President:

The first period of the history of the town, as viewed from the medical stand-point, might be limited by the date of settlement and the advent of the settled physician, that is to say, from 1700 to 1800. Much of the material which would be valuable and interesting for this theme and this occasion, and which might once have been drawn from that period, is irretrievably lost. The doctor dwelt a long distance apart from his Apthorp patients. He had no time to inform the world of his doings. The newspapers did not report his cures, or advertise his skill. He did not anticipate the duty that would fall upon his remote successors on occasions like this. He failed to hand down a convenient journal of interesting dates, experiences and observations, as a country practitioner of ye ancient days. Moreover, the science of recorded observations of disease and of medical statistics found small place in the outfit of the custodian of the healing art in that early day in this region. He dealt with the ills of the flesh according to his best skill and judgment, but had neither the opportunity, nor the facilities, for compiling vital statistics or health reports.

McMaster, in his history of the people of the United States, has graphically described the doctor of this period, his education, his practice, his medicines. No better view of the subject can be found in the space which he devotes to it. The picture is interesting and instructive. It gives us an opportunity for a suggestive comparison of the practice at the extremes of our own centenary, for it is the doctor of 1784, who is described by McMaster. (Vol. 1, pp. 27-36.)

The population was scattered over the river valleys, and was made up of a class that was adventurous and strong. They had no luxuries. If there were any virtue in exercise and ventilation, the human system ought to have come very near perfection in the persons of our pioneer ancestors. They had, of course, the rough life and diet peculiar to new settlements. There was no profit in adulteration of food and rum. Women worked out of doors with the men, and practiced no black art to cut off posterity. We have, in the case of Hannah Caswell, whose story has been so well related by Dr. Rankin, an illustration of the stamina of the women of that time. The people of that generation had a mission to perform, and nature, at the same time generous and discriminating, had given them physical capabilities, equal to all the necessities that were thrust upon them. No doubt they defied many of the maxims of health which we regard as fundamental. Consumption assailed individuals who failed to inherit the average vital power of the race, and fevers brought down the strong in their strength. Disorders of the latter class, were generated, in some instances, from the decay of vegetable matter, which precedes the abolition of swamps, and follows the clearing up of the new land; and in other cases, in neglect of sanitary conditions, in the location and care of stables, out-buildings and places of retirement, and imperfect drainage; in the non-exclusion of filth from milk and other food, and recklessness in exposure to the rigors and vicissitudes peculiar to the climate. The inevitable results of these conditions followed; but the fatal diseases were generally of simple diagnosis, and belonged to a very few classes, as compared with the complex catalogue of physical disorders with which the medical profession has to do in the same locality at the present time.

In the first ten years, the population had not reached a score; in 1790, it is given as 96, and in 1800, it was 381. The dearth of interesting data for an account of the relations of such a population to the subject of medicine is not due solely to the remoteness of the time. Towns about us, equally, isolated in location and sparsely populated, would not, today, yield very much more material for the purposes of medical history, than the Littleton which antedated the days of its first settled physician.

We know something of the early practitioners who came with their saddle-bags, at infrequent intervals, through the town. We know their modes of practice, and we have their books of account, showing what the hardy settlers had to take, and what they had to pay. We know that, owing to the skill of the doctors to cure, or the stamina of the people in resisting the effects of disease, and perhaps of medicine, they increased, multiplied, and were strong. We know that no deadly epidemics scourged the populace, and that they were blessed with health to a degree that is remarkable.

The good old mothers knew the simplest and best of nature's restoratives, and every garret was an honest and reliable depository of the pharmacy of the field and forest.

Patent medicines and the nostrum tramps, who announce their coming in the gorgeous rhetoric of the circus bills, are now the humbug substitutes for the wholesome regimen of health, which, in the absence of professional advice, the good housewives of old prescribed, without money and without price, for the healing of the people. If the doctor could not be called, or was not wanted, the old matrons gave doses from substances, whose properties were understood, and gave them in accordance with the teachings of authentic experience. The good sense of the people in this matter is monumental.

The times have changed. We read of a nostrum; somebody has lied about its virtues; the falsehood is advertised in a thousand papers: on fences and on rocks; without analysis, without knowledge of its constituents, without inquiry as to the skill of its contriver, or the character of its sponsor; its consumers are the millions of all classes and conditions. The stuff is taken in quantities that would turn a thousand mills, and craft is made rich out of folly and ignorance. Butler well says in his Hudibras:

> "Doubtless the pleasure is as great,
> Of being cheated, as to cheat."

There were few medical schools, and few medical societies, at the time of which I have spoken. The doctors were, as a rule, fairly taught, but by private preceptors. The degree of "M. D." was an exceptional distinction. It is difficult, and perhaps impossible, to name all the regular physicians who rode a circuit through Apthorp and early Littleton. We know that Dr. Samuel White of Newbury, Vt., and later on, Dr. Isaac Moore of Bath, were among them. There may have been others, but we do not find their

> "Footprints on the sands of time."

Perhaps the purposes of the subject and the occasion may be as well subserved by giving personal sketches of these men, and of their successors in the profession, in the order in which they have entered into the history of the town, and by showing the relations of each to medical progress in his day and place of action.

In comparing the accomplishments of the early practitioners with their successors, it should be constantly borne in mind, that vast advances have been made in the methods and appliances of medical science since 1770. This is not the occasion for a careful review of this progress, but we may note hereafter some of its more prominent features.

DR. SAMUEL WHITE.

It fortunately happened that all mention of Dr. Samuel White, the first settled physician in the Coos Country, so called, was omitted in Miss Hemmenway's Gazetteer of Vermont. I speak of the incident as fortunate, for it called out a very full biographical account of Dr. White, from his friend, Dr. W. H. Carter, formerly also at Newbury, but now living, at a great age, at Bradford. Dr. Carter was eminently qualified for this duty, as he had from his boyhood known Dr. White, and during the last twenty years of the latter's life was intimately acquainted with him. The lives of these two men cover a long space, and include the whole period of the civilized history of the region in which they practiced their profession. I shall adopt all of Dr. Carter's article that is material to my subject; one item should be added. Dr. White had a large family of children, in which twins were a not infrequent occurrence.

Dr. Carter says:—

"Dr. Samuel White was born in Plaistow, state of New Hampshire, November 10, 1750. He was the son of Nicholas White, Esq., a respectable farmer of that town. He received his early education at the common school where he lived; and he also obtained a competent knowledge of the Latin language to enter upon the study of medicine with facility. At the early age of seventeen, he commenced his medical studies, and continued them four years, under the instruction of Thomas Brickett, M. D., of Haverhill, Mass., who was a man of learning and skill, having enjoyed the advantages of the medical schools and hospitals of Edinburg, in Scotland, and served as surgeon in the British army. The long term of study, under the instruction of an eminent physician and surgeon, was well calculated to fasten in his mind that knowledge which was, afterward, so much needed by him, when, far removed from his professional brethren, and in a new country, he was forced to rely upon his own knowledge and judgment in many difficult cases committed to his charge.

At the expiration of his pupilage Dr. White was well recommended by his preceptor, and entered upon the duties of his profession. He practiced one or two years in his native town with good acceptance, in families of the best respectability. But, at that time, the tide of emigration was fast setting to the north. Many families and individuals from the southern portion of New Hampshire, and from Massachusetts, had located themselves upon the fertile meadows of the Coos Country. Noah White, an elder brother of the doctor, had removed to Newbury with his family in 1763; and Col. Jacob Kent, who married his sister, Mary White, emigrated with his family the same year. Some years after this Samuel visited his brother and sister at the "Coos," and carried with him a proclamation for a day of Thanksgiving, which had been duly observed where he resided, but was received and used by Rev. Peter Powers and his parishioners, as related in the "Early History of Coos." In the spring of 1773 Dr. White concluded to try his fortune with the new settlers on the hills and valleys of the wilderness. This, it will be perceived, was ten years after the first settlement of Newbury was begun, and two years before the Revolutionary war. At that time there were some families in Newbury, Haverhill, Bradford, Orford, and Piermont, and it was necessary that a physician should be located among them. Nor was there any physician between Newbury and Canada, on the river, so that Dr. White was the only one to be called upon for a considerable distance round, at the first commencement of his practice. He was sometimes called to the distance of many miles, through dense forests, to visit the sick; and these excursions were sometimes performed on foot and on snow-shoes, while marked trees were the only guide that led him to his destination. The writer of this, has heard Dr. White relate many stories of his nocturnal rambles to visit his patients, when the darkness was so great that he was obliged to feel for a path to avoid wandering into a swamp, or falling headlong from some abrupt precipice.

Roads and bridges were but few; rapid streams were to be forded and quagmires to be passed through; while the howl of a wolf, or the growl of a bear, were the only evidence given him that the woods were inhabited. The Dr. would often tell of the uncomfortable situation in which he found his patients; many of them in log houses without chimneys, while the only redeeming chance that they had to be warm, was to fill the fireplace with wood, of which they had a plenty. He said he had seen little drifts of snow where the new born infant was lying with its mother. On one or two occasions the doctor travelled on snow-shoes to Lancaster, N. H., to visit some families settled there, while the log huts on the way were few and far between. Most of the inhabitants, at that time, were able to pay him but little for his services; but there was one thing, he said, to cheer him; they were always glad to see him. At the time of the Revolutionary war, Dr. White had fully entered upon the duties of his profession at his new home. With the new settlers, generally, he was well acquainted, and he had his patients in turn among them all. And whether they were active patriots in the American cause, or favored the idea of submission to British rule, he still pursued the even tenor of his way, seeking their best good as their physician. He was ready, at all times, to serve his country in his professional capacity, as occasion required. He acted as surgeon to the Continental soldiers who were stationed at Newbury, under the command of Gen. Jacob Bailey, and dressed the wound received by a Mr. Gates, when a scout of British and Tories made a foray upon the people at the Oxbow, in quest of Gen. Bailey. When Gen. Burgoyne entered the western part of Vermont, Dr. White attended, as surgeon, such troops as could be spared from Newbury and the vicinity, to arrest the march of the British army, and remained with them until ther return from the field of victory. Dr. White was considered a good physician by his employers generally; and the writer of this, remembers of hearing several of his cotemporaries speak in high praise of his success in some very serious diseases: and he continued to sustain the reputation of a judicious and skillful practitioner, as the country became more settled. In the various epidemics which appeared at different times, he manifested a good degree of professional knowledge, and evinced a tact and judgment adapted to the embarrassing and uncomfortable situation in which he frequently found his patients. In the treatment of chronic diseases, the powers of his judgment and discerning were conspicuously displayed, and he always adhered to a regular and scientific course, founded upon true principles of Pathology, as developed in his time. In his intercourse with his professional brethren, Dr. White was quite communicative, and liberally contributed from the stores of knowledge, which a long experience had enabled him to lay up. Hence, he was often consulted with confidence by his juniors, after age and infirmities rendered it necessary for him to relinquish, in a great measure, the regular care of patients. As an operative surgeon Dr. White never made any pretension to fame; although at different periods of his practice he performed several of the minor operations with success. He was of a calm and easy disposition, benevolence greatly predominating, so that he might truly be said to

"Lay his own advantage by
To seek his neighbor's good."

He was not a close collector of debts due to him, and a great part of his earnings were never paid. In his daily intercourse with his employers, Dr. White was of a cheery and facetious turn of mind, and, where danger was not apprehended, his funny remarks and capital stories, would often act as a cordial in cases where there was a depression of the mind from extreme "nervousness," or an unfounded apprehension of danger. He had a peculiar way of relating his anecdotes and short stories, well calculated to diffuse a spirit of mirth and pleasantry among his audience, and cause them for a time to forget their troubles. Many of his capital stories will long be remembered and rehearsed; but his manner of telling them cannot be fully imitated.*

About four years previous to his death, Dr. White united with the First Congregational Church in Newbury. But the sun of his life was fast declining, and his mind and memory soon exhibited but a wreck of what it had once been. The powers of life gradually receded from the worn out body, and on the twenty-sixth day of February, 1847, he quietly fell asleep, aged ninety-seven years."

---

*It was Dr. White who remarked, that he always had poor luck with his patients in their last sickness.

DR. WHITE'S BOOKS OF ACCOUNT.

The worn and time stained books of Dr. White, present to us a most interesting view of the practice of a country doctor one hundred years ago.

Two books, of some 360 manuscript pages, are preserved, which seem to have dated from the beginning of his Newbury practice. In them, are the itemized accounts, written in a hand like copper-plate, of the journeys he took, the drugs he exhibited, the teeth he pulled, and the sums he charged, but often did not collect. There are entries from 1773 to 1790, not always chronologically arranged, and probably not covering the whole of his practice during that period, but presenting doubtless, a good average specimen.

He visited in Corinth, Bath, Haverhill, Mooretown, Barnet, Upper Coos, Piermont, Lyman, Peacham, Ryegate, Topsham, Gunthwaite, Landaff, Morristown, Apthorp, Wentworth, Coventry, Rumney, Groton, Bradford, Riverlamoile and Newbury.

The visit, and each item of treatment, were accounted separately. For instance, we find, at the last of a series of visits to Mr. Abial Chamberlain, the charge made as follows:

"Sept. 10th, 1784. To visit 2s. Physic 1s. Emet. 1s. Bleeding 1s. Sal. Nitre 1s.—6s." The minimum charge for a visit was one shilling; the maximum was 60 shillings—to Upper Coos. While there was usually a regular schedule of charges, there are occasionally great variations, for reasons which do not appear, but the weather and the difficulty of the journey and the urgency of the call, were doubtless taken into consideration; and a very low price may have arisen from other visits to the same place, as well as from the poverty of the patient. To Corinth, it was all the way from one to twenty shillings; to Haverhill, two to six; to Apthorp, two, three and twenty-seven shillings.

Medicine was usually one shilling, sometimes, two; bleeding, always one shilling; tooth pulling, one shilling; dressing a wound, one shilling; lancing a sore, one shilling; setting an arm or leg, six shillings. "Attendance on your wife's Travel" was twelve shillings. The dollar, it appears, was equal to six of the twenty shillings which make a pound, as we find a credit of seven dollars on account, entered as 2£, 2s., or 42s. These two books show accounts approximating 2500£; a large proportion of them have no credit entries, and probably were not paid, as he seems to have entered carefully all payments. Many a large account ran six, eight or ten years, and when settlement is made, it is more frequently by note of hand than by cash.

The good doctor used a wide range in his materia medica. One hundred and fifty-two remedial agents are mentioned in his books; thirty-six of these are used once only, ten twice, and eleven three times. When his patients wanted medicine, they had it. In 4,271 recorded visits only 181 were plain; in all the others something happened, and as we have a record of 8471 doses or operations, frequently much took place.

His main reliance was upon comparatively few remedies. It was "Physic," (some efficient mixture of his own), 1630 times.

Camphor,	994 "
Valerian,	650 "
Bleeding,	504 "
Cream Tartar,	444 "

4222

He gave 228		"vomits"(or "emetic.")
288	doses of	cortex, or balsam Peru.
275	"	myrrh.
258	"	rhubarb.
244	"	bitters.
262	"	tarter emetic.
203	"	nitre.
148	"	antimony, crude or wine.
137	"	lavender.
116	"	"contraery" (contraerva).
93	"	calomel.
83	"	assafœdita.
81	"	chamomile.

2416

2416

6638

He used guiacum, jalap, magnesia, castor, scilla, and

sapo pills more than fifty times each; and paregoric twenty-one; liq. laud. twenty; cascarilla, gum Arabic, oil of amber, elixir vitriol, elixir salutis, annis seed, gum ammoniac, cinnamon, licorice, pectoral balsam, Armenia Bole, and sweet spirits of nitre, twenty or more times each.

He used pill cochiæ, pill æthiops, pill cathartic, sapo pills, female pills, mercurial pills, Hooper's, Anderson's and Locker's pills; elixirs vitriol, astma, solutis, proprieta, stomatica; Bateman's and Thurlington's drops, and British oil.

Most of these drugs are found or known in every pharmacy today. British oil, Bateman's drops, Thurlington's drops and Hooper's pills, greet us with their marvellous cures of over a century upon their imitation antique wrappers.

Less familiar are these others of Dr. White's medicines; sago permeum, sp. sal c. c., ens veneris, Roman vitriol, flos bolostinos, lac ammoniac, mellilot, cinnabar, "contraery," sal mirabile, oculi crancorum, sp. hierapic., flos benjamin, crocus, vorsena, sal cor cerebrini, winter bark and hat case.

One misses from the list many potent chemicals and chemical groups. Iodides and bromides would not be expected. Opiates are little used; alcohols were probably kept in the house, or easily got at the store; aids to digestion appear but little. The remedies apply to inflammatory diseases largely, and to a rugged people. Dr. White bled, in his record, 504 times at a shilling each—about a hogshead all told. He seems to attend to it periodically, as we find entries in different households at the same date. Many a time we find "To bleeding two," and not infrequently "To bleeding three."

His surgical practice seems not to have been large. In the records he has account of seventy-six tooth pullings only, dressing wounds fifty-seven times,—often several times in the same case—setting ten arms and three legs. He records only seven confinements, a number so small that it is difficult to find satisfactory explanation.

I am indebted to Dr. E. J. Bartlett of Dartmouth College, for this excellent analysis of the old books of account. On the point raised by Dr. Bartlett, as to the reason for the limited practice in obsterics indicated by the charges, I have little doubt that the explanation lies in the fact that there were numerous expert midwives in the new settlements, and they attended to this class of cases. It would be on exceptional occasions that Dr. White, the only physician in the country, could be accessible to such calls.

Between 1773 and 1787, the doctor visited patients in Apthorp, as shown by these books of account. Later volumes than the ones now accessible might give us the names of others with whom he had professional relations in Littleton. As a part of the earliest authentic written history of the town, such accounts, relating to our ancient townspeople, are of general interest; and as relics of the beginning of the practice of medicine here, they are worthy of reproduction. We copy them as they are written in the books.

1773   Old Mr. Hopkinson of Apthorp   Dr.

Aug't 23d.   To a visit from Davids to his house,   " 3 "
             To Spt. Lavender, 1s.   Elix. Camphor, 2s.   " 3 "
             To a visit. 20s. Physic. 2s. Gum Camphor, 2s., 6d.   1 4 6
             To Myrrh. 2s.   Sal Nitre, 2s.   Valerian, 3s. " 7 "

     Oct. 20th, 1786. Rec'd the above by his son John's note,   £1 17 6

1774   Mr. Johnathan Hopkinson of Apthorp,   Dr.

Nov'r 8th.   To a visit, 4s. Physic, 1s. Spt. Lavender, 2s.
             Liquid Laud, 1s., 6d.   " 8 6
             To a visit, 20s.   Cream Tartar, 2s. Rhei, 2s.   1 4 "
             To cortex, 3s.   Spt. Lavender. 3s.   " 6 "

     Oct. 20th, 1786. Rec'd the above by his note,   £1 18 6

1775   Mr. David Hopkinson of Apthorp,   Dr.

Aug't 23d.   To a visit, 18s. Spt. Lavender, 2s. Sal Nitre,
             2s.   Valerian, 2s., 6d.   1 3 6

1782		Mr. Samuel Nash of Apthorp,		Dr.	
Oct'r 1st.		To a visit, 24s. Gum Camphor, 3s.		1	10
		To a visit, 27s. Gum Camphor, 3s.		1	10
		To precipitat, 2s. Roman Vitriol, 1s.			3
		To Bazillicum flavern, 2s.			2
July 29, 1783		To a visit, 2s. Pill Cathart. 2s. Cortex Cascarilla, 2s., 6d.			6 4
Aug't 1st.		To a visit, 2s. Physic, 2s.			4
8th.		To a visit, 3s. Gum Myrrh, 2s. Physic, 2s.			7
9th.		To a visit, 3s. Bitters, 2s.			5
17th.		To a visit, 3s. Essence Antimoni, 2s.			5
Sep't 1st.		To a visit, 2s. Cortex, 2s. Gum Camphor, 1s.			5
		To a visit, 2s. Valerian, 1s., 6d.			3 6
				£5	10

1787		Capt.*	Apthorp,		Dr.
Jan. 23d.		To a visit, 26s.————net. 1s. Gum Camph. 1s.		1	8
		Sal Nitre, 1s. Antmi. Vin. 1s.			2
27th.		To a visit, 26s. Cream Tart. 2s.		1	8

DR. ISAAC MOORE.

The town of Bath had no settled physician until 1790, when Dr. Isaac Moore, coming from Haverhill, located in the place. He is supposed to have begun his practice about 1787. He was of rugged Scotch stock, and his youth had been passed in the midst of the hardships and dangers of the frontier in the Revolutionary period. The early record of Worcester, Mass., gives mention of three of this name. One of them, the son of Isaac and Hannah, born March 11, 1741, might have been the father of the doctor. His son John places the date of the doctor's birth in 1765, and the family also have it that it was in Worcester.† While but a boy, he saw the sacking of Royalton by the Indians and Tories in 1780. His wife was a daughter of Col. Timothy Bedel. She was born in Bath in 1771, and was quite young when she married the doctor. They removed to Bath the next year, and for several years occupied the Hurd place, so called, near

---

*The name is obliterated, but was doubtless either Capt. Caswell or Capt. Williams.

†Hon. Nathan Crosby in his History of the Crosby Family, states that Dr. Moore was born and educated in Scotland, but is understood to have had other or additional information after the publication of the book.

the old meeting house. The date of his settlement is taken from the Appendix to Sutherland's Historical Discourse, p. 80. In the same volume, however, on p. 54, there is evidence that the doctor was identified very intimately with Bath, in a professional capacity, if not a resident, at an earlier date. The text is as follows:—" Under date of November 1789, we find the following: Voted, that Dr. Isaac Moore set up a house of Inoculation in this town, one half mile west of Mr. David Weeks." Mrs. Smith states that this movement met with great opposition, and that the first house that he erected was torn down by the disaffected, before it was finished. He succeeded however the next year, in completing one; and a good many persons (she among the rest) went there and had the small pox. But, in a short time it came to a sudden end. In 1793 it took fire and burned to ashes. This account reminds us of the public sentiment recently manifested at Montreal on the same subject. But whatever may have been the temper of the public towards the enterprise, the record shows that Dr. Moore was a sagacious and progressive physician, who early encountered the same difficulties that every man will, who gets ahead of the times in applying the true science of medicine.

This copy of an advertisement in the *Vermont Journal and Universal Advertiser*, No. 391, published at Windsor, January 25, 1791, has been forwarded by Rev. E. M. Goddard of that place, and I give it entire;—

THE subscriber, respectfully informs the public, that he has good accommodations at his hospital, for those who wish to take the benefit of having the SMALL POX by the easy and safe method of inoculation, and on very moderate terms, viz: Inoculation, medicine, attendance, nursing and every thing necessary for each patient, excepting their bed cloaths. for the term of three weeks for thirty shillings; if longer detained, six shillings per week—Inoculation, medicine, and attendance, for fifteen shillings each. The money to be paid at the time of inoculation, or at the farthest at the time of leaving the hospital.—Grain will be received in part payment. The public may be assured that mercurials will not be administered by their humble servant,

ISAAC MOORE.

Bath, (Newhampshire) January 17, 1791.   1&3

It is quite possible that Dr. Moore was the nearest physician for the people of Littleton, for several years after his location in Bath. But, a short time previous, we have found Dr. White coming to his Littleton friends from Newbury. It would not, therefore, be drawing an unreasonable presumption if we assume that Dr. Moore, from 1790 to 1800, a period that evidently was the most effective part of his career, had a principal share of the medical practice in Littleton.

Dr. Ainsworth came here in 1800. Dr. Stanley is said to have been a local practitioner from about 1802 to 1804. Dr. Moore, himself, located at the North part of the town about 1806. He removed from Bath and lived on the Connecticut river, in the house opposite that formerly owned and occupied by T. B. Wheeler. His dwelling-house and all its contents at Bath, had been consumed by fire that year, and this may have been the occasion of his change of location. He remained in Littleton only two or three years. Returning to Bath, he occupied a house near that of Andrew Woods, as it was in 1855. At a previous period he occupied the S. & W. Minot place, and there kept a public house for several years. In politics he was a Federalist. He held various town offices, and was town clerk of Bath several years. He died in 1818, at a comparatively early age. His habits conformed perhaps too strictly to the spirit of the times, and his nervous system became badly deranged a considerable time before the end. His widow remarried and lived to a great age. Her faculties were well preserved, and she was one of the best authorities on events which had come to her knowledge. Thirteen children were born to them. Their descendants hold honorable stations in society, and have been successful in affairs. We have the estimate of two contemporaries on the professional character of Dr. Moore. The Rev. David Sutherland in his Historical Discourse, (p. 16) says :—

"When I settled here, Dr. Moore was the only physician. I believe he was the first physician who ever settled here. Moore was not much of a book learned physician, but had quite a knack of managing diseases. He was a very rough man with a quick perception of the ludicrous ; but his drollery was apt to be offensive to delicacy and modesty. He was superseded by Dr. Edward Dean, who immediately succeeded to almost all the practice in the place."

Says Dr. Adams Moore :—" He was a bold, active, and often very successful practitioner of medicine."

DR. CALVIN AINSWORTH.

The settled physician preceded the settled lawyer and the settled minister in the practice of their respective professions at Littleton. Notwithstanding some vague traditions to the contrary, the distinction of being the first physician to occupy this field belongs to Dr. Ainsworth. He was a young man when he took up his residence here, having been born at Claremont, N. H., June 3, 1777. His father was Edward Ainsworth of that place. His education was academic. We learn from his son Laban, who still resides in this place, that his father studied medicine at Charlestown, N. H. At one time his preceptor was confined in the Charlestown jail for debt, and Ainsworth was permitted to enter the jail limits, recite his studies and get his instruction, without much interruption from outsiders. Professional calls did not interfere with the student's privileges, and he always knew where to find his instructor. Dr. Ainsworth located in Littleton just prior to the year 1800. The population of the place was then small, and the people were just entering upon a moderate prosperity. He was an old school practitioner, and continued in the same field of professional labor for forty years. A good nurse, with tact and a genial presence, he was a favorite doctor in many families. He was vivacious, and fond of amusement and social entertainment. The social element in his nature is understood to have dominated his personal habits in a marked degree. He could play the violin, and sometimes wielded the bow to help on merry-makings. He was, for a time, a Federalist of the Hartford Convention order, but, latterly, a Democrat; but he had no special church affiliations.

He is described as rather stout and short in stature. He

had good physical powers, but was not of a pushing or belligerent disposition. He did not succeed in accumulating property.

Dr. Burns, the only rival who kept the field any considerable time in thirty years, commenced practice in 1806. Burns had many elements of professional success that Ainsworth lacked. The relations of the two were not intimate. On the other had, while Adams Moore was not more like Burns than was Ainsworth, the relations of the latter rivals, if they could be called such, were very close and harmonious.

Dr. Burns did not allow his neighbors to joke him without snug fitting retorts. One story, however, has come to us without his reply to Dr. Ainsworth's sally. Burns had a new sleigh, with runners turned back over the dasher, and birds' heads carved at the ends, according to the prevailing style of adornment. He called Ainsworth's attention to his purchase, and asked him how he liked the style. Ainsworth said it was all well enough except the birds' heads. He would suggest that ducks' heads were more fitting for that sleigh. The ducks would be a great help to him in crying "Quack, Quack."

Dr. Ainsworth married Susannah Howe of New Ipswich, who was a school teacher in Littleton about the time of his settlement in the place. Their children were (1) Americus, lately a farmer in this town; (2) Calvin, a lawyer, here and at Concord, and later, a Municipal Judge at Madison, Wis.; (3) Laban, before mentioned; (4) Sybil P., who married and resided at Townsend, Mass., and (5) Susannah H., who lived with her sister. Both died suddenly and within a few days of each other. The early death of these daughters was a severe blow to Dr. Ainsworth. He sank under his grief, and died at Littleton, July 12th, 1839.

His latest residence was near the first Waterford bridge, though he had dwelt in several other localities, but always in the vicinity of the river. Dr. Adams Moore, for some ten years his contemporary, left this minute in regard to Dr. Ainsworth among his historical papers:—"His disposition was amiable but there was a great lack of self reliance as a physician."

DR. ABNER STANLEY.

Old residents recall a physician of this name who resided here for a short time. He was a tax payer in 1802 and 1803. We have not been able to learn whence he came, where he went, or anything further for his biography.

WILLIAM BURNS, M. D.

William Burns was of Merrimack, N. H. He was born April 15th, 1783. He was of Scotch Irish descent, his family having been among the early settlers of Londonderry. From them he inherited an inflexible will, a biting wit, a proneness to sarcasm which did not always spare his friends, and the sturdy independence which characterizes the race. He received an academic education, pursued the course of medical study usual in his day, but did not take his degree until 1826, when he had been in active practice more than twenty years. He came to Littleton in 1806 and took up his residence at the village, then known as Mann's Mills, and for upwards of half a century enjoyed an extensive practice. In his practice he was conservative, being governed largely by the principles laid down in the books; he was a rigid adherent of his school, and its ardent defender against what he regarded as the heresy of other systems of practice. He was one of the founders of the White Mountain Medical Society, and his name appears in its records more frequently than that of any other member; his interest in its welfare continued down to the closing hours of his life.

Dr. Burns was a public spirited citizen, who gave much of his time to the advancement of every good cause. He was a member of the first board of School Inspectors, the duties of the position being similar to those of the present Superintending School Committee; and for a period covering nearly fifty years was repeatedly a member of the board. It is probable that no man in the state has been so many times appointed to the position. He was among the early members of Morning Dawn Lodge of Masons at Waterford, and with a zeal and fidelity which characterized his life, stoutly maintained the principles of the order under the adverse conditions which resulted from the crusade waged against the order during the period of the anti-Masonic contests of 1826-40. It was his proud boast that at a time when it cost a man his social position, and seriously affected his professional and business standing, he had the courage of his convictions, and stood up and was counted as a member of the ancient order. He was active in securing the charter of the lodge in this town, and, in his honor, his associates conferred his name upon it. He became a member of Franklin Chapter at Bath, in 1823, and, upon the revival of the organization at Lisbon, some forty years afterwards, he was one of the old guard who renewed his allegiance.

In manner, the doctor was a gentleman of the old school. His natural dignity was softened by an unfailing politeness. He was noted as a raconteur, and was long the presiding genius at the improvised club which originally assembled at the old red store, and in later years at the brick store, when under the management of Goold & Balch. Many stories are still current of his encounters with Dr. Ainsworth, in which he sometimes came off second best, as his rival's tongue was nearly as sharp as his own.

Dr. Burns was an apostle of temperance through his long and useful life, and by precept and example never failed to encourage those who were striving to conquer the evil habit; his caustic tongue spared neither saint nor sinner, who transgressed by indulgence in liberal potations. Shortly after coming to town, he was invited by the Parson to join him in a drink of flip, but declined with the remark that ministers must decide upon their own consciences whether they ought to drink, but the physician's responsibilities were such that he must keep his head clear and set no vicious example before his fellows of abuse of his physical system or intellectual powers.

A few years before his death he withdrew from active practice, after having followed it for sixty years, and passed his time in the midst of his favorite books and in delightful social intercourse with friends. He died in September, 1868, honored and respected by the entire community.

ADAMS MOORE, A. M., M. D.

Dr. Adams Moore, son of William and Isabella (McClary) Moore, and grandson of William and Molly (Jack) Moore, was born in Bedford, N. H., October 17, 1799. He was educated at Londonderry, N. H., Phillips Academy, Andover, Mass., and Dartmouth College, from which he graduated in 1822. He was principal of the Academy in Peacham, Vt., 1822-4; tutor in Dartmouth College, 1824-5; studied medicine with Dr. William Burns of Littleton, and took his medical diploma at Dartmouth Medical College in 1827. He commenced the practice of medicine in Littleton; afterwards removed for a short time to Lowell, Mass., then returned to Littleton, where he continued in practice till his death in 1863. As a scholar, he took high rank in college, as is clearly indicated by his appointment as tutor two years after his graduation. The impression of the writer is that he stood first in his class, but efforts to determine this point, positively, have been unsuccessful. As a teacher, he is remembered by one, who, as a boy from ten to twelve years old, was under his instruction in Peacham, as a very pleasant, kindly man. In his chosen profession, his scientific attainments were exceptionally high. He was always thoughtful and studious, and, during his entire professional life, kept himself well informed in regard to the progress of medical science, so that at any time he could tell what was the most approved method of treatment, as well as what was the generally accepted pathology of any disease he was liable to meet with in his practice. In his professional work, the doctor was careful, thoughtful, faithful to every trust, modest, unassuming and unpretentious, and entirely free from all the tricks of quackery, on which by far too much of what is called professional success so often depends.' He was, perhaps, somewhat deficient in energy and professional enthusiasm, and in that nice discrimination and professional tact which is needed to make scientific knowledge most fully available at the bedside; but, taking him all in all, he was certainly a physician of quite unusual excellence.

In his intercourse with other physicians, especially those

practicing in the same field with himself. Dr. Moore was always gentlemanly, courteous, considerate, just and kind, and in some cases certainly very generous, as the writer can testify from his own personal experience. It is not often the case that two physicians, practicing in the same village, live so many years in such perfect harmony as always existed between himself and his old preceptor, Dr. Burns. But he was not merely a good *physician*. Outside of his profession, he was well informed in all matters of general interest, political and moral, educational and social, though too modest and retiring to be, to a very marked extent, a leader of men. His great intelligence, sound judgment, shrewdness, strong will and quiet persistence in whatever he undertook, enabled him to exert a very decided influence over others, and this influence he seemed always to exert in favor of what he deemed to be the best interest of all concerned.

In religious matters, he associated with the Congregationalists, but he was not a member of any church. In politics, he was for many years a Democrat; but in the latter part of his life identified himself with the Freesoil movement. "He took a decided interest in political controversies, and was a frequent contributor to state and local papers. A series of articles in the *People's Journal*, on the subject of slavery, attracted much attention." He was, for many years, associated with the Rev. Mr. Carpenter and others as a member of the school committee in Littleton. He was a Freemason and an Odd Fellow. He had a lively sense of the humorous, and many anecdotes might be given, illustrating this trait of character.

"Dr. Moore's wives were granddaughters of Col. Moses Little of Newburyport, Mass., a prominent soldier of the Revolution, and proprietor of nearly all the land in the original territory of Littleton, which took its name from him; and the doctor became the best informed man in his section, as to the history of all grants, titles, boundaries of townships and private holdings in northern New Hampshire. Before the breaking out of the war he had a history of Littleton well under way, the first chapters of which were devoted to these topics, and constitute a most valuable contribution to local history. Few men had better opportunities for accurate information in such matters, and few could have made better use of them. Had he lived to complete this literary undertaking, he would have placed his name in the list of those to whom our people are indebted for valuable historical work."

Dr. Moore was twice married, first, June 1st, 1829, to Anna Mary, daughter of Moses Little of Newburyport, Mass., by whom he had five children—Maria Little, Isabella McClary, Elizabeth Adams, William Adams and Anna Mary. Second, to Maria Little, sister of his first wife, August 16, 1843, by whom he had one son, James White. Of these children, three survived him, and two are still living. One, the youngest daughter, is the wife of Hon. E. P. Green of Akron, Ohio. James, the only son by the second wife, is a physician in successful practice at Lynn, Mass.

"William, the oldest son, and a young man of much promise, was one of the earliest volunteers when the war broke out, and, after a brief service in a New York regiment of Zouaves, returned to Littleton, raised a detachment and joined the fighting Fifth New Hampshire Regiment, under the heroic Col. Cross. Before he was twenty-one years of age he became a captain, fought with distinguished bearing in all the battles of the Peninsula and Antietam." He was killed, as is well known, at the battle of Fredericksburg, and though great efforts were made to recover the body, they were unavailing. This sad event had a very depressing effect on his father, who died not long after, November 5, 1863. His death is supposed to have been hastened, if not caused, by this great sorrow.

Besides the public positions already referred to, Dr. Moore was Censor of New Hampshire Medical Society in 1860 and 1861; president of White Mountain Medical Society in 1848 and 1849; surgeon's mate of the Thirty-second Regiment, New Hampshire Militia, from 1838 to 1843. He was the author of an epitome of Braithwaite's Medical Retrospect, and many papers read before the medical societies of which he was a member, besides the political and historical writings already noticed.

EZRA CARTER WORCESTER, M. D.

Several members of this family have been identified with the history of Littleton. Two sons of the Rev. Leonard Worcester, Evarts and Isaac R., were successively the Congregationalist pastors of the First church. Ezra, another son, having taken the degree of M. D. at Hanover, in July, 1838, in poor health came to Littleton and opened a select school. He was unable to endure the fatigue of this occupation, and, after a few months, gave it up. Drs. Burns and Moore, who were the only physicians in town, urged him to try the practice of his profession here. His health in a short time again failed. After studying theology a year, and satisfying himself that the labor of that calling would be beyond his strength, he located in the practice of medicine at East St. Johnsbury, in 1841. He was at that point two years; then at Chelsea, Vt., and from 1846 to the present time he has been at Thetford, Vt. He is a member of the Congregationalist church, and of the regular school of medicine. He was married, August 23, 1843, to Ellen H. Conant at Littleton. They have a large family of children, who have been well educated, and some of whom are occupying prominent positions in society and affairs. The scholarly trend may be readily sighted back to the great-grandfather, Noah Worcester of Hollis. Dr. Worcester has engaged to a considerable extent in the culture of small fruits, particularly strawberries, and is a successful horticulturist. He has turned his attention in these directions as a relief from the wear and tear of professional life, which he has never been able to endure for very long periods. He has given much attention to the study of the subjects of chemistry and botany, and taught both these branches for several years in Thetford Academy. He has been prominent in several medical associations. His annual address before the Vermont Medical Society for the year 1845 was published. He also delivered one of the addresses before the Woodstock Medical Society. He was many years examiner of the Woodstock Medical School, by appointment of the Supreme Court, and has been delegate from the Vermont Medical Society to the

American Medical Society. He says, his "life has been one long struggle with ill health and bodily infirmities." Notwithstanding this fact, his brethren know that he has succeeded in making it useful to his fellows and honorable to his profession.*

CHARLES MARTIN TUTTLE, A. M., M. D.†

Another has commented on Dr. Tuttle's relations to the profession of medicine and his part in the history of the town. He was born in Eaton, P. Q., February 18, 1820, where his parents, who were Vermonters, were temporarily residing. He graduated in medicine at the college in Woodstock, Vt., in 1840, and at once commenced his practice at Littleton. Here he has remained, with the exception of the short interval in which he resided at New Bedford, Mass., to the present time. He is thus the earliest and the longest in the profession here, of any who are now his co-laborers.

CARLETON CLARK ABBEY, A. B., M. D.

Another physician whose sojourn here was quite brief was Dr. Abbey. He was born at Middlebury, Vt., in May,

---

*The sketch we have given of Dr. Adams Moore should be credited to Dr. Worcester.

†Dr. Charles Martin Tuttle, son of Horatio and Betsey (Thomas) Tuttle, and a direct descendant of John Tuttle, who settled in Ipswich, Mass., in 1640, died at his home in Littleton, May 13, 1887, while this work was going through the press. Dr. Tuttle was born at Eaton, Canada, February 18, 1820. In addition to instruction received at the common schools of Colebrook, N. H., and Barnet, Vt., he attended the Peacham, Vt., Academy; later, studied medicine with his uncle, Socrates Tuttle, and William Nelson, at Barnet. He attended medical lectures at the Vermont Medical College, at Woodstock, and was graduated from the same in 1840. He settled in Littleton the same year, and commenced the practice of medicine at the age of 21, where he continued, until his death, in the active duties of his profession, with the exception of five years spent in New Bedford, Mass., and a short time in a New York hospital.

Dr. Tuttle was three times married. First, to Mary Place of Littleton, N. H.; second, to Elizabeth Roach Arnold of New Bedford, Mass., and third, to Luthera Moulton of Waterford, Vt. He had five children, Alice Louise, by his first wife, now the wife of Dr. Frank Moffett of Littleton; Alpheus Moulton, Lizzie Arnold, Mary Sargent, and Jennie Hobart by his last wife. He was a member of the Moosilauke and White Mountain Medical Societies, and had been president of both. He was a member of the legislature in 1866. In 1879 he was appointed by the Governor and Council as the Grafton county member of the State Board of Agriculture, which office he held until 1882. In politics, he was a life-long, and consistent Democrat.

His funeral took place at his home, May 17, 1887; Rev. J. B. Morrison of Lancaster officiating. Dr. Tuttle was liberal in his religion, but not a member of any church. He was earnestly devoted to his profession, untiring in his labors, independent in opinion, generous in his impulses, and kind to the poor. As a physician he was able, studious and energetic. He possessed a keen, analytical power in diagnosis, and a sound, discriminating judgment in treating disease; hence he built for himself a wide and honorable reputation as a physician.

1818, and died at San Francisco in February, 1853. His father and grandfather had the same name, Solomon Abbey. He graduated at Middlebury College in 1845, and attended medical lectures at the Jefferson Medical College in Philadelphia, receiving his degree of M. D. in 1848. His practice was begun in this town in 1849, but he remained but one year. He belonged to the order of Odd Fellows, but was not a church member. He married, first, Nancy J. Eile, in 1848, and, second, Fatima Hastings, in 1850. Of their three children, the son died in childhood, one daughter, Mrs. W. S. Hastings, resides, married, in Waterford, Vt., and another, Mrs. W. W. Weller, lives in this town.

Mr. Abbey taught school for a considerable time in South Carolina and Alabama while studying medicine. After leaving Littleton he opened a drug store in Philadelphia, continuing the business a year and then returning to Littleton. This was his residence for two years more. In 1853, he joined a party for California, but died soon after his arrival.

He was possessed of a strong desire for travel. He was well acquainted with general literature ; his talent for writing was marked, and, had his life been spared, he would himself have made his mark in the literature of the time, either professional or general.

ALBERT WARREN CLARKE, M. D.

Dr. Albert W. Clarke practiced his profession in Littleton for a period of about ten months, in 1856, and left this field, intending to practice in one of the western states, one of his brothers having preceded him in that direction. He made an extensive tour in those states, including California and some of the territories. The few months' experience he had in the society then forming, at all points, where he spent any time, convinced the doctor that he was better fitted to practice his profession among a people of higher culture. Perhaps he did not fully anticipate the future of the communities then massing at so many points, since become famous for the enterprise and push materialized in the rise of many a city, where, but a few years ago, was nothing but barren wastes.

The result, however, was that for a few years Dr. Clarke made his home at Woburn, Mass., until called by his country to take position as an assistant surgeon in the Thirty-Fifth Massachusetts Regiment. In the service, he won the deep regard of those under his charge. He was a bold, and, at the same time, a most conscientious practitioner, giving more of his strength and time to his patients than could in reason be asked of him. To this untiring devotion, and these severe demands made upon his strength, particularly by the prevalence of pneumonia at the time of his death, we attribute the great loss sustained by the profession in his death. I am confident that every brother in the profession, so fortunate as to know Dr. Clarke, will join me in saying that his life was one of spotless purity towards both his clientage and his professional brethren. His second residence in Littleton was from 1864 till his death, March 27, 1867. He was born in Lisbon, July 25, 1828. When he was quite young, his parents removed to Lyndon, Vt., where he acquired his education in the common schools and academy. He studied with Drs. Sanborn and Newell of that place, beginning in 1848, and taking his degree at Dartmouth in 1851. Dr. Clarke married Miss Philinda G. Willey, in March, 1852. She, with his three children, two sons and a daughter, survive. Of the sons, one, George A., is a promising artist in Boston, and the other follows his father's profession.

MARTIN LUTHER SCOTT, M. D.

A son of Rev. Nathan Scott (M. E. Church), he was born in Glover, Vt., January 1, 1835. He attended the common district schools, where his parents resided, until, having mastered the branches taught there, he was sent to Lyndon, Vt., Academy, finally finishing his education in Newbury Seminary, Newbury, Vt.

Choosing medicine as his profession, he commenced his studies with Dr. C. B. Darling, an honored and celebrated homœopathic physician residing in Lyndon, Vt., in the spring of 1852, where he remained about a year; when, at the urgent request of his brother, Chester W. Scott, then practicing in

Irasburg, Vt., but now for some years in Lawrence, Mass., he continued his studies under his direction, and graduated in the University of Vermont Medical College at Burlington, in 1856. He commenced practice the same year at Littleton; but, after a few months he removed to Georgeville, P. Q. He has since practiced in Bradford, Vt., Denver, Col., Randolph, Vt., and is now located in North Hampton, Mass., where, we understand, he has a large and lucrative practice.

He is a member and has been one of the board of Censors of the Vermont State Homœopathic Society. He is also a member of the Masonic Fraternity, in which order he has advanced so far as Knight Templar. In 1857, he married Miss Sarah N. Worthington, by whom he has three daughters living. While at Littleton he was regarded as a man of ability, with prospects of large success in his chosen field of professional labor.

RALPH BUGBEE, M. D.

Ralph Bugbee, Jr., comes of a family noted in medical annals. His father, Ralph, Sr., was for more than half a century a prominent physician at Waterford, and three brothers have been distinguished in the profession. Ralph, Jr., was born at Waterford, December 20, 1821, and early began the study of medicine with his father; he took his degree at the Medical College at Castleton, October 4, 1845, and began practice at once in his native town, where he remained nine years. He was at Franconia three years, and, in 1857, came to Littleton, where he has since enjoyed an extensive and lucrative practice. Dr. Bugbee has acquired a wide reputation for his successful treatment of a class of chronic diseases which brings him patients from distant states; he is also noted as a surgeon.

The doctor has been three times married; his first wife was Phebe J. Tift, to whom he was united in 1846. She died soon after, and, in 1847, he married Mary Barker, by whom he had one son, Dr. George Ralph Bugbee of Whitefield. In 1856 he was united to Jeanette C. Batchellor. He is still in the enjoyment of that health which a strong constitution, that has never been abused, alone can bring and guarantee to hale old age. He is a member of the White Mountain, Caledonia and Vermont State Medical Societies.

JAMES LANG HARRIMAN, M. D.

Dr. Harriman was born in Peacham, Vt., May 11th, 1833. He was educated at the academies at Meriden and Exeter, and, in 1853, entered the office of Dr. Albert Winch at Whitefield, where he pursued the usual course of study. He then attended three full courses of lectures at the Medical College at Woodstock, Vt., Albany, N. Y., and Brunswick, Me., and was graduated from the last named in 1857. The same year he began the practice of his profession at Littleton. He remained here but four and a half years, acquiring the reputation of being a careful and skillful practitioner.

In July, 1862, he entered the service as assistant surgeon of the Thirteenth Regiment, Massachusetts Volunteers, and was discharged for disability in January, 1863. He then settled in Hudson, Mass., where he now resides, in the enjoyment of a full practice. Dr. Harriman is a member of the White Mountain, Middlesex Southern and Massachusetts Medical Societies; has represented his town in the General Court of Massachusetts; for many years has been a member of the Board of Health and school committee of Hudson; and, while residing at Littleton, was chairman of the school committee. He married, in 1859, Miss Mary E. Cushman, daughter of Horace Cushman, Esq., of Dalton. They have one child, a daughter.

THADDEUS EZRA SANGER, M. D.

The most prominent representative of the Homœopathic school in Northern New Hampshire is Dr. Sanger. He located here after two years' practice in Hardwick, Vt., in 1858, succeeding Dr. Scott, who had then lately left this field. He was born March 12, 1833, at Troy, Vt., a son of Ezra Sanger. His academic education was at St. Johnsbury Academy, and his medical education, begun in 1850, was pursued under Prof. A. F. Bissel at Toledo, Ohio, and with Dr. Stone at St. Johnsbury, and Dr. Darling of Lyndon. He took degrees in Medicine at Cleveland in 1854, and at Philadelphia in 1856. His marriage with Ianthe C. Kneeland occurred October 22, 1857. They have a family of three daughters. In his twenty-six years of practice here, Dr. Sanger has identified himself with many important interests of a social, business and professional nature. His politics are Republican, and his church preferences Episcopalian. He has been instrumental in organizing the Homœopathic practitioners in local and state associations. In these he has been an active worker, and has been repeatedly president of both bodies. He is also a member of the American Institute of Homœopathy. For a number of years he has held the office of United States Pension Examiner at this place. This office has a single incumbent here, and is not, as is the general rule, committed to a board of three. Notwithstanding the digressions which the doctor makes in general business, Freemasonry or politics, he keeps his profession next his heart.

Our friend Eastman in his remarks has spoken of several of our co-laborers from Vermont, which, as spokesman for the whole, our Green Mountain modesty will not allow us to repeat, and for which we make our most respectful bow to the author.

ADAMS BROCK WILSON, M. D.

Dr. Wilson was a native of Newbury, Vt., a son of Adams Wilson, born March 8, 1842. He prepared for college at the old Newbury Seminary, and was at Wesleyan University at Middletown, Conn., one year. He commenced the study of medicine in 1863; his preceptors were Dr. H. L. Watson and Dr. Dixi Crosby. After taking three courses of lectures at Dartmouth Medical school and the medical department of the Vermont University, he graduated at the former institution in 1866. He entered zealously upon the practice of his profession at Littleton, immediately after his graduation, but in less than three years was broken down by overwork, and died at Bradford, Vt., August 30, 1869. He was of the regular school of practice. His church affiliations were with the Congregationalists. He was a member of the Alpha Delta Phi College Fraternity, and of the Freemasons in Pulaski Lodge at Newbury. His politics were Democratic. In 1866, November 18, he married Miss Lou. M. Little of this place, but there were no children. His widow remains unmarried, and has gained an enviable reputation as an educator. She is at present Superintendent of Public schools at Des Moines, Iowa.

HON. HENRY LYMAN WATSON, M. D.

Dr. Watson enjoys the distinction of being the oldest practitioner in town, and is full of that wisdom and experience which age alone can bring; it is not necessary to state that these are important elements in the successful treatment of many of the ills which flesh is heir to. The doctor's ancestors were among the early settlers of Salisbury, and belonged to the Society of Friends; in that town he was born, February 10, 1811. He received an academic education at Phillips Academy at Exeter, and, soon after attaining his majority, began the study of medicine; he attended three full courses of lectures at the Dartmouth and Vermont Medical schools, and received his degree of M. D. at the last named school in 1838. He then opened an office at Stewartstown; remained but three months, and then removed to Guildhall, Vt., where he was in full practice for twenty years. On account of the superior educational advantages afforded at Newbury, he took up his residence there in 1858, and, in 1865, came to Littleton. His practice here has filled the measure of his desires; the frosty hand of time has been laid lightly upon him; and advancing age has brought its full share of honors and the rewards incident to a life spent in an earnest and successful endeavor to assuage the sufferings of humanity.

Dr. Watson has frequently been called to fill administrative and legislative positions. While residing in Guildhall he was county commissioner, postmaster, twice elected to the State Senate, 1852 and 1853, and, in 1856 and 1857, was elected representative, and was the candidate of his party for the speakership of the House of Representatives. In 1868 he was appointed postmaster at Littleton by President Johnson, a position he resigned within the year. In early life he was an active member of the military; was a commissioned officer in the same; and, for a long time, was regimental surgeon. He married, first, Roxanna Hughes. She dying, he married, second, Mary Jane Hardy. He has three children, the eldest being Dr. Henry P. Watson of Haverhill.

THADDEUS THOMPSON CUSHMAN, M. D.

Dr. Cushman was in practice here but eighteen months, coming in 1868 from Lunenburgh, where he had been in practice for twenty-four years, and gained the reputation of being a skillful and honorable physician. He was fast gaining a practice here when he removed to Randolph, Mass., where his only child, Mrs. Breitling resided. He was born in Sumner, Me., in 1821, took his degree in course at Bowdoin Medical College in 1844, and established himself at Lunenburg, the same year. He is a member of the White Mountain, Vermont and Massachusetts Medical Societies, and has been president of the first named, and a councillor of the Massachusetts Society. In 1848 he married Miss Lucretia W. Gates, who died in August, 1850. Since going to Randolph, he has been a trustee of the Stetson High School twelve years, and a member of the Board of Education. He is highly esteemed, both in medical and social circles.

DR. LEONARD MARSHALL EUDY.

Dr. Eudy practiced in this town but one year. He was a student of the Harvard Medical School, and had received his preliminary education at the common schools in Bethlehem, where he was born, January 8, 1843. He was a son of Capt. William Eudy, who resided many years in Bethlehem, but subsequently located at North Littleton. Dr. Eudy served as a private in the war of the Rebellion during the full term of his regiment, the Fifteenth New Hampshire Volunteers.

He entered upon the study of medicine, in 1865, with Dr. Tuttle, continuing with Dr. Watson, and entered upon the practice in 1870. After his brief location in Littleton he removed to Upper Bartlett, and continued in practice there as long as he lived. He was a practitioner of the regular school; never married, was an attendant upon the Free Baptist church, and a Democrat in politics. In 1877 he was engaged in the care of the small pox cases at the camp established near his circuit of practice, and died in the midst of the epidemic on the 28th of November, at Bartlett. He is entitled to a large measure of credit for the courage and persistency with which, in the face of serious obstacles, he pursued his ambition to acquire a position in the medical profession.

FRANK TIFFT MOFFETT, M. D.

Dr. Moffett is a native of Littleton. He was born August 6, 1842. His father, Col. Alden Moffett, has for many years been prominent in town affairs. His well known military title was gained in the old militia. The son was educated in the common schools of Littleton and the high schools of Barnet, Vt. At the age of twenty he entered the Union army as a private in the Fourteenth New Hampshire Volunteers, Capt. Hodgdon's company. His service extended from August 15, of that year, to July, 1865. He was with Banks on the Red River; was all through the valley campaign with Sheridan; went to Savannah, Georgia, and met Sherman's command as it emerged from the march to the sea; was present when Jefferson Davis was captured, and with the detachment that conveyed him to Augusta, Georgia, and placed him on a government transport.

In 1867, he commenced the study of medicine with Dr. C. M. Tuttle of Littleton; attended three courses of medical lectures, and graduated at the Harvard Medical College in 1870. He located in the practice of medicine at Littleton in 1871, and has since prosecuted his profession with marked success at that place and the vicinity. He married Miss Alice M. Tuttle, daughter of his medical preceptor, in 1873. They have two daughters.

Public matters have received considerable attention from Dr. Moffett. He is a member of the lodge, chapter, council and commandery in Freemasonry, and is active and useful in those organizations. He is a Republican in politics, and was the first representative of that party elected from Littleton since 1858. This office he held in 1883. As a business man, he is one of the most successful in his profession. He is industrious, judicious, conservative. His devotion to his practice, with the exception of a trip to Bermuda in 1875, on account of the impairment of his health, has been practically uninterrupted since 1871. He has received a large part of the professional calls which come to this place from the line of the railway between here and the White Mountain Notch. He will be long remembered by the members of the signal service as the physician who ascended Mt. Washington in mid-winter, 1872, and took charge of the remains of the first member of the corps who died at the summit station.

Dr. Moffett maintains his interest in military affairs as an active member of Marshall Sanders Post, No. 48, G. A. R., and as assistant surgeon of the Third Regiment of the New Hampshire National Guard. The surgeon of this regiment is Dr. I. A. Watson, who, as a resident and student, and by the residence of his family for many years at this place, has been closely identified with its people and affairs. It suggests the time when Dr. William Burns was surgeon, and Dr. Adams Moore, surgeon's mate of the old Thirty-second Regiment of militia.

Like his associates of the regular school, Dr. Moffett is an active member of the White Mountain Medical Society. He is also a member of the State Medical Society, and was one of its delegates to the American Medical Society in 1883. He then became a member of that association.

GEORGE RALPH BUGBEE, M. D.

Dr. George R. Bugbee is the only son of Dr. Ralph Bugbee, Jr., and Mary (Barker) Bugbee, born at Waterford, Vt., February 7, 1849. He received a common school education at Franconia and Littleton, and academic at Newbury,

Vt., and New Hampshire Conference (Tilton) Seminaries. His father was his private medical preceptor, and he attended lectures in the medical department of Michigan University at Ann Arbor, and at the Dartmouth Medical School. He obtained his degree at the latter institution in June, 1872. His first year's practice thereafter was at Littleton. He then removed to Whitefield, where he has since continued in practice. He is Republican in politics, and of the regular school of practice. In 1871, December 31, he married Emma E. Lindsey. They have two children, a son and daughter.

WILLIAM SAGE CROSBY, L.L. B., M. D.

The residence of this physician in town was very brief. He was born in Roxbury, Mass., in 1849; educated at the Roxbury High School, and graduated in medicine at the Harvard Medical Department in 1874. His first location in practice was at Boston. A country practice was afterward deemed advantageous in his case, and Littleton was selected. He had only been in town a few days or weeks when he was stricken with a fatal sickness, and died at his hotel, April 5. 1875. He belonged to the regular school of practice, but had no opportunity to display his ability as a practitioner among us. He was a man of agreeable manners and dignified bearing.

EDWARD JOSIAH BROWN, A. B., M. D.

One of the promising young men, who have been engaged in practice in this place, is Dr. Brown. He is a son of Ira Brown, M. D., a well known Vermont practitioner, and was born at Burke, January 14, 1851. He received a thorough education at Kimball Union Academy. at Meriden. N. H., and at Dartmouth College, from which he graduated in the academic department, class of 1874. He commenced the study of medicine in 1876, his father being his office preceptor. He took three courses of lectures at the University of the City of New York, and at the Dartmouth Medical School, graduating from the latter in October, 1878. In the following February, he located in practice at Littleton, and remained until May, 1880. The next two years he practiced at Haverhill, and in April, 1882, settled in Minneapolis, Minn. There he rapidly came to the front in his profession. The Minnesota State Board of Health gave him service in 1882, as health officer and inspector. From January, 1883, to April, 1884, he held the position of quarantine physician of the city. June 30, 1884, he was appointed to the chair of Preventive Medicine and Hygiene in the Minneapolis College of Physicians and Surgeons. He has also been active and useful in promoting the cause of medical organization. He was a member of the Moosilauke Medical Society in New Hampshire: Hennepin County Medical Society, and Society of Physicians and Surgeons of Minneapolis, and treasurer of the last two named societies; member of the Minnesota State Medical Society, and a member of the American Medical Society.

He is an active member of the Congregationalist church, and an efficient worker in social, philanthropical and religious enterprises. He is unmarried.

GEORGE WILBUR MCGREGOR, M. D.

The youngest present practitioner in the place is Dr. McGregor. He is a son of Willard A. McGregory, late of Bethlehem, a prominent business man and town official. Dr. McGregor was educated at the common and high schools of Bethlehem, and at the New Hampshire Conference Seminary at Tilton. His medical preceptors were Dr. George S. Gove of Whitefield and Prof. L. B. How of Manchester. He attended upon three courses of medical lectures at Dartmouth, and obtained his degree in June, 1878, at that institution. He first settled in Lunenburgh, Vt., and remained there a year and a half; then (in August, 1880), came to Littleton, where he has since practiced. He married E. Augusta Eaton, February 24, 1880. They have no children. The doctor is a Democrat in politics, and has been the candidate of his party for representative. He is a Freemason, and affiliates with the Congregational church.

LOUIS ANTONY GENEREAUX, M. D.

The Canadian element constitutes a considerable part of

our population. Dr. Genereaux was their first representative here in the medical profession. He was a native of Toronto, and a graduate of Laval University, Medical Department, of Quebec, in 1880. He located at Littleton in October of that year, and remained about two years. He subsequently located in Claremont. While residing here, he became a naturalized citizen. He was unmarried, and of the Roman Catholic faith.

BENJAMIN FRANKLIN PAGE, M. D.

Another prophet, not without honor in his own country, is Dr. Page, born in this place, July 7, 1843. His father was Benjamin Page, recently deceased, at Lisbon. Dr. Page is a brother of Samuel B. Page of Woodsville. B. F. Page received an academic education at the old Newbury Seminary. In 1864, he began the study of medicine with Dr. H. L. Watson, and also studied with Dr. C. H. Boynton. He attended three courses of lectures and graduated at the Vermont University, Medical Department, in 1867. For five years thereafter he was located at Lisbon in practice; next, at St. Johnsbury, Vt., nine years, and, since 1881, at Littleton. He is a member of the White Mountain and Vermont State Medical Societies. His school of practice is regular; politics, Democratic; church relations, somewhat Congregationalist; secret society, Masonic. He married Miss Caroline Farr, daughter of John Farr, Esq., of this place, in 1870. They have a family of promising children.

These young men have taken up the burdens of the practice in a field which tries the best temper. Without attempting to place before their own eyes an analysis of their several excellencies as practitioners of medicine, it may be said of them all that they are in manners gentlemanly, in their practice faithful, painstaking, cheerful and successful, and in other relations of life, popular and progressive.

MEDICAL SCHOOLS AND MEDICAL STUDENTS.

Although the Dartmouth Medical College, founded in 1798, is the nearest institution of the kind, a large majority of our practitioners have come from other medical schools. Dr. Burns attended its lectures in 1813, and again in 1834. The College at Castleton, Vt., was instituted in 1818, by charter, as Castleton Medical Academy, and closed in 1862, having been legally designated in the meantime as the Vermont Academy of Medicine, and finally as the Castleton Medical College. Another flourished at Woodstock, Vt., from 1831 to 1854. That year the medical department of the University of Vermont was established, succeeding the Woodstock school, and it has been successfully maintained to the present time. Many of our students and practitioners were educated at these institutions. A few were at Harvard, New York, Philadelphia, Ann Arbor or Bowdoin. A. R. Chamberlain, in 1819, and Harry Brickett, in 1842 and 1843, were catalogued from this place at Hanover. Horace White was a student with Dr. Burns and Albert Winch, and Dr. Ross with Dr. Moore. Edwin L. Farr of Boston, Jas. B. Sumner of Lunenburg, Vt., Dr. Dunbar of New Bedford, Dr. Henry West, Dr. Wheeler of Peacham, Vt., who fell while heroically devoting himself to the treatment of the victims of ship fever in Quebec, Dr. Smillie of Quebec, and many others, have been under the professional instruction of Dr. Tuttle. Francis Towne, now surgeon, U. S. A., studied with Dr. Bugbee. His brothers, Frank and Lafayette, were also his pupils in medicine. With Dr. Watson, since he resided at this place, have been N. Harvey Scott, now of Wolfeboro, Fred Phelps, now deceased, and others. Dr. Sanger's students have been Geo. S. Kelsea, late of Newport, Vt., Moses Whitcomb of North Stratford, Buck G. Carleton of New York, Aaron Bond of Nashua and Ned K. Parker. It is not necessary to repeat here the names of those whose preceptors have been already stated in the personal sketches. The sons of our doctors have, in several instances, followed the paternal profession. James W. Moore is in practice at Lynn, Mass.; Israel J. Clark at Ashland, Mass.; Henry P. Watson at Haverhill; George R. Bugbee at Whitefield, and Alpheus M. Tuttle is now a student of medicine with his father. In recent years, our boys have been more generally attracted in this direction than to the law. Charles E. Thompson, M. D., now of North Stratford, was a native of this town, born April 11, 1856, son of Merrill W. Thompson, a student in medicine with Dr. Moffett, and a graduate of the medical department, Vermont University, and Harvey E. McIntire, M. D., now of Middletown, Conn., a son of Warren McIntire, born at Lyman, September 1, 1859, but reared in Littleton, a student of Dartmouth College; and Dr. McGregor, and a graduate of the Bellevue Medical College, have both been well received in the practice, and have the ability to become useful members of their chosen profession.

Many matters of historical interest relating to this division of our subject must be derived from the annual catalogues of the medical schools. These are not readily accessible. Whoever accomplishes the task of collecting these scattered pamphlets from the nooks and crannies in which they are now mouldering, will be the largest contributor of material for the personal history of the medical profession. No satisfactory accomplishment of that work can be expected without that material.

SHORT CALLS.

The *White Mountain Banner* contained the business card of E. K. Cummings, M. D., now of Claremont, as a Littleton practitioner in 1856. He writes that his sojourn here was in February of that year and for only one day. He treated one patient in the night, but seems to have experienced an unfavorable impression of our climate at that season, for he got his fee, and, the next day, shaking the snow from his feet, he abandoned the field.

Dr. C. Woodward came here in 1842. He was a disciple of Thompson, and advocated the theories and practiced the healing arts of that school. In the few weeks of his sojourn in this place, the doctrines of Hahnemann received his attention, and he adopted them. Subsequently, locating in the practice as a representative of the school of homœopathy at Danville, Vt., he achieved a liberal measure of success and prosperity.

Dr. Eldad Alexander, one of the strong men of the profession in Vermont, proposed to locate in this place in 1854, and established himself at Thayer's Hotel. Old associations were too strong for his new resolve, and he returned to Danville, after a six weeks' residence among us. He was a man of capacious intellect, eminent as a surgeon, and in all the branches of general practice. History will accord him a high rank among his cotemporaries for professional accomplishments and native worth.

Dr. Jonathan Knight made a short sojourn at Littleton, about 1837. He came from Stoddard, had studied medicine with the elder Twitchell, and shortly proceeded to Piermont, where he remained many years. Dr. Spaulding of Haverhill, who knew him well, says he removed to the lower part of the state in his later years.

MILITARY AFFAIRS.

A summary of the items pertinent to this topic may be a convenience in reference, and we include it in that view. Dr. Burns, Dr. H. L. Watson, Dr. Tuttle and Dr. Irving A. Watson have been surgeons; Dr. Adams Moore and Dr. Moffett, assistant surgeons of regiments in the militia organizations. Dr. J. S. Ross and Dr. Francis Towne, who were students of medicine here, became army surgeons, the former in the Eleventh Regiment of New Hampshire Volunteers, and the latter permanently in the regular army. Dr. Harriman, soon after his removal from this town, became assistant surgeon of a Massachusetts war regiment, and Dr. Clark had rendered similar service just previous to his final establishment in this place. Dr. Moffett and Dr. Eudy came from service in the ranks to the study of medicine. The military spirit seems to have been felt in the medical profession, as in other classes of our citizens. It would, no doubt, manifest itself today, as in the past, for the common good and the common defence.

NEIGHBORING PRACTITIONERS.

Littleton has been the abode of a numerous medical fraternity in recent years. Formerly, Waterford, our Connecticut river neighbor, had more settled practitioners than this town. It was convenient for our people to call their doctors from over the river to the neighboring farm houses. Dr. Stephen (?) Cole was probably the first physician to settle in Waterford. Dr. Freedom Dinsmore, Dr. Thomas McDole, Dr. Moses F. Morrison, Dr. Abner Miles, Dr. Beniah Sanborn, Dr. Newell, Dr. Cargill, Dr. Kelley. Dr. Richard Rowell, and perhaps others, might be recalled, who practiced from that town for longer or shorter periods, and ministered to the sick in this place.

The old time leaders of the profession in Caledonia County were Dr. Alexander of Danville, Dr. Jewett of St. Johnsbury and Dr. Bugbee of Waterford. These men were the oracles whose verdict in the hard cases was supposed to settle the question of life or death. A native of Ashford, Conn., and a graduate of Yale Medical School, Dr. Bugbee came to Waterford in 1816, and continued there till his death in 1881. His professional skill gave him a practice over a large region. He was a man of learning and character. At times he encountered strong popular disfavor for his fixed and somewhat pronounced adherence to his principles. He was one of the old Freemasons, and "adhered." This position he maintained against an almost universal clamor, which approached very near to persecution. But opposition, no matter how strong or intolerant, was not one of the methods of moving him from a position. He was also surgeon of his militia regiment. His four sons became regular practitioners, and his daughter became the wife of Dr. Enoch Blanchard of Illinois, who was surgeon of the Seventh Vermont war regiment. A few years since, the doctor found a news item, paragraphed by Charles R. Miller, then of the *Springfield Republican*, and indicating how he was surrounded by the atmosphere of medicine in his later years, in this wise:—"Dr. Ralph Bugbee, Jr., of Littleton, had a little party in honor of his fifty-second birthday, a few days ago, and the gathering was one calculated to inspire terror in the average healthy mind. There were his three brothers, all physicians—Dr.

Abel Bugbee of Derby Line, Vt., Dr. Frank Bugbee of Lancaster, and Dr. Lafayette Bugbee of Willimantic, Conn.; also, his son, Dr. George R. Bugbee of Whitefield. And the venerable progenitor of all these doctors, Dr. Ralph Bugbee, Sr., of Waterford, Vt., gazed on his posterity, with a heavy heart, participating meanwhile but mechanically in the festivities, and wondering what he should do when he got old and sick." In his sixty-five years of practice, he established a reputation which made him as well known in Littleton as in Waterford.

Dalton and Bethlehem have seldom had resident physicians. At Franconia, Dr. Colby, Dr. Wells, Dr. Moody and others, have been acceptable practitioners at successive periods, covering many years. The physicians of Lisbon and Whitefield, being more remote, have not, until recent years, been so frequently called, or so well known, as those who resided on the river, near the western borders of the town.

The medical school at Hanover has brought many eminent medical men within the call of our patients for consultations and treatment. Muzzy, Peaslee, the Crosbys, and their associates, have often given our people the benefit of their great medical and surgical skill in novel and difficult cases. We now call the first authority in the profession from Boston, by telegram, in less time than Dr. White could have been brought from Newbury to Littleton a hundred years ago.

PHARMACY.

This has come to be a separate department in the medical world. Its importance to our profession is beyond computation. In recent years, those engaged in its duties have recognized the necessity of excluding from the ranks of its employes all who have not been found specially qualified by strict examination. Their general associations have thus met a demand made both by the members of our profession and the more general public. Here, the business of vending drugs had a small beginning, some sixty or seventy years ago, in Squire Brackett's store, in which John Farr was a clerk. The drugs and medicines then constituted a small part of the stock of the establishment.

In 1832, Francis Hodgman located in the place, and, within a year or two, erected a building for his jewelry business, with which he joined that of an apothecary; to him, Mr. Brackett sold his entire stock of drugs and medicines. He carried on this dual business, gradually increasing it, and improving its accommodations, for more than thirty years. He then, in the time of the war of the rebellion, retired, and was succeeded by his sons. Upon the death of the younger, the business was sold to Curtis Gates & Co., who were succeeded by Robinson Bros., the present proprietors. The Grafton County drug store was established in 1853 by George K. Paddleford, in the building now owned by Robert Whittaker, on Main Street, which was erected for this purpose in that year. Mr. Paddleford was assisted in the enterprise by Dr. Sabine. S. W. Atwood succeeded to the business in 1854. After about two years, Hovey & Hall purchased it, and, in a short time, Eben L. Hall became proprietor. The advertisement in the columns of the *White Mountain Banner* disappeared in the spring of 1858.

Another drug store was established in the Union Block, in 1867, by Dr. H. L. Watson. He was succeeded by Albert Parker & Co.; this firm by G. & G. F. Abbott, and they by W. F. Robins, the present proprietor. Fred B. Hatch & Co. have recently established a successful pharmacy. These three establishments, by healthful competition and progressive methods, are giving the medical profession and the public good service in an important and exacting calling.

An interesting relic of the drug business, as it was in its early stages in our vicinity, was found among the papers of the late Dr. Bugbee, Sr., of Waterford. It is an advertisement clearly printed by White & Clark of Wells River, Vt., dated probably about 1825. The head lines are as follows:

"MEDICINE.

LUTHER JEWETT,

At his shop on St. Johnsbury Plain, keeps for sale a general assortment of medicines. Physicians and families supplied with genuine articles cheap, especially for ready pay. The following are some of the articles."

Then follows a list of 180 articles, whose names and virtues are familiar to the old practitioners. This is the list of pills :—

" Relfes Asthmatic   Family   Jewett's
  "   Aromatic   Hooper's   Thayer's
  "   Toothache   Anderson's   Sias'
  Lee's   .   Morrison's   Blue."

In the old families, the terms used by Luther Jewett in his list are household words, and they have very little of the mystery that surrounds the voluminous catalogues of modern pharmacy.

DENTISTRY.

This has now become a profession independent of our own. It has its distinct state and national organizations, and its colleges. We are fortunate in obtaining a sketch of its beginnings in this town, from one of its earliest practitioners, Dr. Silas A. Sabine of Claremont, who has long held high rank as a dental surgeon. In a recent letter, he says:

"When I was in the practice of my profession at Haverhill, N. H., in January, 1845, I was constantly receiving invitations from some of the most prominent citizens of Littleton to visit that place, professionally. Accordingly, on the 27th of February, 1845, I took the stage under the guidance of one "Steve" Hale, who landed me safe at the Granite House, kept by J. L. Gibb and Father—afterwards by numerous proprietors—where I continued to make it my home as long as the house was kept as a hotel, afterwards at the White Mountain House, kept by H. L. Thayer, the most popular landlord in the state. My first patient was Cephas Brackett. At the time of my first visit to Littleton, dentistry was comparatively in its infancy. In a place so remote from cities, work was done in a very rude and bungling manner by itinerant dentists, who were just as likely to be tinpeddlers—meaning no disrespect to that numerous and honorable body—who had sold out their stock, purchased a box of instruments, and are on their way home, practicing upon the teeth of their too willing dupes as a means to pay expenses. The first years of my being at Littleton, the best work coming under my observation was from the hands of Dr. C. M. Tuttle, and I think he made no pretentions to artificial work. February 24, 1845, one G. W. Williams advertised to be at Cobleigh's hotel for a few days; further, I know nothing of him, or of any one else prior. In December, 1855, Dr. Cummings, a former partner of mine, with Dr. Smith, opened an office in the Gile building, but did not stay long. About the year 1862 or 1863, A. A. Hazeltine, a student of mine, settled in Littleton; how long he staid, I cannot state. The three last named were good dentists, and, I think, include all who practiced at Littleton during the time I visited there, viz.: from 1845 to 1870. My impression is, now, that I was the first to do artificial work with artificial gums, and the first to use what was then called Letheon."

Dr. E. G. Cummings of Concord adds to our information. He says:—"Dr. W. M. Smith of Claremont and I were located at Lancaster, and used to run down and stop at Littleton a few days at a time, but lived at Lancaster. I think this was in 1856, 1857 and 1858. Dr. Silas A. Sabine of Claremont is the first man whom I know of as practicing at Littleton." Dr. A. A. Hazeltine opened an office in 1861, and was the first permanent resident practitioner among us. He remained until 1867.

Others have had days in town while residing elsewhere, or have located with sojourns of brief duration. We recall, as belonging in this list, Dr. Switzer, Dr. Wood, Dr. Carey, Dr. G. O. Rogers, who has since spent ten years with large success in the practice of dentistry in China, Dr. Robinson, Dr. Patterson (whose former wife, now Mrs. Eddy, is a leading apostle of the so-called Christian science, or mind cure), Dr. Hall, Dr. Bolles, Dr. Cooley and Dr. Hickok. Our time does not permit such detailed mention of these, our allies, in what may be considered a department of surgery, as I could wish to make.

Dr. Samuel C. Sawyer, Dr. E. B. Hoskins and Dr. Millard F. Young, who are now the representatives of this profession here, are in the first rank in their calling. Nothing would be gained in going abroad for dental work while we may command the professional services of these gentlemen.

LOCAL BOARDS OF HEALTH.

As early as 1799, the General Court authorized the inhabitants of the town of Portsmouth to establish a local board of health. By the act of January 3, 1833, this power was extended for the benefit of all the towns in the state. We are not informed as to how generally this act became operative. This town appointed its first board in 1873, and has maintained it to the present time. It has always contained at least one physician. Its work has been preventive of disease, and it is believed that what has been accomplished has been of great value in preserving life and health in our community. Prevention receives little praise as compared with what is accorded for conspicuous cures; but the old maxim, "an ounce of prevention is worth a pound of cure," embodies the plainest statement of the most important of all the laws of health. A tabular statement of the membership of the Littleton Board of Health, since its first organization, has been compiled:

BOARDS OF HEALTH, LITTLETON.

1873	C. M. Tuttle, M. D.	C. W. Rand, Esq.,	John Sargent.
1874	"	F. T. Moffett, M. D.,	"
1875	"	"	H. L. Watson, M.D.
1876	"	"	"
1877	"	"	"
1878	"	C. W. Bolles, Esq.,	"
1879	"	W. H. Mitchell, "	Chas. C. Smith.
1880	"	"	"
1881	"	Fred B. Wright,	John Smillie.
1882	"	E. C. Stevens, Esq.,	Albert H. Bowman.
1883	"	"	G. W. McGregor, M.D.
1884	"	"	"
1885	G. W. McGregor, M.D.	"	Wm. M. Taylor.
1886	"	J. R. Jackson, Esq.,	Fred A. Robinson.

THE STATE BOARD.

The establishment of a State Board of Health, in 1881,

was one of the most wholesome and important pieces of legislation that can be found in our state history. With a code of health ordinances essential to the perfection of the system of which the town boards and ordinances were only branches, a long stride forward was made in the domain of state medicine. The system embodies two ideas, education of the people in hygiene, and enforcement of common sense rules of health, as embodied in law or sanctioned by public opinion. The state board has made its influence felt in every hamlet, and in almost every household. The gospel of cleanliness, as next to godliness, is preached, understood and heeded as never before. In our own community, the physicians and the people are more watchful of the sewage and kindred breeding places of disease and death. We have been warned of our negligence in these matters, and the state board has pointed with the strong hand of authority to the condition of our river beds and our school-houses as they were, and the remedies have been effectually applied.

One of the foremost men, one of the prime movers, in this great field of preventive medicine, has been regarded for twenty years as a son of Littleton, and we may congratulate ourselves on his identity with our people and our interests.

IRVING ALLISON WATSON, A. M., M. D.

Among the solid men attracted to Littleton, when business was adjusted to conditions of peace, and the town commenced upon a new era of prosperity, was Porter B. Watson. This was in 1867. His oldest son was a sturdy young man of nineteen years. He obtained a solid education at the common schools and at the old Newburg Seminary. He studied medicine with Dr. A. B. Crosby and, with his uncle, Dr. Henry L. Watson. He attended medical lectures at Dartmouth and the University of Vermont, taking his degree of M. D. from the Vermont school in 1871. Immediately he located in practice at Groveton, and modestly and laboriously laid the foundation for his future career. He was ten years at Groveton. The observing men in the State and White Mountain Medical Societies gradually came to know his worth. At length his masterly treatment of a virulent and wide-spread reign of diptheria, in his own vicinity, and his no less masterly investigation and discovery of the cause, and his presentation of the history of the case, with his views on the necessity of radical measures in the department of practical and scientific hygiene, brought him before the medical world as a man of ideas, as a man of action, a man with a future.

Upon the establishment of the State Board of Health, his medical brethren looked to him as the man to become the executive member for the medical profession, and his many personal friends of both political parties urged his appointment.

He became Secretary of that board, and a little later (1883) also Secretary of the American Public Health Association. He has left his mark deep in the health organizations of the country and in the literature of the subjects with which those associations have specially to do, and his work is but just begun.

He has also found time to serve in the legislature, to assume the duties of many social organizations, to make his mark as a surgeon in the military organizations of the state, by enforcing his views of military hygiene, and to assume the undertaking of a history of the medical profession in the state, and other important historical work. His wife, Lena A. Farr, was a Littleton girl, and here is still his paternal residence. Here he is always welcomed by a host of friends, who are glad at his success, and who believe in his mission.

THE WHITE MOUNTAIN MEDICAL SOCIETY.

This institution was first organized at White's Inn, at Lancaster, May 17, 1820. Dr. John Willard was made moderator, and Dr. Wm. Burns of this place, secretary *pro tem*. The association procured an act of incorporation, June 23, 1821. Dr. Eliphalet Lyman became the first permanent president. The society has maintained an uninterrupted activity in usefulness to the present time. It has drawn its membership from both sides of the Connecticut river, and has been augmented by the recent union with it of the Caledonia

(Vt.) and Moosilauke (N. H.) Societies. Several Littleton practitioners have been occupants of its presidency. These were, Dr. Burns, 1830 to 1834, 1836, 1842, 1843, 1855 and 1860; Dr. Adams Moore, 1848 and 1849; Dr. T. T. Cushman, 1865 and 1866; Dr. C. M. Tuttle, 1875 and 1876. He was also secretary for six years from 1849. Nearly all the other permanent residents of the profession here have labored in the various official positions of the society, in gathering material for its reports, in its discussions, in its social, educational and remedial work. The meetings are held in the principal towns in the district by rotation. The doctors are always welcome guests in the occasional visitations which the society makes at Littleton.

Only two of our local practitioners have been members of the state society. "I suppose," says Dr. Watson, "the reason that so few Littleton physicians have become members of the society, was the difficulty in attending the meetings, especially prior to the railroad reaching Littleton. It is often very difficult for a physician to leave his patients for three or four days at a time, as would be required of members living so far away from Concord as Littleton."

THE CUTTLE FISH OF THE PRACTICE.

> His knowledge was not far behind
> The Knight's, but of another kind,
> And he another way came by't,
> Some called it Gifts, and some New Light;
> A lib'ral art, that costs no pains
> Of study, industry or brains.
> *Hudibras.*

Our people are regularly called upon to contribute to the support of that numerous class of practitioners who come among us claiming special gifts, such as no one, who is educated for the profession by the best preceptors, and by the best schools which the country affords, and such as no one, but a stranger from afar, is supposed to possess. These itinerants, not to say tramps, find patronage for a time; but, as the novelty of an original advertisement wears off, and the public slowly recognize the old humbug in a new guise, they are gone to greener fields, and a new fraud comes upon the scene. The mystery of the human system is so great, the hope of cure for the incurable is so universal, the multitude of imaginary ills is so vast, that quackery in medicine will doubtless prey upon credulity, until ignorance and superstition are banished from men's minds, and wisdom bears the universal scepter. We ought to know, without a hesitating doubt, that he who has the great art of healing will never need to hawk his gifts from hamlet to hamlet. His fame will bring the sick to him, or they will call him to them, regardless of distance, or of price. Such a physician will not be a tramp or a mountebank. He will stand up in communities as a conspicuous figure. He will be a monument of his profession in some permanent location. He will face the consequences of his acts, and will abide the verdict of his life work among the people who have known him as a man as well as a physician. The tramp doctor, on the other hand, is gone when disaster results to the simple one who trusted him. In his successive places, the lesson of his previous deceptions is lost, for what those like him have done is forgotten in the glare of novelty, and the hope of an impending miracle. The miracle is always paid for, but never delivered. I do not hesitate to say that the mischief of believing that the violation of nature's law can obtain immunity by medical, physical or spiritual magic, is incalculable. There is no wisdom here that does not recognize the law of cause and effect in the workings of the physical system. When science and skill, disciplined together in experience, have done their best for humanity, it is folly to seek in this enlightened age for a suspension of the physical laws of life or health.

CLERICAL MEDICINE.

The relations of the clerical and medical professions in Littleton have generally been harmonious. Their representatives have often been called to minister at the same bedside, and have joined in the effort to alleviate human suffering and comfort human sorrow. Each came in the town's infancy, equipped in accordance with the requirements of the times, for the prosecution of a humane mission. Each now beholds a marvelous change and undoubted progress.

Dr. Worcester was compelled to abandon his theological studies and reinforce the profession of medicine. His cotemporary and present townsman, the Rev. Harry Brickett, then a resident of Littleton, after graduating at Dartmouth, in 1840, prosecuted a medical course in the medical school at Hanover until he was substantially fitted for the practice, but afterwards became a clergyman of the Congregationalist order. These cases may be set off against each other.

A more recent pastor of the Methodist Episcopal church, the Rev. George Beebe, was a graduate of the New York University Medical School, in the class of 1864. He was a warrant surgeon in the United States service in the last years of the war of the rebellion. He entered the ministry in 1867, and his sermons were frequently tinctured with the lore and experience of his former profession. The *White Mountain Echo* of August 30, 1879, contains an abstract of a pointed sermon by Mr. Beebe, at Bethlehem, on the allied gospels of health and prosperity, under the title of "A Prophetic Discourse."

Our townsman, the Rev. Charles W. Millen, was the orator recently at the Commencement of the New York Electic Medical College. His address, which was published, indicates that he might well have squared accounts with Dr. Beebe, as did Dr. Worcester with the Rev. Mr. Brickett, in maintaining the equilibrium of the professions. Whatever may be said of these exchanges of the personnel of the two professions, there is no question that a mutual benefit must accrue from a liberal interchange of ideas.

EPIDEMICS AND CONTAGIOUS DISEASES.

SMALL POX, 1807.—As the town had been quite sparsely settled until very near 1798, the year in which Jenner announced his discovery, the ravages of this disease among the inhabitants, presumably, would not be so general or serious as to make its local features a subject of record. The state had taken such legislative action as was usual at that period, requiring isolation, providing quarantine, authorizing hospitals, and punishing for wilful communication of the infection. It does not appear that there was ever any notable spread of small pox in this town. In 1807, however, it prevailed to some extent, and a pest house was established near Leavitt's pond, on the Charlton place, and another at the house of Joshua Lewis, not far from the Waterford bridge. The site of the house is a part of land of Levi B. Dodge. The buildings are gone. Dr. Ainsworth was one of those who were attacked. One of the isolated patients demonstrated the futility of that method, so far as he was personally concerned, by leaving his place of confinement and posting himself on the bridge in the way of all passers. Another person was incarcerated as a small pox victim, but his symptoms developed into nothing more epidemic than the itch. Vaccination had become so general that our people never knew much of small pox in its ancient virulence. Indeed, statistics now show that its fatality is not one per cent. of that from diptheria and scarlatina. The peculiar dread of small pox, that still exists, is based upon conditions which prevailed before vaccination was practiced; but there is no longer any reasonable foundation for it.

SPOTTED FEVER, 1812.—Spotted fever (cerebro spinal meningitis) was first observed in this country, in Medfield, Mass., in 1806, although it had been known in Europe as early as 1505, when it prevailed to an alarming extent. In April, 1807, it appeared in Connecticut, and continued to prevail in different towns in the state, through the years 1808 and 1809. It is said to have appeared in Deerfield, N. H., as early as 1807, but did not prevail as an epidemic throughout the state until two or three years later, and remained as late as 1815 or 1816. In 1809, 1810 and 1811, it prevailed quite generally throughout Maine, New Hampshire, Connecticut, New York, Pennsylvania and Canada. Its march was very erratic, as may be seen from the fact that the disease prevailed in Bath in 1811, in Walpole, Bethlehem and Littleton in 1812, in Gilmanton and Croydon in 1813, in Boscawen in

1814, while Warren was not reached till 1815, when it prevailed in that place with fearful malignancy. During the period named, it prevailed in other localities in the state than the towns above mentioned, but these instances are given to show the peculiarities of its progress.

SCARLATINA, 1832, 1842, 1874.—This malady is never inactive. In 1832 and 1842, it prevailed with very serious fatality. It has reappeared at intervals in the entire period of the history of the town. A considerable mortality resulted from it in the winter and spring of 1874. Since then we have seen but little of it. It is a noteworthy fact, that at no one of the periods of its severest visitation in our midst, was it as violent or fatal as in other towns of the vicinity. Whether this amelioration of the effects of this affliction was owing to methods of treatment for which our local practitioners should have credit, or to more favorable local conditions, we cannot say. Perhaps it was attributable in a measure to each of these influences. The disease is apparently under better control than formerly. Nevertheless, it has, and deserves, the most serious attention of the best intellect and acquirement of the profession, for we have abundant reason to view its approach with alarm.

DIPTHERIA, 1863.—A lady, who returned here from a visit abroad, had contracted diptheria. In greeting her friends she communicated the disease, and it raged with fatal effect for several months. Many deaths resulted, and it gave the medical profession the most serious test they had encountered since the advent of spotted fever in 1812. Its character was very malignant. Young and old were victims. It recurred in 1869, but with less fatality. The activity of sanitary reforms of recent years is undoubtedly making itself effective in undermining the strongholds of these so-called epidemic disorders. The putrid sore throat of former times is closely allied to diptheria. The accounts of its ravages, as given by Belknap, the historian, and our own experience, would best be forgotten, were it not that they are the whip and spur that must drive on the sanitary reform, which is, as yet, only in the first stages of development, and which science and philanthrophy demand.

ERYSIPELAS. 1842. 1843. 1844.—This remarkable scourge had a beginning here in 1842, when we found a child in the village suffering from erysipelas, attended by marked peculiarities. Dr. Moore recognized the true nature of the case, and gave it consideration in connection with the history of the disease, as it had been known in London. The infection was unconsciously conveyed by physicians in their practice, and otherwise, and an alarming fatality followed. This was especially the case with women in child birth. The epidemic became general in Vermont, and a fatal termination was almost certain with the special class of cases to which I have referred. In this town, it was brought under control, perhaps, in a measure, by favorable local conditions. As this became known, the town attracted many women from Vermont, for the period of confinement. Many lives doubtless were saved by this hejira. The town was, for this reason, regarded as a sanitarium, forty years ago—a "city of refuge" from the epidemic.

DYSENTERY, 1851.—This disorder, peculiar in its epidemic or infectious form, was communicated at Waterford by two children, who had contracted it while on a visit with their mother in Boston. It was violently contagious and fatal to almost every child that came in contact with it. It was communicated at funerals and in clothing. It was a violent dysentery, accompanied by a remarkably efficient element of contagion. Nothing of the like character has before, or since, been known in this vicinity. A peculiar feature was, that it prevailed in the winter months.

No adequate treatment of these topics can be given in this place. It is a subject that well deserves an article extended and in detail. It is, however, apparent from what we have outlined of this branch of the history of the town, that its exemption from special visitations of disease is phenomenal. If our experience has been thus fortunate under the lax methods and habits of the past, we may hope for a more striking immunity under the regimen which the enlightened science of the future will enforce.

STATISTICS OF HEALTH AND LONGEVITY.

The review of the periods in which our people have suffered special visitations of disease, demonstrates that our exemption, if not complete, has been remarkable. The conclusion is justified that our climate and sanitary conditions are very favorable to general health and longevity. The streams course rapidly over our territory, down marked declivities. Nature, therefore, controls the drainage, and scours the surface of our hillsides and valleys with frequent and drenching rain storms and mountain floods. We have the pure air of the highlands, and the mountains break the violence of the winds. The water of our springs is wholesome, some of them having mineral constituents of a medicinal character, and others being of as absolutely simple chemistry as the famous Poland spring. The registration report of 1883 gives the number of births as 101 ; in 1884, 79. The deaths were 56 in 1883 ; in 1884, 51. In view of the conceded efficiency with which the data has been gathered here, as compared with many other sections of the state, we have an average in these important statistics which is very favorable to the health conditions of the town. A careful estimate of the number of residents, who are more than seventy years of age, gives 150 in that class. One feature of our climate, especially favorable to small children and invalids, is, that the nights are almost invariably cool in the mid-summer season. Our people have a daily relief from the strain of the heated term. Other elements of the sanitarium mark the town. Its advantages are becoming known abroad, and its attractions, as a resort for health and recreation, are recognized by increasing numbers of welcome visitors. We cannot promise immunity here from the ills to which the human system is everywhere susceptible ; but this town is assuredly one of the favored spots.

THE CHURCH IN LITTLETON.

ADDRESS BY REV. JOSEPH E. ROBINS.

The President said:—The eighth subject is that of the Church. That the people of Littleton have always maintained churches, and provided means for religious worship, is beyond doubt. We have present one who is a minister of the gospel, a native of Littleton, whose father was born, lived and died here, from whom, I have no doubt, you will all be glad to hear, the Rev. J. E. Robins.

ADDRESS.

Mr. President, Friends and Neighbors:

I deem myself honored to be permitted to stand in this presence, on this occasion, to speak for the Church in Littleton. Though from Portsmouth, today, I am of Littleton, always was, ever shall be. In yonder churchyard, sleeps the dust of four generations of our family. The farm, two miles yonder, over the hills, is now trod by the fifth. Every year I bring my family to Littleton, and tell them that here is our home. It was here that I received my first religious impressions. Here, I dedicated myself to God and the church. My first church-going recollections take me back to the old Congregational meeting-house, where, sitting in the gallery loft, a lad of five, I watched with intense interest the playing of the big fiddle.

Since then, what a change in church edifice, preaching, music, and people! The Rev. Mr. Carpenter—I see him now, tall, dignified, a little inclined to stiffness—scholarly, sympathetic, thoroughly in earnest! Never shall I forget a sermon which he preached in the little red school-house, in district " No. 5." Nor that inquiry meeting for the young, in the parlor at Philander Farr's.

" How do you enjoy your mind, Sister Robins?" said Mr. Carpenter, to my mother, while making a pastoral call. The awful solemnity with which the question was asked, sent a shudder to my child-depressed heart; and I inwardly said, " isn't that awful?" But Parson Carpenter was a good man, made good proof of his ministry, and has gone home to his reward. He rests well from his labors, and with him many of his church and people.

Littleton, with her mountains round about, has a physical situation like Jerusalem, hemmed in by " The Mountains of God." And, if we mistake not, here is to be found " A Remnant of the Elect," not in the one church only, but in all the churches, for we have now the seven.

During the century, Littleton has made rapid strides in material, intellectual, and social interests. Nor have " the Law and the Prophets " been neglected. The Law is of age, and speaks for itself. Of " the Prophets," I will attempt to give a fair interpretation. Though myself a Methodist, through and through, yet I am not such a Methodist, I trust, as to disqualify me for this position. During my brief ministry, I have preached in Calvin Baptist, Freewill Baptist and Christian Baptist churches; in Congregational, Presbyterian, Dutch Reform, Universalist, African, and Methodist Episcopal churches; among the Catholics, I have some personal friends, one of whom is Father Finnegan, known well to some of you.

I believe in catholicity and christian union. As a practical illustration, I, a Methodist, married a Presbyterian, at the residence of an Episcopalian, the ceremony being performed by a Dutch Reform divine. On my mother's side, I was, originally, " Farr " from a Methodist, hence I hope I am one of the elect, according to the free grace of God. Allow me at this point to relate an authentic anecdote: Some years ago, one of Littleton's prominent lawyers was quite intimate with the Methodist preacher, a man of stalwart frame. The two were looking over some business matters that were quite perplexing. The lawyer let slip an emphatic word which the clergyman considered an oath. Said the parson to the lawyer, "why did you swear?" The legal member quickly replied, "I thought somebody ought to swear, and it would not sound well for you."

In my boyhood days, I sometimes heard hard things said of Littleton—that it was a kind of spiritual "Sodom." And the impression was, that if a man died, and came up to the gates of heaven, and it were known that he was from Littleton, that fact alone would be enough to exclude him from the kingdom. I did not believe it then, I do not now. "The Wheat and Tares" may grow together here, but this is not, altogether, bad soil for "the Wheat," after all.

The churches in Littleton have, at least, an average standing. To say more might seem boastful; less, untruthful. Denominations have multiplied; membership increased; the standard of practical piety advanced. This is true in temperance, in general philanthropy, in missionary zeal, and christian unity. Today, you would not permit your minister to enter the sacred desk from the bar-room of the tavern, and to minister in holy things under the inspiration of New England rum. Today, deacons, stewards, even private members, are not allowed to touch the intoxicating cup. What a revelation would the "Old Red Tavern," "The Giles Stand," at the center of the town, make, could it but speak!

In "the olden time," the cheering glass was held as indispensable to health and prosperity; though, often, drunkenness was regarded as a sin. Some of the fathers of the church occasionally took a little too much for the stomach sake, and were compelled to confess their sin in the public congregation. Deacon R—— had a weakness in this direction, which he humbly acknowledged, and pledged himself to correct. Merchant O—— of Waterford, a man well-to-do in the world, had committed the gross sin of drunkenness. (Waterford and Littleton united at that time for the support of meetings.) Deacon R—— was appointed by the church to labor with

Merchant O——, in view to his amendment. A wag, caring more for fun than temperance, gave O—— an "inkling" of the contemplated mission. One cold, winter morning, Trader O—— saw Deacon R—— driving up to his store, and made haste to welcome him. "A cold day, deacon," said Brother O——. After chatting a few moments, O—— brought forward some fourth proof spirit, mixed into a glass of toddy. "Take a little something, deacon," said Brother O——, "it will warm you." The deacon had not the heart to refuse, and soon drained the glass, remarking that he felt much better. A little later, a second and a third glass was disposed of. By this time, the old deacon was pretty well "set up." Then Brother O—— remarked, "the next time the church sends a man to labor with me for drunkenness, please appoint some one not guilty of the same sin."

We will in brief outline the church history of the town.

In the earlier days, the people being few and scattered, highways rough—where there were any highways at all, and the material resources extremely limited, we could hardly expect to find a church edifice and permanent preaching. It is evident that some of the fathers were religious men, and did what they could for the support of religious interests. Their log cabin homes were thrown open to the people; and, from Sabbath to Sabbath, services were conducted by one of their own number. James Rankin, a Scotch Presbyterian, often officiated on the Sabbath, and at funerals. Nathaniel Webster officiated also.

Among the places where worship was held, were the cabins of Thomas Miner and James Williams.

Pioneer preachers from time to time passed through this section, and gave words of exhortation and encouragement. About 1790, a preacher by the name of Atkinson, of much talent, from Portsmouth, ministered to the people for the space of six months. In '91, a vote was passed to hire preaching for two months. In '92, £9 were voted for the gospel. In '96, the town voted " to pay James Rankin for going for the minister." In '99, voted to raise a committee to hire a minister to preach out the money subscribed." March 18th, 1800, voted " to choose a committee to direct the selectmen in fixing a senter place in town, to hold town meetings, and hold meetings of preaching." Voted that "Capt. Williams, Capt. Hoskins, Andrew Rankin, and Mr. Robins be the committee as aforesaid."

In 1802, the town voted $100 for preaching. In 1802 or 1803, John Lord preached for a while in town. The records are as follows:—" March 15th, 1803. Voted to allow Capt. James Williams his account of $7.25 for paying and boarding Rev. John Lord, a minister. Voted to allow Mr. Asa Lewis $5.00, paid to Rev. John Lord.

In 1811, the town subscribed $200 towards a meetinghouse, with the understanding that the town should have the privilege of holding their town meetings here. Two acres of land at the center of the town were given by Moses Little, Esq., for the site of the proposed building. The meetinghouse was completed and dedicated in 1815, with the understanding that it was to be occupied by the several denominations uniting in its erection, in proportion to the amounts which they respectively owned. Hence, we see that, even at this early period, the people did not all think alike in matters of religion. Methodism was already introduced.

The itinerants have followed close in the immigrant's track. In '98, Jesse Lee preached in Lisbon. He was again in the vicinity two years later. In his journal, under date of Saturday, September 6th, 1800, he makes this record. " We set out early in the morning, and rode out to Connecticut river, at Northumberland meeting-house; there I left my traveling companion, and rode down the river, through Lancaster, Dalton, and into Littleton, where I was hailed and stopped by Josiah Newhall, an old acquaintance of mine, who had moved up into the country; I consented to stay all night with him, and was thankful to find a house, though but a small log cabin, where I could lay my head in peace—myself and horses were weary. I was greatly pleased with that part of the country. It was generally level and rich land, near the river, and the rising grounds, at a distance, made a beautiful appearance. The country promises to be very fruitful, and I doubt not but religion will flourish in this country before long. Our preachers have lately formed a circuit there, called Landaff. I rode one hundred and forty-five miles, and preached six times, that week."

In 1800, E. R. Sabine was appointed to "old Landaff circuit," Littleton and all the surrounding towns being included. In 1801, this circuit was reported as being all in a flame with revival, with 100 conversions. About this time, Baptist missionaries visited the town and deeply moved the religious sentiment of the people. Congregationalism was, however, the dominant order, though certain concessions were made to the other "sects" in the building of the meetinghouse. The old Puritanic church naturally and rightly absorbed the others; but it did not assimilate them.

THE CONGREGATIONAL CHURCH.

The Congregational church, consisting of ten members, was organized in 1803 by Rev. David Goodall, a citizen of the town, and Rev. Asa Carpenter, pastor of the church in Waterford. Prior to 1820, the church had no settled minister. The Rev. David Goodall preached for half of the time during one summer. Mr. N. K. Hardy, a licentiate, served the church half of the time for three years, until his sickness and death. In 1820, the church numbered thirty-five members, and the Rev. Drury Fairbanks of Plymouth was installed pastor in May of this year.

PASTORS AND TERMS OF PASTORATES.

From May 1820, to March, 1836, Rev. Drury Fairbanks.

March 14, 1836, Rev. Evarts G. Worcester was ordained and installed. Before many months, consumption cut short his labors, and his life.

September 27, 1837, Rev. Isaac R. Worcester, brother of the above, was settled. After a pastorate of three years, he was compelled to resign because of failing health. The church was then supplied for a time by Rev. William Withington, Rev. Samuel Beane and Rev. Drury Fairbanks.

December 13, 1842, to January 6, 1857, Rev. E. L. Carpenter. Then the Rev. Mr. Russell supplied for one year. September 28, 1860, to December 31, 1878, Rev. C. E. Milliken. The Rev. W. A. Hadley and others supplied the desk for a time.

January 25, 1881, Rev. Geo. W. Osgood, the present pastor, was installed.

The present membership of the church is 204.

CHURCH EDIFICE.

The old meeting-house, at the center of the town, known to the boys as the "old Town House," gave place, in 1834, to the more pretentious structure in the village, costing $2000. This house was dedicated on the 4th of July of this year. In 1852, the church was enlarged, a vestry built underneath, and was furnished with a bell. In 1874, the church was again remodeled, as we now see it, at a cost of $8000.

In 1883, a beautiful and commodious chapel was built.

We have spoken thus at length concerning the Congregational church, since it was the first church, for a long time the only church, and is now one of the most prominent churches in town.

Congregationalists, in the west part of the town, contiguous to Waterford, have, from the earliest period, there made their church home.

THE METHODIST CHURCH.

There was no stated Methodist preaching in town until 1843. Prior to this, Littleton, as a small part of the great Landaff circuit, was occasionally visited by the "Itinerants." since 1801. Services were held a part of the time by local preachers, Elder Burkley, Joseph Robins, Jr., James Rankin, Jr., and others, officiating in this capacity.

Sixty-nine members are reported as the Methodist strength in 1822. In the Shute neighborhood and on Mann's hill the Methodist interests were especially flourishing. Rev. J. P. Williams, a presiding elder, was living in 1845 at North

Littleton, and helped the Methodist cause considerably by preaching in the school-houses round about.

A class was formed, so that, in 1844, Littleton and Whitefield reported 140 members.

PASTORS AND TERMS OF PASTORATES.

In 1843, Littleton and Whitefield—Rev. J. S. Loveland, and one to be supplied; 1844, Littleton and Whitefield, Rev. J. S. Loveland and Rev. A. F. Hewes; 1845, Littleton and Bethlehem, Rev. J. G. Johnson; 1846, Littleton and Bethlehem, Rev. Silas Wiggins; 1847, not reported; 1848, Littleton, Rev. Charles Cowing; 1849, Littleton and Whitefield, Rev. C. Cowing.

After this date, Littleton appears as a separate charge. 1850-1, Rev. Sullivan Holman; 1852-3, Rev. Dudley P. Leavitt; 1854-5, Rev. L. L. Eastman; 1856, Rev. J. P. Stinchfield; 1857-8, Rev. Geo. N. Bryant; 1859-60, Rev. L. P. Cushman; 1861-2, Rev. Geo. S. Barnes; 1863, Rev. S. E. Quimby; 1864, Rev. H. L. Kelsey; 1865-6, Rev. Truman Carter; 1867-8, Rev. A. E. Drew; 1869, Rev. James M. Bean; 1870-1, Rev. John Currier; 1872-3, Rev. George Beebe; 1874-5-6, Rev. George W. Ruland; 1877-8, Rev. N. M. D. Granger; 1879-'80-1, Rev. Geo. A. McLaughlin; 1882-3-4, Rev. G. M. Curl, the present pastor.

CHURCH EDIFICE.

The church was built on the site of the "old Red Store," during the pastorate of Rev. S. Holman, and dedicated by the Rev. J. E. King. A chapel was built in '76, Rev. G. W. Ruland, pastor. The church was remodeled at a cost of $4000, and re-dedicated by the Rev. J. R. Day, in the winter of 1881. A parsonage was bought in 1868. The present membership is 176.

THE CATHOLIC CHURCH.

The Catholics were a mission, depending on Lancaster, from 1854 to 1874; then a mission, depending on Lebanon. Since '82 the church has been independent.

PASTORS AND PASTORATES.

From 1854 to 1876, Rev. I. H. Noiseaux; 1876–8, Rev. F. X. Trudell; 1878–'81, Rev. J. P. Finnegan; 1881–2, Rev. L. M. Laplante; 1882–4, Rev. I. H. Noiseaux, the present pastor.

CHURCH EDIFICE AND MEMBERSHIP.

The church was built in 1876–7. There were thirty-three Catholic families in 1876; one hundred and twenty-five families in 1884.

CALVIN BAPTIST CHURCH.

As early as 1821, there were nine members of the Baptist society in town, connected with the Baptist church of West Waterford, commonly known as "the Snuff Box Church." In 1839 or 1840, a small church was built at the Scythe Factory Village. Rev. Nicholas Bray, who was the first pastor, served the church two or three years. There were twenty members. Anson Alexander was chosen deacon, and Barnet H. Smith was chosen clerk. In 1842–3–4, Rev. Wm. Lovejoy served as pastor. The church, suffering from removals and other losses, was disorganized, so that Mr. Lovejoy was the last pastor.

FREEWILL BAPTIST CHURCH.

Rev. John Colby of Sutton, Vt., speaks of preaching in Littleton at one o'clock on Monday, in the summer of 1810, as he was passing through the town from Waterford to Lisbon. Ever after he passed "around," not "through" the town. There were six members of this church reported in 1821. The Baptist members of Littleton were doubtless connected with the church at Bethlehem until 1869, when the church was built, and the Baptist interests of Bethlehem were transferred to this town. At the time of this reorganization at Littleton, the membership was 27. Its present membership is 113.

PASTORS AND PASTORATES.

From May 29, 1869, to December 27, 1873, the time of his death, Rev. Elijah Gilford. From this date, to July 2, 1874, Rev. Burton Minard. July 2, 1874, to May 4, 1876, Rev. E. P. Moulton. September 1, 1876, to May 1, 1878, Rev. Ira Emery. May 1, 1878, to October 30, 1879, Rev. Burton Minard. October 30, 1879, Rev. F. H. Lyford, the present pastor.

CHURCH EDIFICE.

The church was dedicated, April 29, 1869. It has since been remodeled. The church has a vestry and lecture room. The society owns a parsonage.

PROTESTANT EPISCOPAL.

The corner stone of the church was laid, July 22, 1875. The church was dedicated in November of the same year, by Bishop Niles. Cost of building, $5000.

PASTORS AND PASTORATES.

The first rector was Rev. J. B. Goodrich, who officiated about two years. The Rev. A. R. Graves served three years, ending his pastorate in September, 1880. Rev. Geo. C. Jones acted as pastor until the following May. He was succeeded by Rev. H. M. Andrews. Rev. J. G. Kent, the present pastor, has been rector of the church for two years. The church has a membership of thirty-five. There are funds nearly sufficient for a parsonage.

UNITARIAN.

While the old Union church was used by the several denominations alternately, according to compact, the Unitarians nearly equaled either of the others. Their preachers frequently occupied the pulpit. This added zest to the controversial character of the discourses of the period. At a later period, the Unitarian sentiment was less pronounced.

For three years past the Unitarians have held services in town twice a month. A lot for a church has been purchased. The erection of a house of worship is contemplated at an early day. Rev. J. B. Morrison of Lancaster, pastor.

THE SECOND ADVENTISTS.

The Second Adventists, after several series of successful services in the halls, and holding a vigorous tent meeting at the Factory Village, under the direction of Elder Miles Grant, Elder Couch and others, secured a room in the "Grange Building" for permanent services, where meetings of much interest are held.

The Young Men's Christian Association has been in successful operation for about ten years. It has done good work in the "outlying" districts, and has promoted christian unity and fellowship in the churches.

The churches have sent forth christian workers to various parts of the world. Miss Rankin has organized a mission work in Mexico, and published an account of her labors in that section. Mrs. Lizzie Cobleigh Cole has been laboring as a missionary in Eastern Turkey for sixteen years. The Rev. Nelson F. Cobleigh has charge of Congregational missions in Washington Territory. The Reverends Truman Carter, Warren Applebee, Charles W. Millen, A. B. Carter, Joseph W. Presby and Joseph E. Robins, all sons of Littleton, are members of various Methodist conferences. Other ministers, natives of this town, not already named, were Rev. N. E. Cobleigh, D. D., Methodist; Rev. Andrew Rankin and Rev. John Gile, Presbyterians; Rev. Enoch M. Pingree, Universalist, who have been called from labor; and Rev. Henry B. Mead, Congregationalist, and Rev. John A. Bellows, Unitarian, who are in active clerical work.

IN CONCLUSION.

The churches were never before so near together as today. Many members, but one body. Diversity of gifts, but one spirit. Christ, the head, of whom the whole family in heaven and earth is named. Congregationalism has caught some of the Methodistic fire. Methodism has been touched with Congregational learning. The Congregationalist can now bow the body as well as the spirit. The Methodist can stand in prayer, and yet be as humble as the publican. Election and Free Grace clasp hands and kiss each other. The 'Baptists' holy tone is wholly lost, and water is applied according to the individual liking.

The Episcopalian still clings to his prayer book and robes, lest his individuality be lost; while in spirit, even, he is largely unified with others.

Here it is hard work to keep up the church barriers, and the abler ones occasionally jump over. All are learning the spirit of the Master's saying, "Other sheep I have, which are not of this fold."*

---

*The friends of Liberal Christianity (Universalists and Unitarians), who have been moving heretofore to secure preaching for a portion of the time during the year, and have finally made arrangements therefor, met at the office of C. W. Rand, Esq., on Saturday evening last (June 14, 1873), adopted articles of association, and formally organized a religious society, to be known as the "Liberal Christian Society of Littleton." A board of Trustees was elected for the ensuing year, consisting of the following persons:—Wm. J. Bellows, C C. Smith, Wm. H. Chandler, Mrs. C. W. Rand, and Mrs. F. G. Weller. L. D. Sanborn was chosen clerk and treasurer. C. W. Rand, Esq., and H. H. Metcalf were chosen delegates to the Universalist state convention, to be holden at Manchester, on Wednesday and Thursday of this week. This Society starts with nearly a hundred members, and every promise of success.—*White Mountain Republic, June 19, 1873.*

Rev. J. P. Atkinson (Universalist) of Laconia was engaged to supply preaching for a year, commencing Sunday, June 22, 1873, services to be held at Farr's Hall. Other Liberal Christian clergymen officiated under the employment of this society from time to time.

The decease of some of the principal movers in this enterprise, and the removal of others from town, checked the development of the undertaking. The rise of the Episcopalian, Freewill Baptist, Unitarian and Advent establishments in place, in the meantime, afforded congenial church privileges to many, who, the for various reasons, had not chosen to affiliate with the two elder churches.

The pastorate of Rev. Geo. W. Osgood of the Congregationalist church closed late in 1884. He was succeeded by Rev. Edwin C. Holman, who was pastor till the latter part of 1886. Rev. Fred G. Chutter took charge of the church about the first of 1887, and is the present pastor. This society has a commodious parsonage in the process of erection.

Rev. F. H. Lyford closed his pastorate with the Free Baptist church in 1886, and was succeeded by Rev. Granville C. Waterman, who is now in charge.

The Unitarian society has erected a church edifice in modern style, and with modern conveniences. This parish is still under the pastoral supervision of Rev. J. B. Morrison of Lancaster.

The Methodists recently built a large and convenient parsonage. Rev. M. V. B. Knox, Ph. D., the present pastor, succeeded Rev. George M. Curl in 1885.

Since 1884, Rev. Mr. Kent has concluded his work; Rev. Henry H. Haynes has served a second time as minister in charge of All Saints Protestant Episcopal church, and Rev. Isaac Peck is now in charge.

Father Noiseaux continues as the Roman Catholic parish priest.

The Advent society continues its public services, but without a settled pastor.

June, 1887.   A. S. B.

LITTLETON ABROAD.

ADDRESS BY SAMUEL B. PAGE.

The President said: The next subject is "Littleton Abroad." We have with us, today, Mr. Samuel B. Page, who was born and studied his profession in town, has since resided and practiced elsewhere, with whose general knowledge and brilliant sallies, you will no doubt be both entertained and instructed.

ADDRESS.

Mr. Chairman:

When I rise in response to your kind introduction, I must be pardoned if I make claim to the consideration of this large and intelligent audience, upon other ground than personal desert or merit. I ask your attention, for a brief time, not to the lawyer nor the orator, not the speaker in any other quality or capacity than as a son of Littleton. With a pardonable pride, I trust I may, today of all others, boast of my nativity here, as of a rich inheritance. You will surely permit me not to forget that I am entitled to that honor, although I may be the least among you.

Citizens and Children of Littleton:

It must be a source of mutual gratulation among you that your committee of arrangements have selected the birthday of our National Independence for the celebration of the hundredth anniversary of your municipal existence; and, that the double occasion has brought together here so many of your sons and daughters, not only of those who still keep alive the fires upon the old hearthstones, but scores and hundreds of others, who, for a day, attracted by past memories or traditions, have come up here to bow with you before the old domestic altars, and revive those memories and make real those traditions. We return to you, some more or less bad pennies, more or less debased or worn by worldly attention, but, as a whole, we hope, good current human coin ; not all a discredit to the old town, from whose fostering arms we went forth to seek and conquer fortune. And what shall I say of our reception and welcome? Not content with the immolation of the regulation "fatted calf," supposed to be invariably stall-feeding for the family tramp, you seem to have decimated your herds and depleted your granaries. Every latch-string hangs out, every hand is extended, every voice sounds a welcome, and, friends, "Littleton Abroad," in the embrace of "Littleton at Home," ardently, aye, passionately, responds to every loving word, tender gesture and noble deed.

I suppose that, in response to the sentiment "Littleton Abroad," I am expected to speak of, and as I am able for, your friends and kindred who have sought other homes, who, though of us, are not with us. Some of the most highly honored of these are, today, upon this platform. Listening to their eloquent sentences, you have already given, and will continue to give them your approval and applause. We will not turn ourselves up here in a mutual admiration society.

Others, as honored and honorable, are scattered through the aisles of this grove, receiving glad welcome, hearty handshake and warm embrace. Whilst you stand thus, hand to hand, heart to heart, a more eloquent voice than mine is speaking. I hardly need tell you of the friend once again within the sound of your voice, and in your strong clasp. But there are thousands of our number that, though of us, are not with us. Among them, living or dead, are men and women of not only local, but national fame, whose lives are representative of the highest thought and noblest doing; men and women who have won distinction in letters and in art, in every location and profession, winning and wearing the highest honors bestowed by an appreciative people. I cannot name a tithe, but I must not be deemed to have intentionally forgotten any, by a brief reference to a few out of many whose names now occur to me.

One of the most eminent of these, Benjamin W. Bonney, L.L. D., became eminent in the legal profession, in the city of New York, and was, later, a Judge of its Superior Court. As a wise counsellor and an honest judge, he won esteem and honor for himself and his native state amidst the sharpest rivalry and the most searching criticism.

Calvin Ainsworth was appointed from the bar to act as a Commissioner to compile the Statutes of 1853, and subsequently was a Judge of a Municipal Court in Wisconsin.

Moses A. Dow, whose active and intelligent push made the Waverly Magazine the means of amassing a fortune, deserves wider mention, as a man who, whether in Boston, his adopted home, or in this, his native town, used his wealth nobly and well. His public and private charities, many of which are only known to the grateful hearts whose burdens his wise charity has relieved, entitle him to high rank among the philanthropists of his generation.

Among the first names familiar to me, in my early boyhood here, was that of Frank A. Eastman. I have an impression that he was then identified with a newspaper in this town, but very soon he appeared in the great city of the West, Chicago, leader among her journalists, and potent in her political affairs. Later, in New York, he wielded hardly less influence.

N. E. Cobleigh, D. D., L.L. D., has held high rank in the M. E. church, as a preacher, a journalist and an educator. His pulpit eloquence has been characterized as equally fervid and convincing, and his striking success in the conduct of the denominational journal, and the foundation and maintenance of preparatory schools and colleges, attest a wonderful versatility and capacity.

Hardly less notable appears the life of the Rev. Enoch Merrill Pingree, Dr. Cobleigh's sectarian opponent, but a most brilliant orator, especially upon controverted theological questions. Like Dr. Cobleigh, he could not content himself with a sphere bound by his voice, but sought to reach a whole people through the press.

Among your distinguished daughters, I recall the names of Elizabeth Rankin, pioneer of American (Protestant) Missions in Mexico; Maria Bonney, well and favorably known as an author and teacher, and of extensive experience in travel; and Lizzie Cobleigh, self-denying and earnest missionary to Turkey.

True, tender and loving, christian gentlewomen all, whose lives have been representative of scores of others, whose praises may never be sounded from any public platform or pulpit, but whose good works do live and follow them; whose names may never be written in address or essay, but will surely be written in letters of light in the Book of Life, as of those who loved and lived for their fellowmen. God bless them, one and all. Their sisters are honored in their sex, all humanity in their sweet charity, high intellectuality and earnest christianity.

And now, my friends, I approach, with reverent emotions, with slower step, and hushed voice, the memory of your lost and brave.

Distinguished in civil life, your scattered children in the land were not sluggards in the war. In danger's front, daring, dying, from the beginning to the end of the great struggle of sections, they were true to you, themselves, and their country. Among the best of soldiers, and bravest of men, you must recall the name of Alpha Burnham Farr, who, at forty years of age, left Lowell, Massachusetts, for the front, at the echo of the first gun from Sumpter. Having been alderman and marshal of his adopted city for years, he had naturally identified himself with the local militia. The first note of war signalled the march of the famous Massachusetts Sixth for Washington. Col. Farr, rising from a sick bed, and defying his physician, assumed the post of adjutant, and accompanied his regiment on the historic march through Baltimore, actively participating in all its stirring scenes.

Upon the return of the Sixth, he assisted in recruiting the Twenty-sixth Massachusetts, was commissioned its Lieutenant Colonel, and, after three months, its Colonel. He led his regiment through the series of victories, Forts Jackson and Philip, La Fouche, Baton Rouge and Sabine Pass, and for more than a year was Provost Marshal of New Orleans. Transferred to the army of the Shenandoah, he did gallant service under Sheridan, engaging in the battles of Fisher Hill and Cedar Creek. Returning to civil life, at the close of the war, Col. Farr served his adopted city and the country until near the time of his decease, which occurred at Rumney, N. H., and as if Providence sought especial honor for a brave man in death, even, his last sun rose and set upon this anniversary, July 4th, 1879.

Conspicuous among your brave sons, who early answered their country's call, was Major Evarts W. Farr, who gave his good right arm at Williamsburg, and, returning to civil life among you, was, by the suffrages of his Congressional District, sent into the national councils.

Not a week since, in the southern part of the state, an enquiry brought around me a score of scarred veterans, all eager in their admiration of another Littleton boy, Major Sam Goodwin, whose military tutelage began with Ellsworth, and his Fire Zouaves, and whose stalwart person bore wounds received in almost every battle he fought south of the Potomac.

Capt. Wm. A. Moore, first of Duryea's Zouaves, and, later, valiantly, fearlessly facing every peril by the side of New Hampshire's noble son, Col. Cross of the Fighting Fifth, attained his captaincy before he was out of his minority, and, though boy in years, yet a man in heroism, sank in death under doubly deadly wounds upon the bloody field of Fredericksburg.

Among others, brave men all, I can pause but to name your neighbor and my friend, the unpretentious, high-minded gentleman today, the cool and fearless soldier in service, who bears daily among you the shattered shoulder, pierced at Cold Harbor, Captain George Farr ; also, Captain Marshal Sanders, whose name the G. A. R. here perpetuates, who was with the first regiment to enter Richmond at the close of the war, but who soon slept his last sleep, dying from the hardships of the service; Captain Rennie Richardson, whom I knew, boy and man, who was raised to his rank upon the field of Gettysburg itself for conspicuous gallantry in the old "Second," a regiment of gallant men; Captain Ezra B. Parker of the New Hampshire (not the Rhode Island) Cavalry; Captain George E. Pingree, a native of Littleton, but later a soldier of Lisbon, who won his straps in the Eleventh regiment by his record in the old Second, with Marston; Captain Theron A. Farr, who followed the fortunes of the old Fifth to the end; Lieutenants Davis of the Third, Bemis of the Sixth, Kilburn and Gaskell of the Thirteenth, Hazeltine of the Fifteenth, Green and Quimby of the Artillery, and hundreds of brave men, who, in the ranks, performed deeds of valor, and manly, patriotic self-sacrifice, none the less noble and sublime because unwritten and unspoken.

Your check-list of 1884 bore the names of 915 legal voters, and the enrollment of the town for the same year was 365. Your check-list of February, 1861, gave the names of 582 legal voters. The enrollment for that year is not given, but, assuming for it the same ratio to the number of legal voters that existed in 1884, the enrollment for 1861 should have been 217. From these statements, it will be seen that the number of men actually furnished for the war, by this town, according to Capt. Farr's estimate, exceeded by ten the whole number liable by law to be called to do military duty in 1861. "And it came to pass, from that time forth, that one-half of my servants wrought in the work, and half of them held the spears, the shields and the bows, and the coats of mail."

With such a record, so bestarred with glorious achievements, have you not just pride in "Littleton Abroad?" Have not these, your children, honored their parentage, and left you, in fame, an inheritance passing all price? I know their works will follow them down the generations yet to come, and that their memory will never fade so long as the earth stands and the stars endure.

EDUCATION.

ADDRESS BY DANA P. DAME, A. M.

The President said: The subject, "Education," is assigned to Mr. Dana P. Dame, principal of the high school, whose address will appear in the published proceedings.

ADDRESS.

MR. PRESIDENT:

There is one characteristic which marks the English people as it did the peoples from whom they mainly sprang, and that is their intense love of home. The typical Englishman is comparatively indifferent to society. For the sake of a home, he will cross the sea, and settle in an unbroken and unexplored wilderness. The solitude of a new country has no fears for him. The society of his wife and family is sufficient, and he cares for no other. In this characteristic of the Englishman, we find the mainspring of all his greatness. Love of home, of wife, of children, necessarily prompt him, a man of action, to better their condition. Of such sturdy, fearless stock were the first settlers in the town of Littleton, true hearted men, men of christian purpose and energy. And, although history, and even tradition, have as yet contributed nothing to enlighten us in regard to education in the town for the first few years after its incorporation, as previous to the year 1791, we find no records of schools being taught, school-houses being built, teachers being hired and paid, or of a school tax being raised, yet we must picture each household of such a community as its own little school, with its mistress and pupils, in which were taught, possibly, the three " R's," probably the catechism, and surely how to withstand hardship, and endure many privations.

In 1790, the town voted for representatives to Congress, the whole number of votes cast being ten, but the town had not, as yet, taken any steps toward organizing a school. True, there are many country districts at the present time in our state with less than ten voters which support a school, and, while we might, in this age of enterprise and education, be led to wonder and, perhaps, to harshly criticize the early settlers because, as the public records show, they had not for several years failed to fill such offices as those of hogreeve, pound-keeper and fence-viewer, without so much as taking the initiatory steps toward organizing a school, we see a reason for this course of action in the fact that the inhabitants were few, and consequently the town was very sparsely settled. The distance of the dwellings from each other, and the impoverished condition of the people, owing to the Revolution, rendered it impracticable for them to take measures to establish a school before 1791. At the annual March meeting of that year the town " Voted that sixteen bushels of wheat be raised for the use of schools next winter." At the following March meeting, the town " Voted that sixteen bushels of wheat be raised for the use of schools," and, " Voted that the town be divided into three districts, and that the division be at the parting of the roads at the Wheeler place, so called," a farm now owned by Geo. W. Richardson of this town. These three districts were then designated the Upper, Lower, and Middle Districts. In 1795, the Lower district was divided by a line half way between Lyman line and the crotch of the roads at the Wheeler place. In 1799, it was voted to divide the Upper district into two districts, the boundary line being substantially what is now the line between districts two and three. In the same year, the line which divided Lower district became substantially what is now the line between districts three and four, and was a substitute for the line made in 1795, the latter having proved unsatisfactory. In 1799, at the same meeting at which the new line dividing Lower district was decided upon, another district was created, being bounded as follows: It began at the south line of the land owned by Silas Wheeler (now owned by Gilman Wheeler, his grandson), ran toward Concord (now Lisbon) far enough to include the Jonas Nurse place (now owned by E. Fitch), and thence extended in the direction of the cross road that ran by what is now known as the Douglas Robins place, half way to the Rankin Mills. This district was the foundation of the present No. 5. (We say the present No. 5, because the districts were not numbered prior to 1805.) In 1802, it was "Voted that below Andrew Rankin's and the River settlement be a district for schooling," but, in 1805, this was rejoined to No. 4. When No. 5 was created, in 1802, that portion of the Middle district, so called, not included in No. 5, was called the Ammonoosuc district. In 1805, the Ammonoosuc district was divided by the line which now divides Union district and district No. 6. In the same year the town appointed a committee of eight, David Goodall, John Millen, James Williams, Peter Bonney, Joseph Morse, Andrew Rankin, John Nurse, Sam'l Rankin, who were to divide the town into school districts. The committee reported at a meeting, same year, recommending that the town be divided into six districts, and from this time, the districts were designated by numbers. Numbers 1, 2, 3 and 4 were the same substantially as now constituted. No. 5, was the same as the present No. 6, and No. 6 comprised what is now Mann's Hill and Farr Hill. These six districts were mentioned in the report of the committee, and the town, after accepting their report, proceeded to make more districts. There is a record of a division of No. 6 as defined by the committee's report, and seven districts appear to have been created at this meeting, according to the record of votes, but the meeting immediately proceeded to designate a committee of one from each district to build school-houses, and the record shows that there were eight members of the committee. By a separate vote, they chose eight collectors of the school tax, evidently one for each district. These last two votes indicate clearly that the town at this meeting recognized the existence of eight districts, whereas the constitution of but seven by actual vote is shown. The subsequent records show the existence of eight districts, and give lists of the district offices, showing one from each district. The residence of these officers, plainly designate these districts as they now are, from one to seven inclusive, and the No. 8 of that time included the No. 8 that was merged in Union School District, and several other districts subsequently created, viz. :—14, 15 and 17. It is probable that a vote actually passed at the meeting, the minutes of which present this discrepancy, would set the matter right, had it not been accidentally omitted. The numbering of the districts, as given in the committee's report, was not followed beyond district No. 4. In 1811, by a vote of the town, district No. 9 was set off from No. 4, and district No. 10 was set off from No. 5. No. 10, as then constituted, ran along what was called the cross-road, leading from the present residence of Elijah Fitch, by the Douglas Robins place, to Rankin's Brook. These 10 districts, as then numbered, contain a part of the same territory that the same districts now do, except No. 9, which was rejoined to No. 4, in 1875. In 1814, No. 11 was formed by setting off parts of districts 3 and 5. In 1823, No. 1 was divided through the centre, and the northern portion constituted No. 12. In 1828, district No. 13 was created by setting off all territory south of the Ammonoosuc river, in districts 8 and 6, except the farm of Nathan Applebee. In the same year, No. 8 was extended up river to the Bethlehem line, most of the territory thus added being, prior to this time, comprised within district No. 7. In 1833, a committee, consisting of Ezra Parker, Joseph Palmer and Joseph Robins, recommended certain boundaries for the thirteen school districts, and, at the next town meeting, the town voted to accept the boundaries as recommended by them. With the exception of Nos. 8 and 13, the boundaries were substantially the same as they are at the present time. In 1838, No. 14, now known as the Scythe Factory District, was established, the boundaries being the same substantially as now. In 1840, it was voted that all that part of the district No. 8, lying west of School street, should constitute a new district, No. 15. In 1850, district No. 16 was set off, the territory being parts of districts 2. 3 and 5. In 1877, this district was divided among the districts which originally ceded parts of their territory to form it. In 1844, the farms of Parker Cushman, Jonas Temple and others at North Littleton were set off in a district by themselves, being heretofore parts of 1 and 2, but the district was never organized. In 1853, it was voted to set off all that part of district No. 8, lying south of Ammonoosuc river, into a district, which was No. 17. In 1854, No. 11 was divided, and that portion next to Partridge Pond constituted, and still constitutes, what is substantially No. 18. In 1859, No. 19 was formed by setting off a portion of No. 11, and annexing it to a portion of the town of Lisbon, and since that year, but few unimportant changes have been made until the organization of Union District.

Littleton has been favored with a goodly number of faithful and energetic teachers, of whom, Robert Charlton and Ansel Hatch were the first, both of whom stood high in the profession. We could mention scores of names of other teachers, besides, who have been foremost in elevating, instructing and refining the children of our town, teachers, who have, by their influence and example, developed and rounded out our character, led us on, up the rough path of learning, and left their precious and lasting impression upon our lives. We should not here omit to mention Miss Melinda Rankin, who, at the early age of 14, began to teach, and whose after life has been devoted to missionary work, and charitable and benevolent purposes. Nor can we forget the long and useful career of Warren McIntire, who has devoted the best years of his life to the instruction of the youth of Littleton, and whose efforts in the school-room, and interest in educational matters have contributed largely to raising the schools of our town to their high standard of excellence. Many of us, doubtless, remember John Sargent, the able and efficient teacher, and Mrs. L. M. Wilson, at present superintendent of schools in Des Moines, Iowa. The prominent teachers in the town, also, include Daniel Wise, D. D., Gen. Gustavus Cushman, James Calhoun, Solomon Goodall, Richard Peabody, Smith Ross,

S. B. Page, Geo. Streeter, Harry Brickett, Hiram K. Dewey, Daniel Wilkins, Hannah B. Farr, Susie Brackett, Angie Day, Sarah Calhoun, Sue Moffett, Clementine Calhoun, Luella Calhoun, Mary Calhoun, Josie Millen, Ezra Hall, Dwight Carleton, Joseph Bickford, Hon. William Heywood, Reuben C. Benton, the Misses Peabody, Walter Charlton, the Misses Charlton, Wm. Hadley, Mrs. Walton (daughter of Peter Bonney, at present head teacher in the English department of Mme. Zeitska's Institute, San Francisco, Cal.), and the Misses Cobb.

For the first few years after Robert Charlton and Ansel Hatch began to teach, the schools were kept either in their own house, or some other more centrally located building, sometimes in a mill or a shop, and, in the summer time, often in barns. The first school-house was built near the site of the present house in district No. 3. It was a log school-house, standing back from the highway, with a strip of hard trodden ground in front of the door, which formed the play-ground of the younger scholars, while the play-ground of the older ones extended down the road as far as the "big rock," or as far as they had time to go, and often a great deal farther. Back of the school-house ran a brook, in which swam the trout and minnow, too often the unwary victims of "spools of thread for fishing lines, and bended pins for hooks." Just around the bend in the stream, was the "deep hole," in which the more daring took their noonday swim. It was the style then among boys, as it is now, to venture into the "purling brook" long enough before returning home from school at night for their hair to become dry, for mothers, then, as now, wished their boys to learn to swim without going near the water. The school-house, which was painted red, was fastened on the outside with a padlock, the windows were seven feet or so from the ground, to keep the scholars within from looking out, and rogues without from looking in. Around three sides of the interior were wooden benches running parallel with the walls, while up the center ran an isle, just wide enough for a single file of scholars to pass. At the other side of the room, the end where the scholars entered, was a platform, with its rough wooden desk and bench for the use of the teacher, and any visitor who wished to look wise and assume a *distangue* air. Just back of the desk, which was groaning under its weight of books, ferules, and trinkets taken from unlucky pupils, was the blackboard, which consisted of a single painted board, nailed to the wall, upon which the scholars scrawled their abuse of their committee, teacher or their fellows, and, after exhausting these subjects, they often soared aloft into the regions of poetry.

> "Multiply cation, Is, vexation
> division Is, as, Bad,
> the, rool of, 3, It, pusles Me,
> And, practis, Makes, Me, Mad."

The desks, if we examine them, will have, hollowed out upon their upper side, coarse images of Indian fights, canal boats, tomahawks, fox-and-geese and checker-boards, miniature river systems, and many a cut and hack, made in the mere exuberance of youthful spirits, without any apparent design. A look at the walls reveals to us the stucco work of spit balls and paper quids, fired at flies or imaginary targets, by mischevious boys, and places, too, bare of plaster and whitewash, where some ball or ink bottle has struck, in the absence of the teacher.

A great many people look upon the country school as a very insignificant institution, whose influence, they think, if it has any, is confined to its own district, but, doubtless, the country school will, in the future, as in the past, educate a large per cent. of the people. Two generations ago, the majority of our successful and influential men came from country schools. After attending school in their district several terms in the winter, they would complete their education by a term or two at some academy or high school. Realizing that the chances offered them for obtaining an education were limited, they generally applied themselves assiduously to the performance of duty, and the mastering of difficult tasks, which made them men of great good sense and originality, and men who depended upon self and did not fear to grapple with difficulties. And, right here, we can see a difference between our schools thirty-five years ago, or more, and those of today. Then, "I will," and "I can," were not so seldom heard as now, and by most children "I can't," was considered a sign of weakness; while too often, in the school of today, "I can't" is uttered with the utmost indifference as to the suicidal effect it will have upon the nature and capabilities. Then, much attention was given to the training of the memory, and little to the development of the observation; and, while we cannot say that the opposite is true, today, yet the tendency is to neglect the memory and to devote too much time to the training of the observing faculties, and this results in an education, unsatisfactory and superficial. Then, information was the chief element of education; now, discipline is the chief element. Then, the people were content to commit to memory what others had thought; now, we advocate that we should do our own thinking; and perhaps there is no greater contrast between the schools of that period and the present than the severity then, and the lack of severity, often laxity, now.

The facilities for education, were, in the early history of the town, very meagre. The spelling book and an inferior arithmetic were the only books in which there was any uniformity or adequate supply. There were no readers in use, but each pupil who could read, carried his own book, whatever he happened to have, such as the Columbian Orator, a geography of some kind, the history of somebody's captivity among the Indians, or a volume of sermons. Those scholars who were sufficiently advanced, sat upon the benches in the back part of the room and read around, one after another, the teacher pretending to listen, but having no book to follow the reading, very few criticisms were made. "The monotony of such a dull exercise," says Miss Rankin, a native of this town, and a teacher high in her profession, "often threw our master into a profound slumber, and I remember, one time, I, and another mischievous girl, tried to see how hard we could punch our sleeping pedagogue without awaking him. He was so moderate in returning to consciousness that we had ample time to return to our books with the most intense application, leaving him in entire ignorance as to where the ones were who would presume to disturb his pleasant dreams." About the year 1820, school books began to multiply, and this fact ushered in a new era in educational matters. Murray's English Reader and Grammar, Woodbridge's Geography, with Peter Parley's books of useful knowledge, Whelpley's Compend of Ancient History, and Watts' Improvement of the Mind, all contributed in a marked degree to raise the schools out of the ruts, and gave a great impetus to education. "This impetus to education created a demand for other text books, which continued to multiply as the demand for them increased, and at the present time we ought to rejoice, because we have so many books and other helps to aid in the education of the young." From the educational reports, which run back more than thirty years, we learn that, in 1852, Littleton ranked 27th among 225 towns in the state, and seventh among 37 towns in the county, in the per cent. of school money raised above what the law required. In 1853, Littleton stood second among the towns of the state, and first in the county in the same respect. Judging from the report of the commissioner of schools for Grafton county, 1857, we get the impression that for a few years, at least, our schools had not been in the best condition. "Littleton has reformed. In this town we passed a pleasant day. Found but one poor school. The south school in the village is quite too large to be profitable. It was only a retrograde experiment. I think they will not soon crowd two schools into one room again. On Mann's Hill we found the most advanced common school it was ever our privilege to visit." In the commissioner's report for 1861, we find Littleton mentioned as one of the few towns deserving praise for the character of their schools, and for their interest in education.

Union School District was first organized by a union of the three village districts under the Somersworth act, in April, 1866. As there seems to have been some question as to the legality of the organization, the legislature of 1867 voted "That the acts and doings of the several school districts in Littleton, in uniting and forming what is now known as Union School District, and adopting the provisions of the

Somersworth act, are hereby legalized and made valid." The first superintending committee under the Somersworth act was composed of Hon. G. A. Bingham, Franklin Tilton, Franklin J. Eastman, James R. Jackson and George Farr, the prudential committee for the same time being Hon. G. A. Bingham, Franklin Tilton and Franklin J. Eastman. In April, 1868, a reorganization was effected under the Concord act, and a board of education, consisting of nine members, elected.

In 1868, a new school-house, one of the largest and finest in the state, was erected at a cost of $32,000, and was subsequently ornamented with a beautiful and expensive clock, which daily proclaims to our eyes and ears the generosity of Moses A. Dow. Since its completion, the schools have been in successful operation. The first board was composed of Rev. Charles E. Milliken, James R. Jackson, Col. H. L. Tilton, Hon. Harry Bingham, George Farr, Col. Cyrus Eastman, Maj. William J. Bellows, Hon. James J. Barrett and Hon. Charles W. Rand. Since the organization of the graded school, in 1868, the interest in educational matters, though becoming less and less enthusiastic, has, we believe, become more and more firmly rooted in the affections of the people, and, though we might not think thus, judging from the number of visitors on examination day, for the last few years, and the number on like occasions during the previous history of the school, yet, taking into consideration the number who have been graduated of late, and the number who are at present attending college, who have fitted at our high school, we see an interest among the people, not lively 'tis true, but live and growing.

The first principal of the Littleton Graded School, Rev. C. E. Harrington, D. D., was born at Concord, N. H., 1846, and educated at Colby Academy, New London, N. H. He taught in Littleton one year, 1868, and then in Farmington, N. H., two years. Every inducement was offered to persuade him to remain in the latter place, but, having determined to study for the ministry, he began a course of study at Bangor Theological Seminary in 1872, and was graduated two years after. He was pastor of the Congregational church in Lancaster, N. H., from 1874 to 1878; in Concord, N. H., 1878 to 1882; and, since the latter date, has been located as pastor in Dubuque, Iowa. Rev. Mr. Harrington has always been a zealous worker in whatever field engaged. As principal of our school, he had a hard task for one so young and inexperienced. It was no small matter to grade the school, and classify scholars coming from several districts, but he was equal to the undertaking, and his fidelity and industry in his work won the confidence and respect of the scholars, and founded the school upon as solid a basis as could be expected from one year of service.

His successor, Franklin J. Burnham, was born in Norwich, Vt., in 1842, and was educated at Kimball Union Academy and Dartmouth College, from the latter of which he was graduated in 1869. He taught but one year in our school, beginning in the fall of that year. He then began the study of law in Chicago University, and was admitted to the bar in 1871. He has practiced in Chicago, Glyndon, Minn., Moorhead, Minn., and is still a resident of the last named place, having been president of the First National Bank of that town since 1882. Before beginning his labors in Littleton, Mr. Burnham had had much valuable training as a teacher, having taught five terms in different schools in Vermont, Massachusetts and New Hampshire. This experience as a teacher was supplemented by his previous three years' service in the rebellion, a service which afforded him, as it did many others, an opportunity for getting that peculiar training in managing and governing, which only military discipline can give. This experience in the army and schoolroom, his ability and thorough preparation for his work, won for him success. He was a hard worker, and his pupils made commendable progress, and what he accomplished in his efforts at grading and organizing the school, arranging courses of study and issuing the first catalogue of the school, and other work of like nature, was highly creditable.

The vacancy caused by the resignation of Mr. Burnham in '69 was happily filled by John J. Ladd, who was born in

Newbury, Vt., in 1828. After graduating from Dartmouth, in '52, he immediately entered upon his career as teacher, and held many high and responsible positions before coming to Littleton. He was principal of Black River Academy, Ludlow, Vt., and of Warren Academy, Woburn, Mass., and, after six years of eminent success in the latter institution, he was called to the Providence High School. He was at the head of this school six years, meeting with distinguished success in fitting boys for Brown University and other colleges. Resigning his position there, he founded, in company with William Mowry, the Ladd & Mowry (now Mowry & Copp) English and Classical High School, Providence, R. I., one of the most excellent schools in the country. He then went as paymaster in the army, and received at mustering out the rank of major. Mr. Ladd's experience before beginning work here was of the highest order, and this valuable experience, together with his natural force and energy, and the magnetism of his nature, his generous christian spirit and devotion to duty, foretold and consummated a career in Littleton of which he may well be proud, and which the people have not yet ceased to praise. Mr. Ladd is still alive to the interests of education. After leaving our school, he was made superintendent of schools in Staunton, Va., under the agency of Dr. Bernard Sears, general agent of the Peabody Educational Fund, and has traveled extensively through the South as agent of the Peabody Trustees, holding institutes, organizing schools and lecturing on educational themes.

After Mr. Ladd's three years' principalship, which, up to this time, had proved to be the longest term of service of any of the principals of the school, Frank D. Hutchins was chosen to succeed him. Born in Putney, Vt., 1850, Mr. Hutchins was a graduate of Kimball Union Academy and Dartmouth College, and had taught four terms in Massachusetts and New Hampshire schools. He taught one year in Littleton, beginning in the fall of 1873, and at the expiration of the school year began the study of law with Nathan B. Felton of Haverhill, N. H., but he completed his studies for admission to the bar with Ray, Drew and Heywood of Lancaster, N. H., and, after practicing law in that town from 1876 to 1881, he became cashier of the Lancaster National Bank, which position he now holds. The committee, in their report for 1873-4, say: "Prof. Hutchins, during the two terms in which he has served the district, already has proven himself a thorough, impartial, scholarly, and, in every sense, highly competent instructor."

Frank P. Moulton, a graduate of Bates College in the class of 1874, was his successor. He was born in Parsonsfield, Me., in 1851, and fitted for college at Limington and Limerick Academies, and Nichols Latin School, and was graduated from Bates College with the highest honors of his class. Mr. Moulton was a fine scholar, and in the school room was an apt instructor. Since leaving Littleton, Mr. Moulton has been teacher of Latin and Greek at New Hampton, and associate principal since 1879. The fact that he holds so high a position in such an institution as New Hampton bespeaks a teacher of great ability. He is not only a teacher, but a growing, progressive teacher, one who keeps abreast of the times in his profession by attending, during vacations, such schools as the Summer School of Science in connection with Bowdoin College, and the Summer Institute at Martha's Vineyard.

B. F. Robinson, a native of Gilford, N. H., born in 1853, and a graduate of Dartmouth, was elected principal of the school in the fall of 1877, and held the position for two years, at the expiration of which he resigned to become editor of the *Littleton Journal*, the leading Republican newspaper of Northern New Hampshire. Mr. Robinson was a strict disciplinarian and excellent instructor. The report of the superintending school committee says: "We can truthfully say that he has proved himself an efficient and popular manager as well as a successful teacher." Since entering upon his editorial duties, Mr. Robinson has retained his interest in school affairs, and has twice been elected member of the Board of Education.

Austin H. Kenerson, who succeeded Mr. Robinson, prepared for college at Peacham, Vt., and McIndoes, Vt., Academies, and was graduated from Dartmouth in 1876. Before entering upon his work here, Mr. Kenerson taught one year in McIndoes Academy, and two years in Lyndon Academy and Graded School. Mr. Kenerson was a very energetic and successful teacher, and continued to raise the schools to a higher standard of excellence. He remained in charge of the schools one year, and then resigned to take charge of the high school at Nahant, Mass., and held his position there one term more than two years, resigning to take a position as New England agent in one of the publishing houses in Boston, where he is at present engaged.

Mr. Kenerson's successor was Harry H. McIntire, a graduate of New Hampton Institute in the class of '74, and of Dartmouth College in the class of '79, and the only native of Littleton who has been principal of its high school. He taught seven terms before entering upon his duties here. the last of which was as principal of the Lyndon, Vt., Academy and High School. He proved himself to be an able instructor and a great favorite with his scholars. Mr. McIntire continued to be the principal of the school until November, '81, when he was called to take charge of the high school, and superintend the city schools at Lake City, Minn. This position he held until June, '82, when he resigned to engage in the business of real estate and loans, in which he is still engaged.

A. G. Miller was elected to fill the vacancy caused by the resignation of Mr. McIntire, but sickness compelled him to resign after a few weeks. At present he has charge of the graded schools of Whitehall, N. Y., a very responsible position.

D. P. Dame was elected to fill the vacancy. He was born in Tuftonborough, N. H., 1857, fitted for college at Dover High School, and is a graduate of Dartmouth, of the class of 1880.

Miss M. E. Furber, the first assistant, served but one year, and was succeeded by Mrs. Hattie Meserve Furber, who served for seven years. Mrs. Furber's term of service, as you well know, was one of complete success, and her pupils, one and all, have come to fully appreciate, in after life, her labors, and to feel most thankful that they were blest with so good a teacher. Miss Clara Meserve, Miss Carrie Ross, Mrs. Frank Cofran, Miss Lizzie Cushman, W. F. Gibson and Miss Isabel Parks have, since Mrs. Furber's service, filled the position in the order named. The assistants have, without exception, been earnest teachers, devoted to their work, whose influence upon the minds of their pupils has been the chief factor in training and refining those faculties which go to make up manly and womanly character. Theirs has been the higher education, the nobler work. Long and successful terms of service in the grades below the high school have been those of Miss Lottie Lee, Miss Annie French, Miss Minnie Beebe, and others, whose names are fresh in your memory.

The first board of school inspectors, chosen in 1809, was composed of Rev. David Goodall, Dr. William Burns and Robert Charlton. Dr. Burns never failed to show an active interest in education, and was identified with the schools of our town until his death, in 1868. He held the office of town superintendent as late as 1845. Rev. Charles E. Milliken's connection with the schools of this town has been to their great advantage, and we venture to say that no person, aside from the teachers, has done so much for education in the town as he by his intense interest in educational matters, and words of kindness and encouragement to both teacher and scholar.

School entertainments have played their part for good or ill in the education of the town. There is no doubt that the spelling school, the forerunner of the modern school entertainment, as conducted years ago throughout the town, was productive of good results; the healthful rivalry which sprang up between the scholars of the same and different districts led many to become proficient in orthography, who otherwise would have been content to use a phonetic shorthand of their own invention. The spelling school, besides conducing to the real proficiency, was an intellectual pastime, which did not necessitate great preparation other than the regular school work; but the modern school entertainment, with all its work of preparation, while being a poor substitute for the spelling school, in that it too often overtaxes both teachers and scholars, yet, if sufficient time be taken for preparation, and it being a matter of choice to the pupil whether he participate or not, and the object being to provide for the needs of the school, we fail to see wherein it is injurious or impolitic. The scholars of the high school, with the receipts from a series of entertainments, purchased a piano and Chamber's Encyclopædia, and later, in '82 and '83, the school purchased 200 standard works, the foundation of a library.

The people of this town, like the people in all other towns in which there is a school-house with a teacher, or a church with a pastor, have offered their share of criticism upon these personages. And, though this subject of criticism may not seem pertinent here, it really has a great deal to do with the success and failure of our schools, and, all together, too often the failure. The criticism bestowed upon our schools would lead one to suppose that they had made no progress during the last half century. This carping, and these derogatory assertions, though, perhaps, expressing oftentimes the honest convictions of their authors, are too often due to assumptions which have no foundation, and expectations based upon impossible conditions. It often happens that persons, whose education is wholly due to our glorious public schools, forget that they owe them anything besides their gossiping and unjust criticism. Our school system is not perfect. No one claims that it is. It has not reached the borderland of perfection yet. It has many defects. What if it has? Does it show a mark of manly or womanly character for these self-conceited critics to flaunt their stale and rehashed arguments before the public eye? If they have anything better to offer for the public consideration, why not offer it, and not try to impede the progress of our existing institutions, when their efforts, directed by a right spirit, would do a great deal toward remedying its defects?

But there is criticism which is conscientious, just and true. It is rather in the spirit of the Apostle Paul, who first told all the good qualities of the people whom he rebuked, and then made mention of their faults,—"Nevertheless brethren, I have somewhat against you." Such criticism exalts the soul who offers it, and encourages and rejoices the soul who receives it.

Children who have wished for a higher education than could be found in our Littleton schools attended an academy in Concord, Vt., which was opened in 1823, by Rev. S. R. Hall, a Congregational clergyman. In after years, Newbury Seminary catalogued as many as thirty or forty scholars from this town in a year, while of late years, our town has sent, occasionally, scholars to New Hampton, St. Johnsbury and Tilton Seminary, all excellent schools. Twenty-six residents of Littleton have entered Dartmouth College, one Amherst, and one Wesleyan University.

Our little town has truly been a factory of men. It has contributed legislators to enact our laws, jurists to administer justice, missionaries to spread the gospel, teachers to instruct our youth, doctors to cure the ills of life, ministers to teach us how to live and die, and, we may say, men for all walks in life, who have brought to the discharge of their duties sturdy Saxon principles and sturdy Saxon sense. The men who have grown up among these hills and mountains have had health and robust intellects, capable of being directed successfully upon any of the pursuits in life.

> "Some there are
> By their good works, exalted lofty minds
> And meditative, authors of delight
> And happiness, which to the end of time
> Will live and spread and kindle."

I have only considered the school as a factor in education, but, during the past century, four principal educational forces have combined to mould the character of our citizens; these are the press, the church, the duties and responsibilities of citizenship, and the school.

The duties and responsibilities of citizenship have elevated and ennobled those who have performed and met them with resolute and unselfish purpose. The citizens have had to understand, answer and decide questions of the greatest moment, and the settlement of these questions has been in its true sense a liberal education. It would not be in keeping with my subject to speak of the far reaching influences for good of the press and our churches, but the latter have been the great power in building up manly and noble character. The religion of the first settlers and early residents of the town being of the stern Puritanic order, formed a broad, deep and sound basis upon which to build education—intellectual, moral and spiritual. In the Christian religion, we see the rock upon which is founded our present public school system, the exponent of American liberty and citizenship.

AGRICULTURE.

ADDRESS BY REV. F. H. LYFORD.

The President said:—The next subject is one to which as much is due as any which has been named today. Of course I do not mean to say that all the others are not important. I know that the clergy would say, that of all the subjects, that of the church is the greater, and to it we should give the most attention. And this may be so. But there is another that comes nearer home to us all, our agricultural interest. It is an interest which furnishes the material upon which we all subsist while we are here below.

And as these, the clerical and agricultural, are the two great interests above all others, and should go hand in hand, we will combine them in one, and now present to discuss them the combined wisdom of the pastor and the farmer in the person of the Rev. Mr. Lyford.

ADDRESS.

MR. PRESIDENT, LADIES AND GENTLEMEN:

> "Men are the growth our rugged soil supplies,
> And souls are ripened in these Northern skies."

Agriculture is the oldest of all arts, the parent of all civilication, and the support of all true progress. God in wisdom designed it as the chief occupation of man. Adam was a gardener on a large scale. Cain was a tiller of the soil. But to Noah was given all the acres of the earth.

Elisha was an agriculturalist, we are led to suppose, on a large scale, as we find him plowing with twelve yoke of oxen.

In later times, all classes of people were expected to cultivate the ground, except ministers of religion. It was supposed that their time would be entirely devoted to the duties pertaining to their profession, although, sometimes, ministers may deal in stocks and bonds. It has been averred that among them were some very excellent judges of horses, handling them with great care and skill. How this may be, we do not pretend to say, but, we are told by some of our oldest inhabitants, that, in the early history of our town, when circuit riders traveled on horseback, the youth who proposed a trade with the *Elder* usually paid dearly for his whistle.

We read that our first parents were placed in a beautiful garden of no mean dimensions by their Creator, under the injunction "to dress it and to keep it." We find them here in their innocency, surrounded by all the apparent necessities and luxuries that humanity might desire. But there was forbidden fruit there, too, and the temptation to taste it became irresistible. They ate the fruit. As a penalty for disobedience, the occupants were driven out of the garden, under the sentence "to till the ground," and that, too, by "the sweat of the brow." All this and much more has been painted by John Milton in rich coloring. We are aware that many have considered this sentence entailed on man as severe, but we are inclined to look upon what is termed the primeval curse upon man as among his richest blessings, and that man's highest enjoyment is to be found in the rich field of manual labor. Who has better health, more happy hours, more serene repose, greater length of years, and a happier home than the independent and honest husbandman, who toils on his own lands and reaps the fruits of his own labors?

An ancient philosopher has left a high tribute and encomium upon agriculture, saying—"It is the employment most worthy of the application of man, the most ancient and most suitable to his nature. It is the common nurse and support of all, of every age and condition of life. It is the source of health, strength, plenty, riches, and of a thousand sober delights and honest pleasures. It is the mistress and school of sobriety, temperance, justice, religion, and, in short, of all virtues, civil and military." What more comprehensive language could be employed in praise of agricultural pursuits?

In a town like Littleton, where, from its first settlement, its people have been so largely engaged in agricultural pursuits, much might be gathered of special interest under this head. Its surface is somewhat broken and uneven, and in some parts rocky. The soil is moist and strong, and very productive of all sorts of grain and grass, especially on the hill farms. Its meadows and intervals, naturally of great fertility, are suited to every species of cultivation common to the climate. Littleton has always ranked with the first in an agricultural point of view. The fact that it is a central point of White Mountain travel, since tourists and pleasure seekers commenced visiting these mountains, opens a ready market for the products of the farm at our very doors. This, with the introduction of our manufactories, railroads and other improvements, has very materially aided in the development and improvement of the agricultural interests of the town.

While the outward world has been moving onward, and progress is seen everywhere, retrograde nowhere, our farmers have not failed in making some advance in their line of industry. Since the days of the old "Yellow Store," we have come from pack horses and lumbering mud wagons to palace cars; from three miles an hour, to a continent crossed in six days; from post riders with a mail once a week (if the roads were not blocked by snow) to a postoffice rolling on wheels more than forty miles an hour, giving us a mail four times a day; from muscle and backbone to the tireless steam engine and a patent office doing the hard work of the world; from a contempt of woman, and the idea of her being a weaker vessel, to a recognition of her mind as the leading inspiration of our race, and an acknowledgement of her ability to care for herself, with physical powers so wonderfully developed as to need little or no protection from the "lords of creation." And while all these wonderful achievements have been working themselves out around us, think you the farmer has been idle? I tell you nay. Instead of the old fashioned wooden mould-board and fifteen foot beam, he turns up the soil with a plowshare of finest polished steel. Instead of the spinning wheel and hand loom of " ye olden time," instead of distaff and spindle, water and steam power are made to furnish fabrics for our clothing at the rate of millions of yards of cotton dress and shoddy goods, daily.

Instead of the village cobbler, tramping from house to house, on his annual tour, with a kit consisting of hammer, awl and shoe knife, making up from leather the year's stock of shoes for the family, thousands and tens of thousands of men, women and children are engaged in the manufacture of an article called shoes, composed of wood, iron, paper and straw board, with a very small quantity of cheap leather, flopping these materials together by machinery, with paste and wax, turning out enough in a single day to supply the entire nation until our next centennial were they of any utility for real service.

Instead of the home-made supply of stockings and mittens for the comfort of feet and hands in cold winter weather, we have from an innumerable host of hosiery mills, and the Saranac, Eureka, White Mountain, Granite State, and other companies, articles for such purposes, fearfully and wonderfully made, from sheep's pelts and buckskin. And thus the world is supplied. Although a chill may creep up the spine as we put them on in July, before January we begin to sigh for a pair of our grandmother's mittens, and for mother's woolen footing. The early settlers of Littleton were a hardy race of men and women, rendered doubly so from the fact of their habits of frugality and industry. Here the land-owner was a sovereign. He loved his home, whether on hill-side or in the valley, and was ever ready at his country's call to defend it. True, an improved agriculture has enlarged our manufactures, and greatly increased our commerce. And yet our safety and prosperity depends upon our devotion to our native soil. The farmer who raises the wheat, corn and vegetables that supply his table, who feeds his own domestic animals, drives his own team, rides in his own carriage, reads his own books, supports his own church and school, is every inch a man, " in mind, body and estate," and is as nearly independent as one well can be under a government like our own. "No rich broker can lock up his gold; no speculator can withhold his supplies; no railroad king can dole out his rations; no aristocratic millionaire can take his children's bread and cast it to the dogs; no scheming politician can command his vote. Surely this is a goodly heritage, where, with honest toil and contented minds, we may be healthful, hopeful, happy and prosperous. For—

> "By him are all mechanics fed,
>   Of him the merchant seeks his bread,
> His hand gives meat to everything,
>   E'en from the beggar to the king.
>
> Milk and honey, corn and wheat,
>   Are by his labors made complete;
> Clothes from his efforts first arise,
>   To deck the fop and dress the wise.
>
> All hail! ye farmers, young and old,
>   Push on your plows with courage bold;
> Your wealth arises from your sod,
>   Your independence from your God."

In the early days of our agricultural history, each farm was a little world by itself. It was good economy then for each farmer to raise, as far as possible, everything which was consumed upon the farm. He fatted his own beef, pork and mutton, made his own butter and cheese, grew all the wheat, corn and other grains used, tanned his own hides, from which his shoes were made, and the good wife and daughters spun the wool and flax, and wove the cloth for family wear. In those days, the idea of making any one branch of farming a specialty would have been received with ridicule. As there were no markets where a surplus could be exchanged for cash, it was the wiser course for each farmer to raise, as nearly as possible, everything that was needed for home consumption. And thus our fathers wrought, toiled and lived, in their day a power for good. Then let us, with reverence, cherish their memory and render to them the meed of praise so justly due them for the work they accomplished.

But now a wondrous change has come over the spirit of our farmers. Few, if any, raise their own food or clothing. The railroad has done so much for the farmer by affording ready facilities for transportation, thus aiding in building up our great markets, that it seems the part of wisdom for the Littleton farmer to give attention to such specialty in crops and products as are best adapted to the soil and climate in which our lot is cast. Our farmers are no longer contented with homespun garments, or home-made shoes. The same carriage is no longer suitable for going to mill, to market and to meeting, nor is the old box sleigh, attached to the team with husk collar and rope harness, the most desirable turn-out for the farmers' sons and daughters of the present day. If thus we continue to cultivate the lands our fathers have cleared for us, we must make them yield larger profits than they ever dreamed of. This we cannot do without making some radical departures from the course pursued by them. We must bring the business of tilling the soil down to a business foundation, by learning the crop or product best adapted to our locality and soil, and then making of such crop or product a speciality. One of our enterprising farmers on the meadow, near where the first house was built in Apthorp, informs me that during the present season, on a small parcel of land, by way of experiment in the raising of grass, he has harvested at the rate of more than four tons of hay to the acre; another on one of our hill farms, that he has harvested thirty-four bushels of wheat per acre.

The Jersey cow, "Hilda 2d," bred in this state, has just obtained a record of 23 lbs., 5 oz. of butter in seven days. In other crops, in beef, mutton, pork, trotting horses and working cattle the stories are simply marvelous, all going to show, at least, the truth that very great improvements have been, and may yet continue to be, made in the products of the farm, where intelligence and skilled labor are combined to develop the resources thereof.

But, gentlemen, let me say to you in all earnestness and candor, it will not do to depend on "luck" for such results. We often hear the exclamation, "oh! he is one of the lucky ones; his corn does not rot; his wheat never winter-kills; his sheep never get into his rye; his cows never get into his mowing or orchards; his crops are better than his neighbor's; his butter brings more in the market, and even his wife and children have a more contented look than other people; everything he touches thrives; what a lucky man he is!" Now, the fact is, luck has nothing to do with his success in farming. If you watch the man you will find that every result he reaches is anticipated and planned for, and comes from his own wit and work. It is the legitimate reward of his labors. It would have been bad luck had it turned out otherwise. His corn always comes up because he always selects the seed himself, and hangs it up in the trace in his garret, where it is kept thoroughly dry. He does not plant until the sun has warmed the soil enough to give the germ an immediate start. His wheat fields are properly drained, and the water that used to freeze and thaw on the surface, and throw the roots of the wheat out and kill them, now runs off, thus giving the roots of the tender plants a chance to grow. His fields are green and beautiful in the spring, when his neighbor's are russet, brown and desolate. His fences are in good repair, and his animals are not made breachy by continual temptation of dilapidated walls. His wife and children are comfortably clothed and fed, and are not kept in a continual fret and worry by a husband and father who has no system or energy in his business. "A time and place for everything" is his motto, carefully carried out. The shoemaker is always called in when his services are needed, and none of his household get wet feet, catch cold, have lung fever, and run up the doctor's bill of twenty dollars, for want of a cent's worth of leather at the right time in the right place.

Now that man does not believe in luck. He knows that health in the family and thrift upon the farm depend upon a thousand little things that many of us are too lazy or careless to look after. So, while others are at the tavern, or loafing in the village, running from place to place, talking politics, he is looking after these things and laying his plans for next year. He has good corn, even in the poorest year, because the soil has the care and tillage necessary and requisite to bring out good, long, plump, well-filled ears. He meant to have sixty bushels to the acre, and he has it, good measure pressed down and shaken together. Don't talk about luck in farming; it's all nonsense. Bad luck is simply a man with his hands in his breeches pockets and his pipe in his mouth, looking on and seeing how it will come out—waiting for something to turn up. Good luck is a man of pluck to meet difficulties, his coat off, sleeves rolled up, working to make it come out right by turning something up.

Among the many intellectual agencies, which combine to add new interest and fresh impetus to the agricultural interests of our people, our state has an Agricultural college, fairly endowed, and ably equipped with a corps of efficient professors and a farm of nearly four hundred acres, for practical experiment. The doors of this college are open to any son of New Hampshire who wishes to enter. More than two hundred of the young men of our state have already availed themselves of the benefits of this institution. The State Board of Agriculture has done much by lectures and discussions to impart information and awaken increased interest in husbandry. Littleton once had a fair—we infer from appearances in and around what is called the "Old Fair Ground;" but, as its officers and managers appear to have passed from our borders, we are unable to state definitely how much of agricultural progress grew out of its management. The only information we are able to gather in relation to the same, from our oldest inhabitants, is that the institution resolved itself into an agricultural "horse trot," and being run on the narrow gauge principle, failed for want of patronage. A farmers' club on Mann's Hill flourished for some years, and was well sustained by practical farmers. But more recently the Grange has come into being and is doing an excellent work for the farmers of our town. The work of the Patrons of Husbandry is apparent to everybody, and commands general approbation. It recognizes in a broad way a great truth, which most of us recognize in a way more limited, i. e., that woman is an important factor in social life, and that the limits of the church and the household alone should not circumscribe her sphere. It has been quick to see that our agricultural communities need social stimulus, and has adopted the very best means to afford it. It has probably done more to bring scattered people together into a cordial and friendly association with one another than any other agricultural agency. It is ever and constantly alive to all efforts for the dissemination of useful knowledge among its members, and to the elevation of the Patron to a higher plane of manhood.

Taking thus into consideration the moral, social and intellectual agencies, by which we are surrounded, we ought most assuredly to show some good farming. We should double our hay crop, increase our root crops, raise more and better neat stock, a finer and purer bred stock of horses. In fact, friends, in the use of means at our hands, and the information lying around loose, ready to be gathered up, we ought to double the value of our stock and farm products in the next ten years. *Will you do it?* If so, then we may rejoice more over the ten, than, today, we do over our hundred already past.

An hundred years have passed, and joyfully today
We to our native town a tribute pay:
The girls and farmer boys of native birth,
Mark this among the lovely spots of earth.
Beautiful Littleton, well may we love her,
He who loves her not, loves not his mother.

MANUFACTURES.

ADDRESS BY DANIEL C. REMICH.

The President said :—There is one important interest, one which has done much for the town of Littleton, and has caused the growth and prosperity, to a large extent, which we are now aware of and can see ; and that is manufactures. Mr. D. C. Remich was assigned to speak upon this subject. But the hour is so late, and the subject so extended, that he proposes to omit it. And you will look for whatever he might have said upon this occasion in the report of the meeting when it may be printed.

ADDRESS.

Mr. President :

To me has been assigned the task of saying a word in relation to the manufacturing interests of Littleton during its first century. I assume, in view of the brief time allowed for the purpose, that nothing more is expected of me than a hasty and incomplete sketch of their rise and growth, for to give anything like a full history of their inception and progress, and the men engaged in them, would require hours of your time, and, I might say, would make a volume by itself, and this you would not care to listen to at this time when there is so much else to engage your attention.

Littleton is not, strictly speaking, and never was, a manufacturing town ; that is to say, the business and prosperity of the town does not depend, and never has, upon its manufacturing interests alone. Because of its situation, it has been a commercial center of importance, and has large and valuable agricultural resources. For these reasons it has not been materially affected by depressions in any particular branch of industry. Owing to the division of capital and business, the progress of the town has been much more rapid and continuous than it otherwise would have been, and there has been no long and serious depression in its manufacturing interests, such as have affected other communities, because if one man failed there were others arising from its commercial, professional or agricultural classes ready to step into his shoes and prosecute the business, or start something else in its place equally beneficial to the community. This ever present demand in our midst has rendered our progress constant, and, today, we boast of our town and its manufactures as among the soundest, best and most complete of their kind in New England, and, what is better, they are, substantially, owned and controlled by men born and reared among us, or who have been identified with the history of the town from an early date. The manufacturing interests that have been built up and prosecuted in the town during its history, so far as I have been able to learn, are as follows;

1, saw mills; 2, grist mills; 3, carding and clothing mills; 4, starch factory; 5, foundry and machine shop; 6, mill machinery; 7, carriage shops; 8, flannel and woolen mills; 9, scythe and axe works; 10, bobbins and spools; 11, watch factory; 12, hatters' shops; 13, pail and tub manufactory; 14, furniture and chairs; 15, cabinet maker; 16, sash, blind and doors; 17, bedstead factory; 18, linseed oil mill; 19, box shop; 20, gloves and mittens; 21, stereoscopic views; 22, varnish; 23, potash manufactory; 24, tannery; 25, distillery.

SAW MILLS.

The first saw mill was built on Rankin's brook, near the grist mill, in 1787-8, by Jonathan Eastman. The frame was up and the saw in running order early the next year. Moses Little traded with Mr. Eastman and got the saw mill in 1788, giving therefor the land now constituting the Russell Steere farm, and Mr. Rankin purchased it of Little the same year, and ran it until his death, in 1802, when it became the property of his son David, who operated it, together with the grist mill, for about forty years. Gen. David Rankin did a large business for those times, sawing the lumber, drawing it to the landing below the "fifteen mile falls," from which point it was rafted down the Connecticut river to market. This was the only saw mill in town until 1792 or 1793.

A second mill was built on the brook, near the postoffice at North Littleton, by Samuel Larnard, Jr. It was a small mill, with small power, and did a local business only. Larnard ran the mill until 1808, when he went to Canada and started, with others, a large lumber business which ended in financial ruin. After Larnard left, the mill was run by Providence Williams for a time, and went to decay between 1825 and 1830.

The next, and third, mill was built by Solomon Mann in 1799, on the site of Fitzgerald & Burnham's lumber shed. Mann ran the saw mill a few years, when, together with the grist mill property, it passed into the hands of Deacon Lewis. The deacon continued its owner until his death, in 1815. From 1825 the mill was owned by John Bowman, and operated by him a part of the time, in company with his son, Curtis C., until 1861. at which time Mr. Bowman died. After his death the mill was run but little, and was soon after torn down, the power having been purchased by joint owners. During Mr. Bowman's occupancy, the ground now covered by Union Block, Dow Brothers' store and Dunn's carpenter shop was used as a mill yard.

In 1824, a small mill was built on Caswell brook, nearly opposite the Hudson place, now occupied by Mr. Cocking. The power was not large and the mill but little used. It soon tumbled to decay and entirely disappeared about 1850.

About 1812 a mill was built by Michael Fitzgerald at South Littleton, on the west side of the Ammonoosuc, opposite the mill now operated by The Littleton Lumber Co. It was at one time owned by Hamlin Rand, and also by Capt. Isaac Abbott.

GRIST MILLS.

Only three grist mills have ever been erected within the limits of the town, and one of these, that built by Eastman, Tilton & Co., on the site of the saw mill of the Littleton Lumber Company, was never put in operation.

The first grist mill was built by Jonathan Eastman for Messrs. Little, Dalton, Phelps, Morey and other proprietors in 1787, on the site of the mill now standing on the Rankin brook, not far from where it empties into the Connecticut river. This mill was first operated by Jonathan Eastman, and afterwards was purchased by James Rankin, together with eleven hundred acres of land, lying in West Littleton, before he moved his family from Thornton. It was owned by Mr. Rankin until his death, and by his son, Gen. David, until his removal to the West in 1846, at which time it passed into the hands of George and Sylvanus Milliken, who ran it until 1863.

The mill in the village was built by Solomon Mann in 1799. He ran it for a few years, when it passed into the possession of Deacon Asa Lewis, who sold it to Noah Farr and Moses Hazen; they passed their title in the property to John Gile, in 1818. At one time this mill was owned by Timothy Gile. It was rebuilt by John Gile in 1825, and by John and Ida Hodge in 1856, who had previously purchased it of the John Gile estate. It subsequently passed into the hands of a firm made up of Eastman, Tilton & Co., and Samuel A. Edson. It is now owned by C. & C. F. Eastman, and leased by Ezra Gates. At one time it was run, under lease, by Curtis and Horace Gates.

TANNERY.

The tannery was erected in 1800 by Peter Bonney, who had but recently moved here from Charlestown. It was run by Mr. Bonney alone, or in partnership with Sewell Brackett, until 1828 or 1830, at which time Mr. Bonney disposed of his interest to Mr. Brackett, who conducted the business but one or two years, when the establishment passed into the possession of Otis Batchelder and Rufus Whipple. Mr. Batchelder soon purchased the interest of Mr. Whipple, and continued the business for many years. A part of the time he had, as a partner, Roswell H. Curtis, the son and heir of old Major Curtis. Sometime in the sixties, Calvin J. Wallace bought the property, and he sold to Silas Parker, whose son Ira was, for a time, his partner, and subsequently James Parker purchased an interest.

CLOTHING MILL.

The first carding or clothing mill was erected on the site of the mill now owned by Tilton & Goodall, by Penuel Leavens in 1801. It was subsequently owned and operated by Ebenezer Cushman, 1811-1814; David Richardson, 1814-1815, when it was burned. A new mill was erected on this site by Ebenezer Cushman, and operated by him until it was purchased by Timothy A. Edson and Josiah Kilburn. It passed successively into the possession of Jefferson Hosmer, Sylvanus Balch, Joseph Roby, Bellows & Stevens and John Gile. In 1851, Deacon James Hale put in a set of machinery and manufactured flannel. Soon after, it ceased to be used for the manufacture of textile fabrics.

The mill now owned by the Saranac Glove Company was built by an association of enterprising citizens in 1839, and was operated by them as a stock company for three or four years, with John Herrin as agent. The company failed prior to 1846. E. J. M. and Joseph W. Hale of Haverhill, Mass., then operated it with great success, until 1867, when it became the property of a stock company and was run with indifferent financial success until 1874.

FOUNDRY AND MACHINE SHOP.

In 1848, Josiah and Benjamin W. Kilburn started a foundry on the site of the old mill on Palmer brook. The power was found insufficient for their purpose, and they built a shop on Saranac street, opposite the Brackett & Abbott saw mill, where they did a flourishing business, manufacturing stoves, plows, harrows and mill machinery. Their expanding business soon outgrew the premises, and, in 1854, they bought the mill then lately occupied by Deacon Hale, and transformed it into a commodious foundry and machine shop. Here the firm remained until 1884, when advancing age led the senior member of the firm to seek rest from business cares which had occupied him for more than sixty years. The junior member of the firm had, some years before, engaged in the manufacture of stereoscopic views with his brother Edward, and his enterprise had so grown under his skill and energy as to demand all his time. So the old firm was dissolved. They had acquired a competency and the respect of every one, and when they pass away, Littleton will lose two of the squarest and best men who ever did business within its borders.

CARRIAGE SHOP.

James W. Merrill came from Conway in the thirties, and built a carriage and repair shop on the site of S. P. Nurse's dwelling. He continued the business for nearly a quarter of a century, when he retired to a farm at North Littleton. In 1854, Lucius A. Russell built a shop on the corner of Main and Brook streets, and here the Quimby brothers (Daniel and Albert H.) began the first thoroughly equipped carriage business in town. They came from Lyndon, and brought with them Asa Weller as trimmer, and Frank G. as painter, all superior workmen. They soon found their accommodations too limited, and moved to the shop now occupied by their successors, Ranlet & Harris. The Quimbys were predisposed to consumption, and that dread disease soon carried them off. Daniel died in 1862, and was succeeded by a new firm, consisting of A. H. Quimby and F. G. Weller. Mr. Quimby died in 1866, and the firm then became Ranlet & Weller, and this firm was succeeded by N. W. Ranlet.

POTASH.

The manufacture of potash was one of the first industries engaged in after the settlement of the town. Buildings for this purpose were early erected in different parts of the town, the largest being located where Ranlet & Harris' carriage shop now stands, by Roby & Curtis, early in the present century. A very considerable business was done here for nearly forty years.

HATS.

The manufacture of silk plug hats was, at one time, an item in the manufacturing industries of the town. In 1836, Prescott White carried on this business in the building now occupied as a bakery. Later, he was followed by —— Miner, who removed from town in 1851.

STARCH.

The manufacture of potato starch has been carried on with varying success since 1850. Aaron Gile built a factory for this purpose, near where the sash and blind factory now stands, and ran it for a few years. Another was built in the sixties, at the mill privilege owned by the scythe company, and still another was carried on by the farmers at West Littleton, under the co-operative plan.

SCYTHE FACTORY.

Among the early industries, which gave an impetus to the growth and prosperity of the town, was the manufacture of scythes. This business was founded by Ely, Farr & Co., in 1835. The unnamed partner in the business was George B. Redington, who has been from that date to the present time one of the most public spirited business men of the town. This business was continued for many years, mostly by the Redingtons (G. B. and Henry C.), and often under discouraging circumstances. They were three times burned out, and had as many times passed through depressing commercial crises, but were never disheartened. Their last attempt in this direction was made in company with Cyrus Eastman, Charles Hartshorn, Otis G. Hale, Luther T. Dow, and others, by the establishment of the factory, now in idleness, but which, it is hoped, more prosperous days may soon start again.

There are other industries that have contributed largely to the growth and development of the town, which deserve particular mention, among which are the following:

The sash and blind factory, formerly owned by Wm. H. Chandler and Ai Fitzgerald, and now in the hands of Fitzgerald and Henry B. Burnham, has, for about twenty-five years, been a leading industry in town. It was built by John Gile, and first operated by Kimball & Wallace, who came here from Manchester in 1837.

D. P. Sanborn's tool factory, during the lifetime of Mr. Sanborn, added largely to the reputation of the town. Being a man of remarkable skill and ingenuity, the tools of his manufacture soon became famous, and were ordered from all parts of the country.

The chair factory of Enoch and Frederick Hazeltine, established in a small way by the elder Hazeltine about 1835, will be remembered as a growing and thriving industry. Both father and son were intelligent and worthy men, much esteemed for their strict integrity and fair dealing. Nevertheless, the father was eccentric and absent minded to a degree that often, as was the case with "Dominie Sampson," occasioned him "disasters," serious to himself, but amusing to his neighbors. These mishaps were of so frequent occurrence with the old gentleman that the recital of one of Hazeltine's "terrible disasters" became a common topic of conversation.

B. W. Kilburn's extensive stereoscopic view manufactory has, for many years, been a prominent feature among the industries of the town. For number and variety of subjects, and perfection of manufacture, his views are unsurpassed by any in the country, and have acquired a world-wide fame.

The Littleton View Company (successors to F. G. Weller and G. H. Aldrich), who continue to publish "Weller's" celebrated Treasures and Allegoricals, together with new and original subjects, both foreign and American, fully sustain the reputation for first-class views which Mr. Weller had acquired. The proprietors are Wm. H. and George S. Bellows and John Ready. Mr. Ready has charge of the manufacturing.

In the line of photography, the two establishments of E. F. Hall and George H. Aldrich are producing work of unsurpassed beauty and perfection, fully sustaining the reputation of the town in that department of art.

The large furniture establishment of Leach & Smith, on Pleasant street, is conducting a business highly creditable to itself and advantageous to the public.

Tilton & Goodall, manufacturers of underwear, are supplying the trade with goods of a superior quality in considerable quantities.

The spool and bobbin factory of M. A. Bowles & Co., the wooden box factory of H. C. Redington & Co., and the paper box factory of Chandler & Little, are important items in the trade of the town.

The woolen factory was purchased about six years ago by Ira Parker & Co., and converted into a glove factory, and is now, together with another building of equal dimensions, besides offices and store-houses, occupied by them for that purpose. It is said to be the largest establishment of the kind in the world, and the superior quality of their gloves is unquestioned. The establishment of this industry, on a scale of such magnitude, was a notable event in Littleton history, as it gave a prestige to business which caused rapid advancement in all branches of industry and trade. And to Mr. Ira Parker is due the credit of having, by unusual energy and perseverance, earned a success almost without parallel in that branch of manufacturing. Following Mr. Parker's lead, three other extensive glove factories have been started, and are steadily increasing their production and extending their field of operation — The "Eureka," "White Mountain" and "Granite State." The former, which has its headquarters in Tilton's Opera Block, occupying, with its workmen, the entire second story of that large building, is managed by Charles and Nelson Parker (brothers of Ira) and Henry Merrill, all of whom are practical men, of large business experience, Mr. Merrill being the traveling member. The "White Mountain" Glove Co., was started by Alonzo Weeks and Robert Meiner, with whom was subsequently associated Geo.

H. Whittaker. Mr. Weeks is an old resident, and for many years was a large dealer in boots and shoes. Mr. Meiner, a native of Germany, is a thoroughly educated glove maker, and has charge of the manufacturing, and Mr. Whittaker attends to the sales. The " Granite State " Co., consisting of Charles and Sherared Clay, Thomas Carleton and Henry C. Libbey, commenced operations at the Scythe Factory Village about four years ago. The Messrs. Clay are both practical glove makers, and Mr. Carleton is a first-class salesman, which position he occupies. Mr. Libbey is a large lumber manufacturer at the Alder Brook Mills, to which business his time is devoted.

The importance of this branch of industry to the trade and prosperity of Littleton can not be overestimated. Since its commencement by Ira Parker & Co., and as a result directly attributable thereto, a large number of neat and commodious dwellings have been built for the use of employes in the different glove factories, the majority of which are owned by them, and large improvements have been made in many other buildings, which, together with the workshops, storehouses, offices, tanneries and out-buildings, erected for the use of the different companies, aggregate at least one hundred buildings, either entirely new or thoroughly remodeled. Nor does this estimate include the three beautiful and costly residences erected by Ira Parker, Charles Parker and Charles Eastman, all of which are in the Queen Anne style of architecture, and for beauty of design, thoroughness of workmanship, modern improvements and homelike arrangements, are unsurpassed by any in the state.

But I am admonished by the fleeting hours that I must draw these remarks to a close. The men who have in the past built up and maintained the manufacturing industries of Littleton, have been among the noblest and best of our citizens, and they have never been in better hands than they are today; and the pluck and industry of the Parkers, Tiltons, Redingtons, Kilburns, and the host of others now engaged in manufacturing, are a sufficient guarantee that our next centennial will find this business second to none in the state.*

---

*In 1880 there were thirty-eight manufacturing establishments in town.

MERCHANTS AND TRADE.

ADDRESS BY WILLIAM J. BELLOWS.

The President said :—Littleton, as a mercantile center, is and has been one of the best in Northern New Hampshire, and its merchants have been equal to the opportunity. The subject, "Merchants and Trade," is assigned to an old resident and merchant, Mr. William J. Bellows. Not being present, his address will appear in print.

ADDRESS.

Mr. President:

To our respected former townsman, Mr. F. J. Eastman, has been assigned the task of showing to what extent Vermont has contributed, through the emigration of her sons and daughters, to the growth and development of Littleton. And as, in the discharge of that duty, he must necessarily embrace in his sketches a majority of the leading and prominent men engaged in mercantile and other pursuits in Littleton during the last fifty years of its existence, I shall attempt mainly a brief outline of the trade and characteristics of the few more prominent men, not natives of Vermont, whose mercantile career commenced during the early history of our town, and continued nearly, or quite, up to and, in some instances, beyond the first half of the period we celebrate.

Samuel Learned, Jr., and James Jackson were the first who embarked in trade in town. They commenced at North Littleton, about five miles from the village, on the road to Lancaster, about the year 1800. They were men of considerable note, and Jackson was a man of fine presence and very gentlemanly. About this time there were about fifty names on the tax list, consequently, their trade, to say the least, must have been limited. Being men of some means, and more ambition, they invested somewhat largely in " Ottawa Lands," which proved disastrous, and caused the failure. How long they continued in trade cannot be ascertained, but as Tillotson Wheeler appears to have established himself, in 1805, in the same store that had been occupied by Learned & Jackson, it is probable their mercantile career in Littleton was a short one. They afterwards moved to Vermont.

Tillotson Wheeler continued in business about nine years, until 1814, at which time the superior facilities afforded by Major Curtis and William Brackett had drawn the trade to the village, and made it unprofitable for Wheeler to continue longer. From what little can be learned of the extent and character of Mr. Wheeler's trade, I can think of no more fitting illustration than the account which "Petroleum V. Nasby" has given of his friend Bascom's business at the " Confederate X Roads," during the war, which, according to his authority, consisted principally in dispensing rum, molasses and tobacco to his patrons, on the strength of promise to pay when something favorable should " turn up."

Major Ephraim Curtis was a native of Charlestown, N. H., and came here in 1804. In connection with Doctor Joseph Robie, who was also from Charlestown, and became, for a short time, his partner, he built what was long known as the " Old Red Store," on the site of the present Methodist church. It was a large and somewhat rambling building, with a basement opening on Main street. Dr. Robie soon retired from the partnership, and Mr. Curtis continued alone until his decease, in 1824. Mr. William Brackett was employed by him for a time as clerk, and afterward, his brother Aaron took his place, and, eventually, bought out Mr. Curtis, and carried on the business at the old store, under the firm of W. C. and A. Brackett.

In connection with his store, Major Curtis manufactured potash in a building standing where Noah Raulet's carriage shop now is, and the large quantity of ashes taken from his customers in exchange for rum, molasses, tobacco and other articles of traffic, enabled the farmer, even at that early period, to convert the forests into a paying medium, quite as passable as the silver dollar of today. In fact, ashes and pig iron, manufactured at Franconia, were substantially " legal tender " between Major Curtis and his customers.

Connected with the " Old Red Store," are doubtless memories and associations that have furnished topics for many a fireside gossip among the older inhabitants of Littleton. There were but few places of public resort at that time, and none where business and pleasure could be more naturally combined than at this store; and, moreover, as Mr. Curtis kept constantly on hand all kinds of liquors, and a plentiful supply of T. D. pipes and tobacco, was naturally social and convivial, knew how to mix a " mug of toddy," that even the fastidious " Tony Weller " would approve, for which the modest sum of " four pence ha' penny," only, was exacted, his store soon became the point of attraction, during the long winter evenings, for a good portion of the worthy male members of the community. On these occasions, it became a matter of etiquette for every one present to " pay " a mug of that delicious beverage, sing a song or drink a pint of salt and water, and there being few that could sing, and none that preferred salt and water to toddy, it is not difficult to imagine that at the close of the sitting his customers carried home more toddy than " four pence ha' pennies," a result which Major Curtis regarded with remarkable equanimity.

Major Curtis also built a large, and for those days, stylish residence on Main street, which is still standing, although remodeled to conform to a more modern style of architecture. It is now owned and occupied by Josiah Kilburn, a native of Walpole, N. H., one of our most respected citizens, who, for a period of sixty years, has been a resident of the village, and, until within a few years, actively engaged in business and largely identified with its interests. Although eighty-four years of age, he is still hale and hearty.

Major Curtis was a man of undoubted energy and perseverence, although disease and bodily infirmity impaired his usefulness during the latter part of his life. He had no competitor in trade in the village while in business, and it is not, therefore, to be supposed that his profits were less than remunerative, and yet the moderate fortune which he left to his family would indicate a reasonable regard for the interests of his customers.

Mr. William Brackett left Major Curtis' employ about 1805, and located himself in trade on what has long been known as "the meadows," about two miles distant from the village, where he built a store, which was also painted red, a handsome residence, and large and commodious out-buildings. The store was taken away many years since, but the dwelling-house and many of the out-buildings still remain without material change, except the natural wear and decay incident to a long period of time. His estate, at that time, embraced a large and valuable meadow farm, lying on the banks of the Ammonoosuc river, well cultivated and productive. A portion of the farm, together with the old homestead, is now owned by Mr. Frank McIntire.

Mr. Brackett was eminently a merchant of the old school. Systematic, strictly upright, cautious, persevering, devoted to business, and not inclined to speculate or take risks outside his legitimate business, he preferred to rely upon the comparatively slow, but sure, gains, resulting from a well regulated business, for success. The wisdom of his course was clearly demonstrated by the ample fortune he was enabled to leave to his family. As to the character and extent of trade during the time Mr. Brackett was in business on the meadows, and Major Curtis at the village, it might be remarked that money was an article but little known in those days, the possessor of a ten dollar bill being regarded by his neighbors as one of fortune's favorites. Consequently, the merchant sold his goods almost entirely on credit, and that of so extended a nature that the heirs of the purchaser often found themselves encumbered with the debts of their ancestors. But the necessaries of life must be had at all hazards, and, as the merchant kindly supplied them on the strength of their prospective crops, it is by no means strange that, in the course of time, the merchant held large claims against his customers, secured by mortgages on their farms. Major Curtis and Mr. Brackett were no exception to this rule, but, to their credit, be it said that their leniency toward their debtors enabled them, as a general rule, to meet their demands without being subjected to a course of law.

At that time, merchants were few and far between, and it was no uncommon thing for customers to come a distance of ten or fifteen miles, over roads by no means "macadamized," to make their purchases, on which occasion supplies for several months would be "laid in," consisting of the usual variety of articles which are now regarded as necessaries, with almost the invariable addition of one commodity, now so generally considered "contraband" as to find no place in the stock of our modern merchant. Judging, however, from the very general use of the article at that time, without apparent detriment to the health of the consumer, it is evident that the New England rum of those days, in point of purity and healthfulness, would easily "discount" the manufacture of the present time, a fact which does not seem to sustain the theory of progression. As to the quantity of that article vended by Mr. Brackett, it may be pertinent to quote a remark made by him to a friend, while riding past his old homestead, which was, that he had sold rum enough in that store to carry his saw mill two weeks.

In 1841, Mr. Brackett moved to the village and built a handsome residence, now, after some alterations, owned and occupied by his son, Cephas. He also built a large store on Main street, where, for several years, he was in trade with his brother, Aaron, to whom the management of the store was principally intrusted, while William attended to lumbering and outside matters, in which they were largely interested. Aaron (familiarly called the "Little Major," from the fact of his being small in stature) was a man of good business qualifications, an excellent accountant, of sterling integrity, and generous to a fault. His memory will long be cherished by those who knew him.

About the time of Major Curtis' decease, in 1824, Major George Little, a native of Newburyport, Mass., came here and embarked in trade in the "Yellow Store," so called, which, together with the dwelling-house, now owned and occupied by F. T. Moffett, one of our leading physicians, was built by him. The store has been moved back from its original site, remodeled, and is now the residence of Mrs. E. S. Woolson, whose husband, now deceased, was, for many years, engaged in business as a merchant tailor, and prominently identified with the growth and prosperity of Littleton village.

Of Mr. Little, it may be said that his like is rarely met with. Well educated, of gentlemanly instincts and address, with strong convictions, and fearless to express them, and with a knowledge of the world, acquired by mingling with all classes, both socially and in a variety of business relations, he could readily adapt himself to any position with credit. But with all these qualifications, he was eccentric and absent minded to a degree that rendered him unsafe in the management of details in small matters incident to the keeping of accounts in a retail business, the reason apparently being that his mind was constantly occupied by matters of large moment, leaving minor considerations unheeded. He would often walk the entire length of the street, earnestly talking and gesticulating to himself, without recognizing his best friends whom he might meet. These moods, however, disappeared when the matter in hand was of sufficient importance to command his attention. Although nominally in trade, therefore, it can hardly be said that he was practically identified to any considerable extent with the buying and selling of merchandise in Littleton, yet he was far from being an unimportant factor in the growth and development of the town. His ancestor, Moses, from whom the town took its name, was at one time the proprietor of the whole township, and to George was entrusted the management of the same interests. In matters of this kind, his judgment was good, and through his energy and skill farms were soon parcelled out, the forests subdued, and the settlement of the town rapidly advanced. Mr. Little, at a later period, became a member of several business firms, not connected with his father's interests, among which may be mentioned George Little & Co., Bellows, Redington & Co., the former of which purchased of Messrs. E. & T. Fairbanks & Co., of St. Johnsbury, the right for the sale of their celebrated hay scales for the state of New York, Upper and Lower Canada, and Great Britain. Mr. Little was selected to go to Europe and make arrangements for their introduction there. This he did in a manner highly satisfactory to his partners, and creditable to himself, and but for the lack of good faith in the parties with whom he contracted, it would have resulted in a fortune for all the members of the company. Bellows, Redington & Co. purchased a large and valuable tract of land, known as the Ottawa Lands, in Canada, upon which they erected mills and commenced the manufacture of lumber; but a crisis in the money market and a rebellion in Canada occurring about that time, business was prostrated, and they, with others, were large sufferers. Although the results of the operations of these companies were unremunerative to them, yet, as their headquarters were here, an impetus and prestige was given to the business of Littleton which was, on the whole, beneficial. After a few years of not very remunerative business, George Little sold out to George B. Redington, who subsequently took his brother, Henry C. Redington, and later his brother-in-law, George W. Ely, as partners. Remaining in the old yellow store a few years, they afterwards built the brick store on the opposite side of the street, which, after several years occupancy by them, was occupied successively by Farr & Goold, Goold & Balch, The Farmers' & Mechanics' Company, John W. Balch, Frye W. Giles, George F. Batchelder, and Otis Batchelder, during which period the number of merchants and aggregate of trade were constantly on the increase.

This store, like the old "Red Store" (bating the liquor), will be remembered by many as the scene of many a jovial winter evening gathering, when nuts and raisins, candy and apples, were dispensed by the proprietors, at a reasonable rate, to whomsoever should be adjudged to pay for them as a penalty for conviction by the "court" of some misdemeanor charged against him, and, as the "court" received their full share of the "penalty" awarded, the culprit seldom escaped punishment, so long as the "court" had occasion for more nuts, raisins, candy, or apples. As "cases" were constantly occurring, the "court was obliged to meet in session nearly every evening, and it is worthy of remark that that honorable body, as also the proprietors of the store, especially John W. Balch and Otis Batchelder, invariably discharged their duties with a degree of cheerfulness seldom surpassed. Unfortunately for the interests of jurisprudence, these cases have never been reported. The case, however, of Goold v. Batchelder, affords a fitting illustration. In this case, the defendant sold the plaintiff a "white oak" cheese for a new milk cheese, and afterwards "made it up" to him by selling him a razor for one dollar and fifty cents that could not be made to cut, and was, consequently, a worse "shave" than the cheese. It was decided against the plaintiff on the ground that, having known Mr. Batchelder many years, he was a big fool for believing anything that Batchelder told him, and therefore ought to suffer the consequences. In justice to Mr. Batchelder, it should be said that he afterwards offered to Mr. Goold to "make it up" again, and Mr. Goold said he "did not see it."

The Redingtons were natives of Walpole, New Hampshire, and came here about 1830. George B. was a thoroughly educated merchant, having served his time with Josiah Bellows, 3d, of Walpole, whose mercantile qualifications were of the highest order. In addition to a thorough training in every department of mercantile pursuits, Mr. Redington possesses an easy and gentlemanly address, strict integrity, quick and keen apprehension, remarkable industry and perseverance, and a tenacity of purpose which yields to no obstacle, and, like the renowned Zachary Taylor, "knows no defeat." Few men can be found who, for a period of about sixty years, have devoted more time to business, and less time to recreation, than Mr. Redington, nor can it be said of him that his efforts have been actuated solely by selfish motives, as few public enterprises calculated to advance the growth and prosperity of Littleton have been attempted in which he has not been an earnest and efficient participator. Success in whatever he has undertaken has been his moving principle, and though not always fortunate in his endeavors, it has been from no lack of persistent and well directed energy that he failed. Mr. Redington rendered valuable aid in the establishment of the Littleton National Bank and the Littleton Savings Bank, of which institutions he has been a director from the commencement. He was also a director in the White Mountains Railroad at its start, and to his untiring effort is largely due the successful termination of that enterprise in 1853. On the completion of that road, rendering Littleton for several years the terminus of all the roads below, an impetus was given to business that resulted in placing our town on so substantial a basis that when the road was extended north the effect proved to be an advantage rather than a hindrance to its continued growth.

Henry C. Redington, for many years a partner with his brother George, under the firm of H. C. Redington & Co., was also largely identified with the business interests of the village, and has devoted his time and talent to that firm, leaving outside matters more especially to George, whose fondness for grappling with affairs sufficiently formidable to be " worthy of his steel " is proverbial. That they have succeeded in acquiring a comfortable fortune is, perhaps, due quite as much to Henry as to his brother, owing to the fact that during all the reverses and vicissitudes through which the firm has passed, he has kept a sharp lookout for the " main chance." Among a variety of other good qualities, Henry C. possesses in a remarkable degree the ability to tell a " good story," precisely adapted to the ocasion, and the wonder is that notwithstanding the frequency of those occasions, his stock increases with the demand, so that a repetition of the same story is rarely necessary.

In order to judge of the degree of credit to which these pioneer merchants are entitled, it is necessary to consider the circumstances under which they commenced their career, and the obstacles they had to overcome. At the time Major Curtis and William Brackett laid the corner-stones of their stores and dwellings, the valley of the Ammonoosuc river was comparatively a wilderness, with here and there an unpretentious dwelling reared by some sturdy and courageous New Englander, whose sole ambition to make for himself and family a home, induced him to leave some more populous locality and incur the hardships and privations incident to the life of a "backwoodsman." These primitive settlements were for the most part on the banks of the Ammonoosuc, and are now mostly gone to decay, or so thoroughly remodelled as to bear no resemblance to the original edifice. They were, in some instances, near enough together to be regarded, in those days, as neighbors, but often were several miles apart. In the vicinity, however, of Major Curtis' store, and within an area of perhaps less than a mile, the village boasted five dwelling houses, a tavern, blacksmith shop, saw mill, and school house, constituting a settlement of not less magnitude than many at that early period that now rank among the foremost of New England villages. Coming from older settlements, therefore, it must be that Major Curtis and William Brackett were influenced in their choice of location mainly by the superior water-power afforded by the Ammonoosuc at this point, which they judged would in time render it a business centre for a large surrounding territory. Under these circumstances, it required men having convictions and the courage of them to embark in and carry forward to a successful termination mercantile enterprises like those of Messrs. Curtis and Brackett. Nearly the same may be said of George Little and the Redingtons. Although commencing at a later period, the way had partially been opened, new buildings had to some extent clustered around the little nucleus, the water-power was being improved, a grist mill, tannery, and another tavern had been erected, and the tourist to the "White Hills," so called at that time, already regarded the village as the starting point of his excursions among the mountains. In fact, from the time the Redingtons were fully embarked in business, the growth of the village was steady, though not rapid, and as early as 1835 it had evidently taken its place among the comparatively few New England villages whose facilities for expansion gave assurance of a size and importance much beyond the average.

From this period dates its more rapid growth. It had become the business centre for all the surrounding towns and settlements embraced within a radius of ten or fifteen miles, being attracted here by the mercantile and other facilities afforded them at this point. The advent of the Messrs. Eastman at about this time was, therefore, the natural result of an investigation of far-sighted men, who were seeking to establish themselves where the natural advantages of the locality gave assurance of future advancement. To these men, together with those who became their partners during the existence of their various firms, a period of more than forty years, may properly be attributed, in a large degree, the impetus to business at that time.

Rapidly following their lead, many other enterprising merchants, from time to time, embarked in trade, and contributed largely to the development and prosperity of the town. Among the more prominent of these, who commenced business about the time of the Messrs. Eastman and subsequently, and continued in trade a sufficient length of time to become identified with the interests of the town, may be mentioned Truman Stevens, who came here in 1824, and, with the exception of a few years engaged as traveling agent for E. and T. Fairbanks & Co. of St. Johnsbury, Vt., has remained in town ever since. Mr. Stevens is well known to all this section as an extensive dealer in saddlery, harness, and trunks, and, possessing a high degree of intelligence, unswerving honesty, and a gentlemanly address, he has been regarded as one of our leading citizens. Being a native of Vermont, he has been mentioned more particularly by Mr. Eastman.

Francis Hodgman, watchmaker, jeweler, and druggist, was one of the old settlers, commencing business about 1831. In a small way he gradually built up a large and thriving trade, and at his decease, in 1864, left a handsome fortune to his two sons, Charles and Francis F., the latter of whom continued the business of druggist for several years, when he was compelled by ill-health to give it up. The store and business, much enlarged and increased, has passed into the hands of Robinson Brothers.

John Farr, a native of this town and a prominent citizen, was, for a time, clerk for W. and A. Brackett, afterwards in trade for himself, and later with M. L. Goold, an old and much esteemed citizen. Later still, Mr. Farr studied law, was admitted to the bar about 1852, and became a law partner with William J. Bellows. After the dissolution of that partnership, he became a director and president of the Littleton National Bank, which position he now occupies.

Frye W. Giles, son of John Gile, one of the oldest settlers, was in trade for a time in the brick store, and afterwards in the McCoy block. Emigrating to Kansas early in its history, when it was a hard struggle to " keep the wolf from the door," he eventually made a fortunate purchase of real estate, enabling him at a later period to establish a private banking institution, which, proving a success, has made him a wealthy man.

Royal D. Rounsevel, a native of Charlestown, N. H., commenced trade in 1851 in the McCoy block, in general merchandise; afterwards in the store recently occupied by Nelson Farr, which he built, and, being a man of excellent business capacity and unusual energy, built up a large and successful trade. Subsequently he purchased a large farm at North Littleton, and also the " White Mountain House," near the Fabyan House, both of which, together with a tannery in this village, he is still running successfully.

C. W. Brackett, son of William Brackett, Esq., commenced trade about 1862 with Henry L. Tilton. Afterwards William J. Bellows became a partner, under the firm of Henry L. Tilton & Co. Tilton, three years later, retired from the firm, and Bellows and Brackett continued together until 1872, when they dissolved partnership, and Brackett has since continued alone, and Mr. Bellows, with his two sons, established the business in which they are at present engaged.

John W. Balch, son of Sylvanus Balch, one of the old residents of the town, for several years occupied the brick store in partnership with M. L. Goold, who had been clerk for William Brackett on the Meadows. They were dealers in general merchandise, and commenced about 1845. They afterwards organized a stock company, under the name of the Farmers' and Mechanics' Company. At a later period, Mr. Balch was in trade by himself a few years at the same store. Mr. Goold also established himself in the boot and shoe trade in the store now occupied by Mr. Pennock as a barber shop.

William Bailey, now of Claremont, N. H., was for many years a leading merchant of this village. He occupied the store now occupied by Royal P. White, dealer in stoves and tin-ware. He left here about 1865. Soon after Mr. Bailey left town, Mr. H. H. Southworth, who had been clerk for Mr. Bailey, commenced for himself in the same line of trade, which was general merchandise. He took the store that had for a long time been occupied by the Messrs. Eastman, where he has continued to the present time, having had several different partners. George Farr was his first partner; afterwards, Charles Taylor took his place, and, later still, George E. Lovejoy, with whom also became associated Fred H. English, now of the firm of Eaton & English. Mr. English retired from the firm about two years since, and is now in company with Charles Eaton. Mr. George E. Lovejoy still remains with Mr. Southworth, under the firm of Southworth & Lovejoy. They are enterprising merchants, and occupy a prominent place in the business of the town.

Charles Eaton, of the firm of Eaton & English, has long been identified with the trade of Littleton. They occupy the store built by William Brackett, in 1841, much enlarged and arranged with every convenience requisite for their extensive trade in groceries, flour, grain, and produce. C. D. Tarbell and Isaac Calhoun, members of the Littleton Lumber Company, and Henry F. Green, book-keeper for Ira Parker & Co., have at different times been connected with Mr. Eaton in the store. Mr. Eaton is a native of Landaff, and Mr. English was born at Woodstock, Vt.

Nelson C. Farr, recently deceased, began in a small way in the old yellow store, about thirty-five years ago. Being industrious and prudent, and having a natural turn for " getting ahead," characteristic of the Farr family, he soon acquired sufficient capital to embark in general merchandise on a much larger scale. For about fifteen years previous to his decease he was a prominent and leading merchant of this village, and by a course of uniformly fair dealing, had obtained the confidence of the community and a large patronage.

Tilton Brothers (John F. and Fred A.), sons of Franklin Tilton, a former partner with the Messrs. Eastman, dealers in clothing, boots and shoes, and family goods, have a fine store in the Union block, carry a large stock, and rank among the leading firms in town.

The extensive establishment of Dennis O. Wallace, dealer in toys, small-ware, books, and stationery, is quite a feature in the trade of the town. His competent, ladylike, and accommodating assistant, Miss Mattie Eastman, is a daughter of Ebenezer Eastman, Esq., now deceased, who was formerly of the firm of E. & C. Eastman, and the oldest member of that and other firms into which it merged. He was a man of remarkable business ability, universally esteemed, and whose death in the prime of his manhood was generally deplored as a loss to the community.

Dow Brothers (Arthur F. and Robert M.), sons of Luther T., and grandsons of James Dow, a veteran of the War of 1812, are large and leading dealers in general merchandise. Young, ambitious, and enterprising, they have built up a thriving trade.

Charles A. Farr, son of John Farr, was for a time in partnership with John Tilton, in the store formerly occupied by Henry L. Thayer, and now owned by Truman Stevens. Mr. Farr is now by himself, two doors east of the postoffice, and dealing largely in dry goods and groceries.

Bellows & Sons (William J., William H., and George S.), occupy the store on Main street formerly owned by Charles A. Sinclair, of whom they purchased it. Their business consists of carpets, clothing, paper hangings, crockery, curtains, furnishing goods, boots and shoes, and draws largely from surrounding towns.

The watchmaking and jewelry establishment of E. Flint, in Tilton's new brick opera block, is probably the handsomest of its kind in the county, and the extensive and comprehensive stock which he carries invites attention far and near. His fine display of oil paintings by our own artists, is quite an attraction.

Charles C. Smith, son of Hiram B. Smith, one of the old settlers, has for many years been prominent as a dealer in stoves and tin-ware, carrying a large stock of everything in his line, and attracts trade from all the towns in this vicinity.

Royal P. White, a competitor of Mr. Smith, although but a few years in town, has established a thriving business in that line. He is also the champion orator of this section for the Fourth of July.

O. Martin Fisher, who was clerk for Nelson Farr for quite a number of years, is now established in the dry goods line in the store formerly occupied by S. W. Atwood, jeweler, and more recently by William H. Whiting. Mr. Fisher is a native of the town, well and favorably known, and has a liberal patronage.

John Smillie, confectioner, supplies the country, far and near, with candies, in all varieties and forms, of superior quality, and of his own manufacture.

Henry Merrill, son of Deacon John Merrill, one of the oldest citizens of the town, much respected, was for several years, previous to 1872, largely engaged in the clothing trade in the store now occupied by Royal P. White. He is now a member of the Eureka Glove Company of this place.

Otis Batchelder and his son, George F. Batchelder, were at different times in trade in the " brick store." George F. afterwards emigrated to Minnesota, where he was in trade several years. From there he went to Chicago, where he now resides. He is now largely interested in " Leadville mining," which is reputed very successful.

Stephen Ouvrand came here from Lebanon, N. H. In connection with his son, Philias F., he is conducting an extensive grocery and restaurant on Main street, which, for neatness and good order, will compare favorably with any establishment of the kind in the state.

Robert H. Whittaker has two stores in the same building on Main street, one a " small-ware " store with five and ten cent counters, and the other a grocery, both of which are well patronized.

The two druggists, Robinson Brothers and Wilber F. Robins, one at each end of Main street, are fitted up in modern style, and are ready at all times to supply the trade, with a panacea for every ill to which flesh is heir.

Carlos P. Day, merchant tailor, has an extensive trade in the Opera Block.

J. S. Brownlow, dealer in pianos, organs, and other musical instruments, has a store on the corner of Main and Mill streets. Mr. Brownlow has been in town but a few years, but is apparently building up a satisfactory trade in his line.

Lane & Stocker's clothing store, in the Opera Block, is very handsomely furnished. Though comparatively new comers, they are enterprising business men, and have already established a successful trade. Mr. Lane was formerly with his brother at Lancaster, and Mr. Stocker came from Windsor, Vermont.

Edson, Bailey & Eaton, successors to Messrs. C. & C. F. Eastman, in the store known as the " depot store," deal in groceries, hardware, and all kinds of heavy goods. Carrying a very large and comprehensive stock, their trade is large, and extends to all the towns in this vicinity.

Andrew W. Bingham, son of George A., has the store formerly occupied by Alonzo Weeks, and carries a nice stock of boots and shoes.

There are doubtless others whose names through inadvertance have been omitted, that during the last fifty years have, from time to time, been connected with the trade of Littleton, besides those who have been alluded to by Mr. Eastman as contributions from Vermont.

In concluding a somewhat difficult task, imperfectly accomplished, I cannot refrain from expressing great satisfaction, in view of the fact, that whatever of prominence, as a leading town of Northern New Hampshire, may be accorded to Littleton, is due entirely to the sterling qualities of those whose names have been mentioned, and their successors, rather than of the unhealthy growth incident to a sudden influx of capital.

It is this fact, together with the substantial basis upon which Littleton is the acknowledged centre of several thriving towns, that gives assurance of its rapid advancement, until it ranks among the foremost towns of the "Granite State."

THE TOWN AND THE RAILROADS.

ADDRESS BY JOHN M. MITCHELL.

The President said: In early times it was hard coming to Littleton and harder getting away; but now it is easy. The subject, "The Town and the Railroads," is assigned to Mr. John M. Mitchell, a former resident. If present he would inform us how the change come about; but, being absent, we must wait till his address is printed.

ADDRESS.

Mr. President:

Through the partiality of friends and former neighbors, for whom I entertain the highest regard, to me has been assigned the privilege and duty of speaking, on this occasion, upon the subject, "Littleton and the Railroads." This, as I interpret the subject, does not involve any question save the means which have led to the development of the railroad system in which the town is interested, and which became necessary for the transportation of products to market, and bringing supplies in return. This question, in the early settlement of the town, was destined to increase in importance and difficulty, and certain to become, as it has, one of the great, if not the greatest, economical question of our time. When the subject was first considered here, the means of marketing products and obtaining supplies were so primitive that for several years it seemed that a total failure would attend any attempts at settlement under existing conditions; but the energy and good sense of the people at length provided means of travel and transportation. There was laid a substantial foundation, the results of which have given us the commercial facilities now enjoyed. Without them no community can achieve permanence. The situation of the place, in the region of two important river valleys, gave it manifest advantages in a commercial point of view. Through these valleys, the county roads, the great stage lines, the canals, and the railroads would necessarily pass. The future of the place depended upon the sagacity of the people in utilizing these natural advantages.

It is my purpose to outline briefly what the people of this town have attempted, and what they have accomplished, in this direction. Men of foresight soon found that the common highways, and the limited means of transportation they then enjoyed, could not keep pace with the demands of a moderate progress. They tried to develop a canal system, and to make it the conduit of the overflowing products of the country.

The nearest projected canal to Littleton, was the one surveyed over nearly the whole line of the Connecticut river. It served a purpose afterwards in fixing the railroad routes of that valley.

Another scheme, which was put in partial operation, and which promised to be part of the machinery of commerce for this town, was the steamboat line which was operated for a time between Hartford and Wells River. This undertaking, of course, was not a permanent success. I take a brief account of it from the *Records of the Governor and Council of Vermont*, vol. 4, page 452, under the subject " Steamboats on the Connecticut River : "

" While General Schuyler was endeavoring to push on the work of his company in New York, the men of enterprise in the Connecticut river valley were not idle. By companies chartered by Vermont, in one instance, at least, by lottery, means were raised for clearing the bed of the river and constructing the necessary canals and locks. Massachusetts and Connecticut co-operated in the work, and finally the river was made available for transportation by flat boats and rafts, much to the advantage of the inhabitants in the valley of Vermont and New Hampshire. These improvements were especially advantageous to those engaged in the lumber trade; and the canal still furnishes water-power for manufactories of great value. In 1830, a small steamboat ascended the Connecticut to Wells River village; in 1831, five additional boats were built, and put on the river at different sections between Hartford, Conn., and Wells River village, and were run about a year; but, in 1832, the company failed, and the boats were withdrawn."

One of these boats was named the Ariel Cooley. At the same time your jovial fellow townsman, Ariel Holmes, was in business at Wells River. These facts may account for the second name, by which Mr. Holmes has been familiarly known for half a century.

Presumably, the traffic of this vicinity was affected by the advent of this mode of communication with the lower New England.

The scenery of the White Mountains had early attracted a special class of travel through this town. Its taverns and stage lines stimulated an annually increasing number, and the village of Littleton became a popular point on the main line. This was a powerful stimulus for the extension of railroad enterprises in this direction. Lines to this point were contemplated by the early charters.

BOSTON & ONTARIO, 1832.

The charter for the Boston & Ontario, granted by the legislature, in 1832, was the first in New Hampshire. It gave authority to the corporation to adopt a route through this state, from Dunstable to some point on the Connecticut river.

PORTLAND & CONNECTICUT RIVER, 1839.

This contemplated a line from the eastern boundary of the state to some point on the river between Haverhill and Colebrook.

BOSTON, CONCORD & MONTREAL, 1844.

This road had power to proceed from some point on the Connecticut river, opposite Haverhill or Ltttleton, in this state, or any town on the river between those towns, thence in the direction of the Oliverian route to Plymouth, and thence to Concord, or Bow, by way of the river valleys, so as to connect with the Concord railroad. Construction was commenced in 1844 at Concord, and was completed to Woodsville, May 10, 1853.

WHITE MOUNTAINS, 1848.

The charter line was from some point on the Boston, Concord & Montreal, in Haverhill, up the valley of the Ammonoosuc river, through Haverhill, Bath, Lisbon, Littleton, Bethlehem, Whitefield, Dalton, Lancaster, to some point on the Atlantic & St. Lawrence, in Lancaster, with power to connect with that road.

The first board of directors was chosen Feb. 6, 1849. They were, Ira Goodall, Bath, president; A. S. Woods, Bath; David G. Goodall, Lisbon; Ebenezer Eastman, Littleton; Morris Clark, Whitefield; Levi Sargent, Manchester; John Pierce, Bethlehem. The clerk of the corporation was William J. Bellows, then and now of this town. Our member, Mr. Eastman, was one of the most unselfish, sagacious, and enterprising men on the board. No single person can be named to whom the town owes a greater debt of gratitude for untiring and well directed efforts to advance its material interests, than to Ebenezer Eastman.

The history of the road under its own corporation is found in the annual reports of the directors, in the reports of the railroad commissioners, in reported cases in the supreme court, and other court records. The first year, from August, 1853, to August, 1854, the road was operated by the Boston, Concord & Montreal. In August, 1854, the contract with the Boston, Concord & Montreal expired, and subsequently the White Mountains was operated by its own corporation.

Robert Morse, John E. Chamberlain, and their associates, procured for themselves an act of incorporation, in 1855, as the Ammonoosuc Valley Railroad Company. This corporation was authorized, within a limited time, to buy the White Mountains Railroad; but the purposes of the act were not accomplished. The trustees, to whom the road had been mortgaged in February, and again in December, 1853, obtained from the legislature, in 1857, a confirmation of their power of sale under the mortgages, and, by the same act, the purchasers were made a corporation, to hold and manage the railroad, and carry out the purposes for which it was originally incorporated. These measures promised to relieve the court, stockholders, and contractors, from some of their troubles, responsibilities, and contentions with reference to the property.

For the first six months of the year ending April 30, 1858, the road was run under the direction of the supreme court, and the earnings were to be paid into the hands of the receiver. August 16, 1858, it was advertised for sale by the trustees, at public auction, at Bath, November 3, 1858. It was then sold to Messrs. Reed, Hale and Minot, for the bondholders of the road, for $24,000. At a meeting of the White Mountains (N. H.) Railroad, which was the organization of the bondholders, at Littleton, November 23, 1858, B. T. Reed, E. J. M. Hale, George Minot, F. J. Eastman, and C. Brackett were chosen directors. Another confirmatory act of incorporation was given these parties, the following June session, the corporation taking the name of the White Mountains (N. H.) Railroad.

This new corporation, on the first day of February, 1859, effected a lease of the railroad to the Boston, Concord & Montreal Railroad corporation, for a term of five years, the rent being fixed at the sum of $10,000 per year, the road to be kept, in all respects, in as good condition as at the time of the lease. This management was continued, with occasional modifications. The transaction placed the new corporation in a very favorable position, when compared with all previous experience with the old White Mountains Railroad.

In June, 1866, the charter was amended so as to allow the extension of the road to Northumberland. In 1871, an act was passed authorizing the White Mountains (N. H.) Railroad to unite with the Boston, Concord & Montreal, and become a part of the same; and the union, under this act, was consummated in 1873, the owners of the former receiving

$300,000, six per cent. consolidated bonds, for their property

After Mr. J. E. Chamberlain relinquished the superintendency of the White Mountains Railroad, it was under the supervision of the officers of the Boston, Concord & Montreal. The best known of these were Mr. Lyon and Mr. Dodge. The latter's connection with our business men and their interests, in his official capacity, was long and intimate. Mr. B. H. Corning was superintendent of the White Mountains Division for several years, previous to the transfer of the road to the Boston & Lowell Company, last month. His acquaintance with the road, its history and connections, is extensive, and I am indebted to him for efficient aid in collecting facts.

In the same year, with the incorporation of the White Mountains Railroad, a charter was granted, under the title of the Connecticut River & Montreal Railroad. The route was through some point on the Boston, Concord & Montreal Railroad in Haverhill, up the Connecticut River, to some point in the town of Lancaster, to connect with the Atlantic & St. Lawrence Railroad. This expired by limitation of the charter, in 1853, and was not, in any event, to be a rival of the White Mountains Railroad.

There was a time, it is said, when the Passumpsic Railroad might have taken the White Mountains property at its own price. The management of the former seemed to regard it as poor property, at any price, and left it to drop into the basket of the Boston, Concord & Montreal as a matter of necessity. It is hardly profitable now to speculate on what might have been, had the Passumpsic, at the earliest possible moment, taken this road. It certainly would have been for some years a cold country for the Boston, Concord & Montreal this side of Plymouth.

Mr. James L. Hadley was one of the original contractors for the construction of the road, and he has kindly furnished me with a sketch of the road, in its early years, wherein he says:

"Morse, Chamberlain & Co. (Robert Morse, John E. Chamberlin, James L. Hadley and Joseph Coburn of Rumney), were the contractors for the construction of the road,

They began in Bath, in May, 1851, and pushed the road along, making temporary termini at the several points. They completed it to Littleton, in 1853. The first temporary station was just below the present one, and near the house now occupied by Lorenzo Burton, and owned by Cyrus Eastman, on South street. Patrons of the road had to climb up the bank at that place. And the cut was meantime completed, which enabled the company to establish the station at the depot now used for freight. There was no formal opening of the road, only an excursion from places below, and a large concourse of people gathered ' to see the cars.' "

Mr. Hadley was, himself, superintendent of the trip, while Mr. Leavitt of Meredith was the conductor of the first passenger train that came into Littleton. Peter Duncklee was the engineer. He came from Rumney, and had been engineer of the locomotive on the iron train. The name of the locomotive that brought in the first train was the Reindeer. After this, the first regular engineer was Henry A. Cummings of Rumney, and his fireman was Walter Farnham of Plymouth. Mr. Hadley became the regular conductor, and continued in this position until the road was sold at auction on the mortgage bonds. The Granite was the name of the first locomotive regularly used after the opening. That was run about a year. The next year the engine named the Boy was procured from the Passumpsic Railroad. Brooks Palmer served as engineer, and Si Kingman as fireman. The next year came the engine Hillsboro, and afterwards the LaMoille. Another was the Chicopee. The White Mountains Railroad never owned any locomotives. Those they used were always either hired or borrowed from other corporations. The Rumford was the name of one used later, when the Boston, Concord & Montreal took the road. Ike Sanborn and James H. Smalley became, respectively, engineer and fireman, and run for a number of years. Dick Wiggin was the freight conductor, for a little while, the first fall; Edwin Abbott was freight conductor at times. Seth Greenleaf and J. Sidney Russ were conductors under the new regime, and so continued down to a comparatively recent time. During the time Mr. Hadley was conductor, he also acted as roadmaster, and was freight conductor for a time on the Boston, Concord & Montreal. He was on the board of directors of the old White Mountains Railroad. The first brakeman was Asa Sinclair, the next, Ward Cobleigh, the next George Eastman, and then John Cleveland. The mail agents, under President Pierce, were James F. Langdon, George W. Hoyt; under President Buchanan, Langdon, two years, Jeremiah Blodgett, Col. T. A. Barker, Jedediah T. Clough; under President Lincoln, Jesse Mann and Harvey Greenleaf; afterwards, Harvey P. Ross, George W. Little, Gen. J. M. Clough, Maj. Samuel G. Goodwin and C. L. Morrison.

At first, and for several years, the arrangement of trains was, in summer—about eight months in the year—a passenger train down to Woodsville in the morning, a freight train back in the forenoon, a freight train down in the afternoon, and a passenger train back at night. In the winter season, only one train down and back was run each day, and it was a mixed freight and passenger. The work was all done by the same set of trainmen.

The early history of the White Mountains Railroad is made up largely of insolvency and litigation. The company agreed to pay the contractors one-half cash and one-half stock. The cash failed the second month. Mr. Morse and his associates were in trouble. They seriously considered whether it wasn't foolhardy to proceed with their undertaking. Mr. Morse judged that they would certainly fail if they did not go on, and it could not be more than that if they did. So the contractors pushed ahead. The corporation pursued the subscribers for the stock vigorously to raise money to meet expenses. That source of revenue was soon exhausted, and preferred stock was issued. Still, when the iron was called for, the corporation could not get funds on stock of any kind, and they could not borrow money, nor get credit for the iron. They issued bonds for this emergency, and mortgaged the road to secure the bonds, and so the iron was bought and laid. Meantime war raged between the contractors and the company. The contractors claimed a lien, and under various rights. The directors, or factions of them, and a number of the stockholders, claimed to have rights. Harry Bingham was the principal counsel for the contractors. Charles W. Rand was the legal manager for the other party, with George B. Redington as their principal engineer. The contractors held a large amount of stock, and, with their friends who held stock, managed to keep "an under hold." The court, at length, appointed a receiver, and in this the contractors scored a point by the selection of Daniel Patterson, their candidate, for this trust. This litigation, in one form or another, occupied the courts constantly down to the termination of the recent case of Sinclair et als. *v.* Redington et als. (58 New Hampshire Reports, page 364).

When the White Mountains road went under the control of the Boston, Concord & Montreal, in 1859. Mr. Hadley was in its employ for a short time, and then went to Barton, Vt., which was then the terminus of the Passumpsic Railroad, and there acted as station agent. In 1861, he became a partner with Hartshorn & Gibb, in the Crawford House, and lost the investment he made there. In 1863, he went west, and obtained a responsible and lucrative position as roadmaster on the Pittsburgh & Fort Wayne Railroad in Indiana. He continued in that business until 1869, and then went to Kansas and engaged extensively in farming. Quite recently, he moved to Kansas City, and is now enjoying a well earned season of leisure. He was born in Nashua, N. H., October, 1817.

The early employes of the road remember Mr. Hadley as the conductor who had a regular system in punching and collecting tickets, which he declined to modify even on occasions when he had but one passenger from Woodsville to Littleton.

Among the other railroad men, connected with the business of the road prior to its extension from this point, who have become prominent in their calling, were Horace E. Chamberlin, now superintendent of the Concord Railroad, John E. Dimick of the same road, who holds a responsible position in Portsmouth, and Hon. Edward F. Mann, who takes high rank in the affairs of the Boston & Lowell, in their new northern connections. These gentlemen have given us the benefit of their information on the subject in hand.

Mr. Mann and Mr. W. A. Haskins, the veteran express messenger and agent, add several names to the list we had of those who became known to us as "railroad boys," when Littleton was the terminus. The list is given, not as complete, nor as correct in the order of time, but for the reminiscences which the mention of the names may suggest:

Conductors— H. E. Chamberlin, J. S. Russ, Seth Greenleaf, E. P. Fisher, W. M. Rollins, H. E. Sanborn, Dave Ferguson, Charles James, O. M. Hines, Geo. W. Eastman, Geo. W. Little, J. M. Wardwell, and Tom Robie.

Baggage Masters—Geo. W. Eastman, Asa Sinclair, E. P. Fisher, W. M. Rollins, J. C. Holmes, H. E. Sanborn, E. B. Mann, E. F. Mann, Charles H. Simpson, O. M. Hines, and Geo. V. Moulton.

Engineers—John L. Davis, H. A. Cummings, Brooks Palmer, Hiram Judkins, Ike R. Sanborn, Geo. C. Eaton, Charles Green, J. W. Lyon, William Clement, and C. M. Burleigh.

Firemen— Henry Simpson, J. K. Hatch, James B. Smalley, Walter Farnham, J. W. Lyon, Will Moore, and Will Martin.

Express Messengers—Harvey P. Ross, Lewis Baxter, Dan. Green, J. W. Wardwell, John Church, J. M. Stevens, W. A. Haskins and Rob. Dewey, Jr. Uncle Jim. Langdon and W. A. Stowell were also well known in this department.

The station agents have been, in the order of service: Robert Nelson, John A. Harriman, Horace E. Chamberlin, John E. Dimick, up to 1871. Since 1871, Alden Quimby has served in that position.

In passing, it may be noted that telegraphic communication was established in Littleton, in the fall of 1862, and William R. Brackett, now of the Boston & Lowell Railroad, was the first permanent operator at this point.

THE ATLANTIC & ST. LAWRENCE.

This road is now merged in the Grand Trunk Railroad.

It was incorporated, in 1847, to go through Coos county. It was opened to Island Pond in January, 1853. The route contemplated was through Gorham, Jefferson and Lancaster, and thence up the Connecticut River, being part of the through line from Portland to Montreal. It was actually constructed further to the northward, and the compensation credited to Lancaster for the change of route was a hotel, since burned, which was sold, and the proceeds invested in the establishment of their academy. The Grand Trunk took this road by lease in 1853.

The extension of the White Mountains Railroad from Littleton, as originally contemplated, was not commenced until 1869. In November, 1870, it was completed to Lancaster, and to Northumberland in August, 1872. Thus a connection with the Grand Trunk, which had been in the minds of the managers from the beginning, was effected.

The line called the Mt. Washington Branch was constructed to Fabyans in July, 1874, and completed to the base of Mt. Washington in July, 1876, making the connection with the Mt. Washington Railroad to the summit, and constituting the only all rail route to that point from Boston.

MT. WASHINGTON RAILROAD.

This road was chartered in 1858. Construction began in 1868. Sylvester Marsh, then of this town, was the master spirit of the enterprise. He pushed the scheme to completion, in 1872, in the face of obstacles which seemed to the public insurmountable. His undertaking was, at first, with the general public, a subject of ridicule, and when he did vindicate his skill, sagacity and enterprise by the success of his great work, through which so much has been realized for this section of the state, there were those who denied to him the full credit for that which was conceived and accomplished by the final construction and completion of the Mt. Washington Railway. It is but just to Mr. Marsh, who was so long an enterprising citizen of this town, and whose energy and labor are so well deserving of recognition, that we give his own statement of the matter, which he made, under oath, before the United States Senate Committee of Labor, at Boston, October 22, 1883.

In the printed report, we find the examination of Mr. Marsh by the chairman of that committee, in the course of which he says: "From Chicago, I came back to Jamaica Plains, near Boston, in 1855; was there six years; went back to Chicago, and staid there three years, until 1863. In 1863, I went to Brooklyn, N. Y., and was there from 1863 to 1864. I went from there to Littleton, N. H., for the purpose of building the railroad up Mt. Washington. I lived there 15 years, and then came to Concord, where I now live.

Q. You are the inventor and constructor of the Mt. Washington Railroad?

A. Yes sir.   *   *   *   *   *

Q. I wish you would give us some account of the invention and construction of the Mt. Washington Railroad?

A. I got my charter from the state, in 1858, for a railroad up Mt. Washington and Lafayette. Nobody believed in it, and it created quite a burst of laughter when the man in the legislature read the bill for a charter. Another man got up and moved to add to it, "a railroad to the moon." I did not commence the railroad until 1866. We were three years in building it. The railroad now pays 10 per cent. dividend on its stock, and during the summer of 1882 carried up eleven thousand people.

Q. You never proposed to build it as far as the moon yourself?

A. No, I did not propose going any further than I could find a foundation.

Q. And you concluded to keep your head level all the time?

A. Yes. I have got a little book containing scraps of all the editorials that were written upon it for seven or eight years, and you would laugh if you could read some of those editorials.

Q. The editors are not always right then?

A. Well, these have been written since the road was built.

Q. After you had got to running it?

A. Yes, since it started, and after we had got two-thirds the way up, and so on.

Q. How came you to build that railroad? What put the idea into your mind?

A. Well, I built it for a pastime and to cure the dyspepsia more than anything else. I retired from business in 1855. After living a few years doing nothing, I had the dyspepsia very bad, and was compelled to do something to save my health. I got this idea and worked upon it, and built different models of it, until I worked it out. It was ridiculed a great deal, and was laughed at, but it cured the dyspepsia.

Q. And you and your family have been realizing the effects of that idea, ever since, and you have made quite a fortune by it, have you not?

A. Well, I have done pretty well. It is paying pretty well now. It has been a good thing for my native state, and brings a good many people into the state.*

PORTLAND & OGDENSBURG RAILROAD.

To this corporation the right of way was granted, in 1869, agreeably to the provisions of its charter, to build a line of railroad from the west line of the state of Maine, through Conway, Bartlett, White Mountain Notch, Carroll, Bethlehem and Littleton, provided, that in case the corporation found it impracticable to locate and build a railroad on account of the grades between Littleton and St. Johnsbury, Vt., and not otherwise, they might locate and build the same via, Carroll, Whitefield and Dalton, to the eastern line of the state of Vermont. This line was completed to Fabyans, from Portland, August 7, 1875, making a connection with the Boston, Concord & Montreal and White Mountains Railroad at that point. This route through the heart of the White Mountains was opened from the east side, notwithstanding the ultimatum of

---

*Report of the committee of the United States Senate on the relations of labor and capital. Vol. 3, pp. 606, 607, 620, Washington Gov't Print. Office, 1885.

the committee to procure the charter for the White Mountains Railroad, in their report, February 6, 1849, p. 21. "In addition, this is the only route which really approaches the White Mountain range, or ever can, and hence our name— The White Mountains Railroad."

It having been decided by the manager of the Portland & Ogdensburg Road that it was impracticable to build by the Littleton route, very much against the interests both of our town, and of the road itself, as we believe, they constructed two miles and a half of railroad, from Scott's Junction to Lunenburgh, Vt., making a western connection there with the St. Johnsbury & Lake Champlain Railroad, using the track of the Boston, Concord & Montreal and White Mountains Railroad from Fabyans to Scott's, an arrangement which still continues. Had the managers of this enterprise begun their line at Littleton, as soon as they had authority, opening it to Fabyans with reasonable expedition, they would have had the full control of the White Mountain travel on both sides of the Notch. They would have had the freight of this town to a large extent, by giving it the shortest possible independent line to the seaboard. Their control of the summer travel by the Notch routes would have been supreme. They would not have suffered from the loss of a section of their backbone, as was inevitable when the distance from Scott's to Fabyans was covered by the iron of a hostile corporation. The same delay that enabled the Boston, Concord & Montreal to seize the approaches to the mountaints on the west side, was utilized by the managers of the Vermont division, in pushing the completion of the road over the Lunenburg line to a point of no commercial advantage to anybody else on the river at the present place of connection. Thus, the western terminus of the Portland & Ogdensburg in New Hampshire was forced to the northward from the chartered route, and the supposed local interests of the Vermont parties were conserved at the expense of New Hampshire and Maine. Construction at the outset from the Connecticut River, at West Littleton, through Littleton village to Fabyans, must have compelled construction by the Vermont division of a corresponding connection over the Waterford line. It is fair to presume that an independent line over such a route, anticipating all rivals in control of the White Mountain portion of the summer traffic, would have saved this corporation from the loss of its Vermont feeder, which is now imminent, from its dependency upon concessions from one of its principal rivals for existence on the west side of the mountains, and from other disasters which have overtaken it. To prevent the consummation of these fatal errors, and to compel, if possible, the construction of the road upon the charter line, this town instituted proceedings in equity, in 1875. Having made the survey, which proved the line practicable in grades, and more feasible than the one finally adopted, the town's case before the courts was a very strong one. The Portland & Ogdensburg directors, in 1878, referred to the proceedings (report 1878, p. 8) as persecution, instigated by rival corporations. This was not the case with the litigation instituted by this town. It would seem that the interests of the Boston, Concord & Montreal were identical with those of the town. The company, however, made no sign, indicating any readiness to aid the town in its struggle against the Portland & Ogdensburg Railroad; and the town understood that, while it was strong before the courts, in the legislature, to which the matter would ultimately go, it would be no match for the railroad. Therefore, with but partial indemnity for its outlay in the matter, proceedings were discontinued on the town's part.

After their discontinuance, it was learned that the officials of the Boston, Concord & Montreal contemplated a tender of support, but the information came too late to be of any benefit to the town. In 1877, the Portland & Ogdensburg were confirmed by the legislature in the right to the piece of road from Scott's to Lunenburg.

Previous to the extension of the White Mountains (N. H.) Railroad, in 1870, the summer travel to the mountains was by stage from Littleton. The stage line from this place to the Franconia Mountains was maintained, and continued to divide business with the Plymouth line to the same point, until the construction of the narrow guage railroad from Bethlehem

Junction to the Profile House, which was opened July 1, 1879, and the Bethlehem (Highlands) Branch, which was opened in 1882.

The present system of completed railways enables our citizens, and a large number of tourists, who sojourn with us in the summer months, to make the trip, either to the summit of Mt. Washington, the Crawford House, Conway, Profile House and Flume, Plymouth, Lancaster, St. Johnsbury, Hanover or Concord, enjoying the luxuries of first-class coaches, and return to Littleton in reasonable hours the same day. These facilities have made Littleton the summer home of five hundred guests, which can but remind us, by contrast, of those ante-railroad days, when our summer visitors were few in number and "tarried but a day."

In 1854, the entire earnings of the White Mountains Railroad approximated only $20,000, as shown by their official reports. This year, the receipts at Littleton alone are nearly four times that amount. The movers in our first railroad enterprises, among the inducements offered, spoke of the "Franconia Notch, where the Old Man of the Mountains draws his twenty-five hundred pleasure visitors yearly in the hot summer months." Within the range of their vision, which was enlarged to the fullest measure, as they offered their stock to an incredulous public, they had no conception of the vast army of tourists, who, by thousands, view that old stone face, and load the trains that pass hourly over the sides of mountains which were pronounced impassable.

Although from bankruptcy and the construction of air castles, these men were compelled to accept their only recompense for labor, losses and anxiety, they, nevertheless, cherished the fond and, as it then seemed, delusive hope, that the time would come, when the journey from the sea board to the mountains could be made in twelve hours. We can now see that this was no extravagant claim, but the conservative estimate of future development by sensible, persevering, and enterprising men, to whom, not only Littleton, but this whole region is much indebted. We can see now that the legitimate and logical sequence, the development of the ideas conceived by these men, not only enable us to make that journey in twelve hours, but we know it can be done in five hours, and in twelve hours the span from the mountains to the great metropolis, New York City, can be passed by rail.

Littleton, although never the pet of any railroad corporation, has, nevertheless, furnished from among her citizens, those who have contributed in no slight degree to the honest development of all railroad enterprises looking to the substantial benefit, not only of Littleton, but the entire state of New Hampshire.

THE WOMEN OF LITTLETON.

The President said: — The sixteenth subject is "The Women of Littleton." I see it is to be responded to by Harry Bingham. All I can say about it is that he is not present. It is not the first time that he has neglected a golden opportunity in this direction. He never was spry in making up his mind on the woman question in days past, and now that he has sinned away his marriageable opportunities, and, unmarried, is midway in the abyss of irredeemable old bachelorship, it is a matter of grave doubt whether he will ever make the effort to write for publication what he should have spoken here, to-day, in commendation of Littleton women. But if he does not, I will say for him, in his place, God bless the women of Littleton. (Applause.)

ADDRESS BY REV. CHARLES W. MILLEN.*

Congenial theme! And as important as congenial. The history of no community can be justly written, any more than it can be enacted, without woman's share in the work. And, especially, is this true of local history, where, more than upon the wider stage of public life, woman's moulding influence is constantly felt and manifest. And in the present case, this task of paying a tribute to the women of Littleton is the more welcome to me, because my mother is practically a Littleton woman. What is the mere accident of birth, com-

---

*This address of Rev. Mr. Millen, which has a place in this volume, was delivered by him in the Congregational church, subsequently to the centennial celebration. Mr. Millen is a native of this town, and was, at the time, supplying the church temporarily.

Owing to a press of engagements, Mr. Bingham has been unable to furnish the manuscript of an address on the subject assigned him, in season for publication, and Mr. Millen's address is, consequently, inserted here, with his consent.

pared to the deliberate choice of a life? Born just across the line, in Lisbon, she early came to this town, and with one of its sons, vowed a wedlock that God has blessed and continued more than fifty years. Here, she has lived, and, with industrious hands, not yet folded, she has contributed to the wealth and well-being of this town ; and, at last, her ashes will be laid to rest in its soil. And my mother represents a large number of noble women, whose lives have been woven, as warp and woof, into this fabric of a hundred years, which we contemplate with so much pride today.

And, then, the first women I ever knew, the *matronly* women, who seemed to me like queens, the embodiment of dignity, purity and grace ; and the *young* women, who arose upon my boyish fancy, sweet, charming, and full of mystery— beautiful enough to have been dropped down from heaven— these were Littleton women, such as a maturer vision never meets, but who still live in memory as the goddesses of a boyhood reverence. But I am to speak, at this time, not so much of personal memories and impressions, as of those facts which form substantial history, and make the Centennial celebration of this town of deep and permanent interest.

One thing to be considered, in connection with this subject, is the fact that the worth of the great mass of our women cannot be represented by speech or pen. When Madame Campan once asked Napoleon, "What is the great want of the French Nation?" he appropriately replied, "Mothers." The most of our women have been the wives of humble farmers and mechanics in heroic conflict with the poverty and limited advantages of a new settlement; but they have been mothers ; they have reared families, and often large families, and by self-denying industry and frugality, united with Christian faith and grace, have trained in knowledge and virtue, their children, some of whom stay to perpetuate their name and continue their work; while others have gone out from us, and are foremost in trades and professions the wide world over. Who shall estimate the value of the influence of these quiet, patient, hard-worked and devoted women, who made their homes the support of the government and of the church, and fostered all those associations that give blessing and vitality to social existence? It is of such that Hannah More so sweetly sings :—

> "As some fair violet, lovliest of the glade,
>   Sheds its mild fragrance on the lonely shade;
> Withdraws its modest head from public sight,
>   Nor courts the sun, nor seeks the glare of light.
>
> So woman, born to dignify, retreat,
>   Unknown to flourish, and unseen be great;
> To give domestic life its sweetest charm,
>   With softness, polish, and with virtue warm :
> Fearful of fame, unwilling to be known,
>   She seeks but heaven's applauses and her own."

All honor to these worthy women, these unsceptered queens of our early homes, these priestesses ministering in the inner sanctuaries of human life, consecrating, annointing, and inspiring their offspring for the performance of the world's great work. In the words of Gray's immortal elegy,—

> "Let not ambition mock their useful toil,
>   Their homely joy and destiny obscure;
> Nor grandeur hear, with a disdainful smile,
>   The short and simple annals of the poor."

Many of these women were possessed of superior natures. They were models of fidelity, gentleness, and affection, and as capable and worthy of higher positions as the Livonian peasant girl who shared the heart and succeeded to the throne of a Russian czar.

In 1849, there was organized in Littleton a sewing society, for benevolent and philanthropic purposes. It was composed of energetic ladies of various classes, including the most refined and cultivated in the community. That organization has ever since been closely identified with the progress and history of this town. By subscriptions, mite societies, sociables, etc., they raised money with which they purchased materials, and made clothing and bedding for the poor. They also furnished the Congregational church—the only church then in town—with its first carpet, organ, and bell. In 1851, the ladies of this society began to talk of a new cemetery. The town was increasing in population, and the only place for burial was a forlorn and neglected one on the meadows, two miles from the village. After much deliberation, they purchased a portion of the present Glenwood. Mrs. William Brackett and Mrs. Otis Batchelder were among the most active in the enterprise ; and it is worthy of mention, in this connection, that the first burial which occurred in the new and unimproved grounds, November 18th, 1852, was that of a grandchild of both these women. The remark was made at the time, " Those two women little knew for what they were working when they gave so much time and thought to those grounds." In 1855, the cemetery society was incorporated as " The White Mountains Cemetery Corporation," and Mrs. H. S. Carpenter was its first president. In 1877, the name was changed to Glenwood. Twice since the commencement of the enterprise it has been necessary to make additions of land to the original purchase. In 1871, a hearse was procured. In 1877, a receiving-tomb was built; and, yearly, the hand of Taste passes over the luxuriance of Nature in beautifying and improving this resting place of the departed. And to the women of Littleton is due this entire work—this village of the dead, in such convenient proximity to the village of the living ; this hallowed place, where affection may erect its monuments, and utter its tributes, and indulge its meditations.

It was the women, also, who, in 1860, broached the subject of a village library ; and who, the year following, made their first purchase of books—the nucleus of a library now grown to respectable proportions. In 1867, the library association was incorporated. This worthy enterprise the ladies have carried forward almost alone, and, by fairs and other means, involving not a little labor, securing the necessary funds.

About the time the ladies began agitating the library, the gentlemen began to discuss the project of a new school house, with a view to consolidating the several school districts in the village, which was greatly needed. Meetings were held, opinions were freely expressed, and, at length, unable to agree respecting its location, the whole subject was dropped. Then it was that the ladies of the library society took up the matter.

They raised, by their own peculiar methods, a fund of $200, and, in 1865, appointed a committee to select a location. Mrs. Charles Hartshorn, Mrs. John Farr, and Mrs. Elliott Thayer composed the committee. They selected the site on which the school house now stands—a location unequaled, not only in respect to its accessibility, but especially in the extensive and inspiring view of natural scenery which it commands. A committee of ladies was also sent to St. Johnsbury to examine a school building that had just been erected there. These, and other efforts, aroused the public, and waked up the men. And so the women turned over their work, and the little fund in their hands, to the citizens, now enthused and ready for harmonious action. And, in the summer of 1867, was erected the beautiful building that overlooks the village and forms its fitting crown.

But, during the greater part of these years of effort in furnishing proper reading for the people, and proper facilities for the education of the young, there was other work also being done of no less importance.

Rebellion and secession, long threatened and determined upon by the slave-holding section of the United States, became realities in the winter of 1860. The bombardment of Fort Sumpter, April 12, 1861, was the actual commencement of civil war. Three days later, the president of the United States issued a proclamation calling for 75,000 volunteers to maintain the Union and coerce into submission belligerent states. Littleton was not wanting in patriotic ardor, and joined in the great uprising of the loyal people of the country. Recruits were immediately enlisted, and the patriotism of the women in giving their husbands, brothers, and sons, was only equalled by the patriotism of the men who were willing to be given as a sacrifice on their country's altar. Even the young ladies of the high school organized themselves as the Dewey Guards (Prof. H. K. Dewey being their teacher), wore rosettes of red, white, and blue, attended in a body the war-meetings which were held, and often marched in line with the recruits, keeping step with them to martial music. On the 25th of April, only ten days after the call of the president for volunteers, the soldiers being drawn up in line on Main street, near the post-office, the Dewey Guards impressively presented them with Union badges. Misses Jennie M. Jackson and Ellen M. Applebee made the distribution, and Miss Georgiana A. Hadley delivered a presentation address, which glowed with the spirit that made our soldiers, not only heroes and martyrs, but trimphant conquerers. A fund of $80 was collected, principally by Misses Luella Goold and Elizabeth Moore, for the purpose of providing the soldiers with revolvers; but, on more mature reflection, it was agreed that the "sword of the spirit" was a more fitting weapon for gentle women to place in the hands of noble men, whom the government would arm with carnal weapons, and who might be called to languish in hospitals, or starve in rebel prisons, or fall in death upon the field of battle. And so, on May 7th, 1861, when the first recruits mustered in this town were about to take their departure to the scene of conflict, it was a touching sight when the Misses Elizabeth Goold, Elizabeth Moore, and Helen Morse, in the presence of a vast assemblage who had come to exchange affectionate adieus, placed in the hands of each soldier a beautiful copy of the New Testament—a gift of the ladies, a gentle reminder that they should be faithful soldiers, not only of their country, but also of the Lord Jesus Christ. All through those terrible years of civil strife, the women of Littleton, in common with patriotic women throughout the North, responded to every call from camp or hospital, working and giving with unwearying devotion to alleviate the sufferings and contribute to the comfort and efficiency of our nation's brave defenders. It has been observed as a remarkable fact that, while the volunteering enthusiasm died out in the first year of the war, so that drafting and large bounties became necessary to keep up the armies in the field, the liberality and self-sacrifices of the women continually increased, so that the sanitary and Christian commissions were able to multiply their agents and extend their operations up to the hour when peace was declared, and harmony again spread her soft atmosphere and beautiful light over all our land.

 The women of the nation were not merely the rear guard,

or reserved corps of the army of the Union—they were the working, praying, and weeping battalion in active service. Every stitch they took helped to close the rent made by secession; every prayer they offered entered into the ear of the God of battles, and their hot tears mingled with the life-blood of the nation to form a holy cement that should bind together forever the sovereign states of the Union. On woman's brow, as on her brother's, we place the martyr's crown. It is no exaggeration to claim that, all through the loyal North, woman was fired by as pure a patriotism as ever burned in mortal breast. Her devotion was not surpassed even by the heroism of woman of old, when :—

> " In ancient days, she buckled armor on,
> And graspt the sword, and sprung the battle-bolt,
> And wore the martyr's scarlet shroud of flame."

It cannot be expected that a small rural town, in the first century of its existence, would produce any considerable number of women, who, in any public sense, would be eminent. But of at least three of our women I may properly speak :

MRS. REV. ROYAL M. COLE

Was born in this town, May 6, 1848. How well we remember her as Lizzie Cobleigh, the merry, bright-eyed, fair-faced girl, with abundance of flaxen hair, and a step as light and graceful as a sunbeam on the water. She was converted and trained in one of our own churches. She married a clergyman, and unitedly they heard the cry of the heathen : " Come over and help us." Responding to the call, they were sent by the American board and stationed at Erzeroum, in Eastern Turkey, where they still labor. On arriving in the country, Mrs. Cole immediately learned the language of the people— the Armenian—and for fifteen years has been one of their most efficient missionaries.*

---

* Miss Clara M. Cushman, who was a school girl in this town during the pastorate of her father, the Rev. L. P. Cushman, is a missionary in China; and Mrs. Ardelle Knapp Mead, who was many years a resident here, is a missionary in the Congo country.

MRS. ELIZABETH M. WALTON.

Now of San Francisco, a daughter of Peter Bonney, Esq., one of the early residents of this town, and a sister of Judge Benjamin West Bonney of New York, was born here on the 12th of October, 1815. She was educated in New York, and afterward taught school in New Orleans and Galveston. She married, for her first husband, a Mr. Wills of Virginia, then a Mr. Parker of San Francisco, afterward a Mr. Walton, and is now a widow. In 1850, she went from New Orleans to San Francisco as correspondent for the New Orleans *Picayune*. She had been there but a short time, when she was requested by the city to write an ode on the admission of California to the Union, which took place October 9th, 1850, and was celebrated in San Francisco on the 9th of November following. A grand procession was formed, and the ode which, by request, was written to the air of "Star Spangled Banner," was distributed from a hand-press to the 10,000 people on the plaza, and sung by them under the lead of a fine band of wind instruments. The city council honored themselves, as well as Mrs. Walton, by presenting her a large and beautiful gold medal.

A little book published in 1852, entitled, "The Sandwich Islands as They Are, Not as They Should Be," was from her pen. In this, she freely criticised the conduct and management of the missionaries then in power in those islands. Whether she wrote with a full knowledge of all the facts involved, has been a disputed question. At any rate, the appearance of the book created no little feeling, both at the islands and in this country. If there were abuses, no doubt her caustic utterances had the effect to correct them.

A woman of great intellectual penetration and power, of wide observation of the world, and possessing remarkable force of character, she has impressed her personality on every community where she has lived. And, though now in the mellow years of life, she is still vigorous, and the columns of the San Francisco papers are frequently enriched by the contributions of her pen.

MISS MELINDA RANKIN.

See her! tall, stately, intelligent, self-possessed; her blue eyes burning as with some hidden fire; her brow too lofty for feminine weakness; and a force of will and character outmatching the sternest difficulties in the way of duty. She was born in the western part of this town, on the 21st of March, 1811. Her childhood was marked by a fondness for adventure, a delight in nature, a love of books, and, at times, a far-away sort of contemplation. For the exercise of all these peculiarities, there were ample scope and abundant facilities, except for a liberal education; for this, only indifferent teachers, scarcity of books, and uncomfortable school houses. But she grasped knowledge in spite of unfavorable circumstances, and, at the age of fourteen years, she was presented with a teacher's certificate. A new era now dawned upon her thought. Her life began to assume unspeakable significance. She became possessed of an ambition to serve, in some high capacity, her day and generation. Her experience at that time is best expressed by these lines of Bonar:—

> "Not many lives, but only one have we—
> One, only one:
> How sacred should that one life ever be—
> That narrow span!
> Day after day filled up with blessed toil,
> Hour after hour still bringing in new spoil."

When she was young, girls were brought up to work. Industry was one of the cardinal womanly virtues. Good housekeeping, spinning and weaving, sewing and knitting, were indispensable accomplishments for every rising young woman; and in all these branches, she became proficient. But she also found time for reading the books of her father's small but valuable library. In Rollin's Ancient History she reveled. Religious works and biographies of good men she eagerly devoured. At that time woman was scarcely known in the public capacity which is now awarded her by general public sentiment. But Harriet Newell had lived, and her memoirs had been published; and, in perusing these, her attention was first attracted to the distinguished usefulness a woman might attain by a simple life of piety and devotion. Inspired with the grandeur of the missionary cause, her highest aspiration was to become, herself, the bearer of the Gospel message to some heathen shore. The various opportunities of home missionary work were improved, in the belief that, if she was "faithful over a few things," God would make her, in due time, "ruler over many things." Teaching in day and Sunday schools was her special delight. Among her studies she took up some of the modern languages, especially the Spanish, not knowing that the Spanish language would be what she would want to use in her future lifework. In 1840, an urgent appealf or missionary teachers came from the valley of the Mississippi, which was then the far west, and fast becoming settled with a foreign Roman Catholic population. She went to the state of Kentucky, opened two schools, and sent for her two sisters in Littleton to come and occupy the positions. She then went to Mississippi where she taught two years, when, procuring another teacher from the North to take her place, she accepted an invitation to Mobile, Alabama, to take a position in the Barton Institute, at that time the most popular female institution in the south. Here she labored one year with much satisfaction.

But, as yet, her proper life-work had scarcely begun. Hitherto, what she had done was only the necessary first chapter of what was to be a magnificent history. War between the United States and Mexico being in progress, her attention became especially directed to that country. She learned of the terrible moral destitution of the Mexican people. The thought of nine millions of immortal souls shut up in the prison-house of papal superstition moved her with profound commiseration. She wrote to missionary boards, and implored them to move in the interests of Mexico, our nearest neighbor. But they replied, "We can do nothing for the people of Mexico until her laws are changed, and a liberal government is established within her domains." This only deepened her anxiety for the spiritual welfare of that oppressed people. Resolved, if possible, on an indirect contact with the country, she went to Texas. Here, by urgent solicitation, she accepted a position in the female academy at Huntsville. Besides teaching, she established schools in different parts of the state, labored in Sunday schools, and wrote for religious and educational periodicals.

A little book entitled "Texas, 1850," was the product of her pen, in which she presented the great need of evangelical laborers in Texas, not only on its own account, but on account of its prospective influence over its neighbor, Mexico, for whose salvation she had become specially exercised.

In the spring of 1852, though unable to enter Mexico as a Protestant missionary, she felt that the time had come to commence her labors for the Mexicans, several thousand of whom were in the valley of the Rio Grande. So she went to Brownsville, about sixty miles up the Rio Grande, opposite Matamoras, and opened a school for their children, and distributed Bibles in their own language among the adults. She felt God's presence with her in the very beginning of her work, and repeated the words of Madame Guyon:—

> "To me belongs nor time nor space,
> My country is in every place;
> I can be calm and free from care
> On any shore, since God is there."

In 1854, with funds personally raised in the states, she erected in Brownsville, by the side of a French Catholic convent, a Protestant female seminary, in which she gathered Mexican girls. And here, on the Texan side of the Rio Grande, she remained till the success of the revolution for religious freedom in Mexico was accomplished by the triumph of the liberal party over the church party—Juarez entering the capital from which Miramon was fleeing, December 25th, 1859. With the exception of occasional evangelistical tours in Mexico, she continued at Brownsville till September, 1862, when she was obliged to leave her seminary (built through her own efforts), and her work in it, by the peremptory orders of a Southern Presbyterian minister; because, as he said, "You are in communion with a country called the

United States, and are not in sympathy with the Southern Confederacy; and no teachers not in sympathy with us can be permitted to occupy that institution."

These were times of great trial. Taking a tearful departure from Brownsville, where she had trained more than two hundred Mexican girls, and from which she had sent out more than 1,500 copies of the Holy Scriptures, she went across the river to Matamoras. But no door of opportunity opened before her, and to go further into the country was unsafe; for Maximillian, sent by Napoleon III, was there to subject the country to the dominion of France. Between the French intervention in Mexico and our own civil war, she seemed to have no standing place in either country. Accordingly, in March, 1863, she concluded to go to New Orleans, which was then occupied by the Federals, and proceed to the North. Perils were on every hand, but providences, as gracious as mysterious, opened up and guarded her way. Reaching New Orleans, she found that Union ladies were greatly needed there at that time, and was persuaded to remain. For nearly two years, when almost every house in the city was a hospital for wounded Union soldiers, she went like an angel of mercy from couch to couch, administering cordials and delicacies, speaking words of heavenly sweetness, and catching the last messages of the dying to convey to their distant loved ones. When the necessities of this work had ceased, she was appointed principal of one of the first schools opened for the freedmen. But she kept an eye on the struggle going on in Mexico. Soon, the French invasion was overcome, Maximillian captured and executed, and the country again open for evangelical missionary labor.

In 1865, after a perilous journey, she arrived in Monterey, as the representative of the American and Foreign Christian Union, under whose auspices she had labored since 1856. Here, she purchased a building, which she enlarged and remodeled for church and mission purposes, at an expense of $10,000, and opened school and Bible work generally. Scores of converts were won to Christ; and soon, she had the co-operation of a body of native workers, eager to proclaim the message of salvation. And when, in 1873, failing health compelled her to resign her work, she passed over to the American Board a valuable mission property; more than a dozen schools in which the Bible was daily taught; numerous Sunday schools, fully equipped for their work; and six Evangelical churches in Monterey and surrounding towns, all the fruits of her "weeping and bearing precious seed."

On returning to the United States, her health greatly improved, and she went among the churches awakening an interest in the Mexican work, visiting, in this way, every state, from the Atlantic coast to the Missouri River. She also published a volume, "Twenty Years Among the Mexicans," which has already passed through several editions, and which is rarely equalled in interest as a record of missionary labor.

Bloomington, Illinois, is now the residence of this pioneer heroine of Mexican missions; and, although considerably past her "three score years and ten," she still rejoices in opportunities for usefulness, "bringing forth fruit in old age."

No presentation of this subject is complete without sketches of some of the pioneer women of Littleton; but these, no doubt, will be furnished by the historian of the town, who has far better opportunities than any one else for making original researches.

There are many women, also, deserving honorable mention, among whom is Mrs. Charles W. Rand, who has been a leader in nearly every enterprise carried forward by the ladies of this town, and to whose accurate information this address is greatly indebted.

There have been women in the homes; women in society; women in the schools; women in the churches;* they cannot be named, but they have left the impress of their sterling qual-

---

*There are but few such illustrations of the importance of woman's church work as that furnished by the ladies of the Protestant Episcopal church of this place. Their church edifice and parsonage have been built mainly, and the establishment almost entirely supported, by the efforts of a few ladies. At the outset of the enterprise, Mrs. Charles Hartshorn and Miss Anna Brackett were among the most active, and the work has been continued and sustained, in a large measure, by the same, or other devoted women, among whom should be named Mrs. Bingham, Mrs. H. L. Tilton and their associates, who are known by their good works by the people of Littleton. In the other churches there has been less disparity of the sexes in the membership, but the same spirit of devotion has distinguished the efforts of the ladies in all our church organizations.

ities in their respective spheres of operation, and have largely contributed to a century of marvelous prosperity and progress.

But let us turn, for a moment, from the secure past to the conditional future. What shall be the record of the second century of our beloved town? We have an inspiring history. We have a goodly heritage. We have splendid opportunities. One hundred years ago there was poverty; to-day, there is wealth. Then, our territory was only a wilderness; now, it is transmuted into rich and blooming fields; then, there was no steam-engine, no telegraph, no railway, no photograph, no spinning-, sewing-, or knitting-machine, no power press, no agricultural machinery; now, mechanical power and the forces of nature relieve every department of useful labor. Then, there were no schools and few books; now, there are magnificent schools with every appliance, and books of every description are scattered like the leaves of autumn, and we have only to peruse them at our leisure in order to become familiar with history, discovery, science, and religion. Then, the homes were rude and rudely furnished—no carpets on the floors, no pictures on the walls; now, in respect to elegance and comfort, they are palaces in comparison. One hundred years ago there was no opportunity for the young people of this town to acquaint themselves with the fine arts, and secure the accomplishments of highly refined and cultivated society; to-day, every avenue of social life is open to our youth; every art may be practiced, and every accomplishment may be acquired.

These splended opportunities—the inherited accumulation of the first century of our town—lay in a heavy burden of responsibility upon those who must make the record of its second century.

The production of noble women has by no means ceased among us. But shall we be able to transmit to the third century a heritage as much in advance of what we receive, as those of the first century were able to transmit to us, compared with what they had in the beginning? The answer to this question must be given principally by our women. It is peculiarly theirs to train and make the men. By their mild virtues they tone society. Intellectually, woman is not inferior to her brother. In sculpture, painting, medicine, science, literature, oratory, business, she has already achieved success, and opened these employments to women everywhere. The cardinal moral virtues she presents in their highest earthly perfection, and the church, in calling for her activities, is saying to her, with a greater emphasis than ever before, "There is a robing of righteousness more comely for a beautiful woman, even, than gold, or pearls, or costly array." But her special empire is home. It is in the holy relations of wife and mother that she exercises her greatest power. The word wife means weaver. "The true wife," as Ruskin says, "weaves and embroiders her husband's fortunes." We are told that, when Mr. Disraeli retired from the premiership of England, he was offered a place among the hereditary aristocracy with the title of earle. He declined it with the intimation that, if there was any reward thought to be deserved, he wished it conferred upon his wife, to whom he attributed all his success. On the day he retired from power, his wife took her place among the noble ladies of England by the title of Viscountess Beaconsfield.

But, as mother, her power is even greater than as wife. She has the early training of every human being that comes into the world. To a greater or less extent she can make her children either angels or devils. Would she carry the world higher, let her carry her children higher in intelligence, in temperance, in a virtuous Christian life. Then coming generations shall rise up and call her blessed. Long after the sensitive heart and weary hands of his mother had crumbled into dust, and climbed to life again in forest flowers, Abraham Lincoln said to a friend, with tears in his eyes, "All that I am or hope to be, I owe to my angel mother; blessings on her memory." She went to heaven when he was only ten years of age, yet the principles she inculcated, and the influence of her life, were not lost; they shed a halo over his life, and elicited this tribute of honor to her memory :—

> "The mother in her office holds the key
> Of the soul: and she it is who stamps the coin
> Of character, and makes the being who would be a savage
> But for her gentle cares, a Christian man."

Let the womanhood of this town be consecrated to high purposes; to the carrying forward of all the elements of material, social, and moral progress; and the interests of Littleton are safe for a second century.

LITTLETON AND THE WAR OF THE REBELLION.

ADDRESS BY CAPT. GEORGE FARR.

The President said: The next and last subject on the programme is, "Littleton and the War of the Rebellion." We have to respond to it a person whose service in that terrible conflict is so well known that he requires no introduction from me. You are acquainted with him, we all know him, Capt. George Farr. (Cheers.)

ADDRESS.

MR. PRESIDENT AND FELLOW CITIZENS:

I am not exactly in the condition that some of the previous speakers have been, who have prepared lengthy remarks to be delivered on this occasion, and, the time being so fully occupied, could not present them. Knowing full well that before it would reach me you would be completely tired out, I did not prepare remarks at any length. You undoubtedly are extremely tired. You have sat here for hours in this hot and smoky air, and have shown much patience.

I think it would have been proper if there had been someone to respond in behalf of the soldiers of the Revolution, and the War of 1812, and the Mexican war. And yet, as you have heard from the orator of the day and other speakers, this town was not settled until just about the time of the Revolutionary war; and, consequently, there was hardly anyone here who could go to war. In the War of 1812, there were few that had an interest, and few that went. Consequently, Littleton took but little part in the wars of the country until the last great and terrible War of the Rebellion. In that war, let me say to you, that she was not behind any of the sister towns of the state, and she was ahead of a large part of them. As soon as the first call, in April, 1861, was issued, the young men of Littleton, some at home and some abroad, rushed to arms. They laid aside their civilian's dress. They donned the blue, either of the navy or army, and they went forth to battle for their country's right. When the call was issued, it was only for three-months men. And when the delegation from this town reached their rendezvous at Portsmouth, they found the First Regiment of three-months men full, and learned that, if they went at all, they must go in the Second. They did not believe in going down there and then turning around and coming back, and the result was that nearly all the men that started for the three-months campaign, put their names on the rolls and went forth, as the boys used to say, "for three years, unless sooner killed."

Twelve went from this town in the Second Regiment—a regiment that probably saw as much fighting as any during the war. But there was not a regiment that went from the state of New Hampshire that ever in any respect disgraced its colors or the state from which it came. The larger part of those who went in the Second Regiment served their full three years. A part of them then re-enlisted and served until the war was over. Eight men went in the Third, one in the Fourth, fourteen in the Fifth. The Sixth Regiment took the largest number of any up to that time—twenty-seven responding to the call. The Seventh took thirteen; the Eighth, nine men. These regiments all went in 1861 and in the winter of 1861-'62. When the call came, in 1862, for more men, the Ninth Regiment was raised. Twenty-three men responded in the fall of 1862, and went into the Ninth Regiment. During this exciting period, when they were holding war meetings all over the state, they had several in this town, at one of which, called at Rounsevel's hall, there were so many people present that all could not get in, and the meeting was adjourned to the Congregational church. This town did not furnish any men for the Tenth, Eleventh, or Twelfth Regiments, but a company was raised here for the Thirteenth

Regiment, fifty-one enlisting from this town, three in the Fourteenth, six in the Fifteenth, two in the Seventeenth, two in the Sharp-Shooters, and fifty-six in other organizations. In 1863, there were some men drafted, but I am unable to find that any drafted men went from this town. There were but very few, and with them all, as the saying was when they were drafted, it was either the blue or the green—either the uniform or the greenback. Those that were drafted preferred to furnish the green rather than to don the blue. I find, on looking over the adjutant-general's report, that the town furnished twenty-nine more men than the quota. There were but two other towns, and two wards in the city of Concord, that furnished a larger number beyond their quota than did the town of Littleton. No other town in Coos or Grafton county furnished a larger number in proportion to its inhabitants. In 1860 less than 300 men were reported for military duty in the town of Littleton, yet 227 men, during the four years of the war, responded to their country's call, and did valiant service in the field. Still, the soldier is not entitled to all the honor in fighting the battles of his country. There is as much or more due the fathers and mothers, wives and sisters, who sent their sons, husbands, and brothers to fight for the preservation of this glorious Union; for mental suffering is said to be worse than physical suffering, and while those in active service were not free from mental suffering, those at home suffered continually, knowing full well that any mail might bring them tidings of a great battle fought, and some loved one left dead or wounded on the battlefield. But at last, on the banks of the Appomattox, the army of northern Virginia lays down its arms, and the great Rebellion is crushed. Nowhere in the world's history can there be found an instance of so large a number of men being so quickly disbanded and scattered throughout the length and breadth of the land, and taking up the implements of peace. They have literally turned their swords into plow-shares, and gone forth working for the prosperity of the country they have labored so hard to save: and never has the United States made such progress in the arts and sciences, in manufactures and wealth, as it has for the last nineteen years since the close of the Rebellion. Most of that great army of the North are getting on the shady side of fifty, and are constantly dropping away. And I bespeak for them the same kindly feeling you have always shown ; and I hope and trust that none of them will ever disgrace the name and record of a Union soldier.

The President said : I would say one thing further, and that is, that, upon the adjournment of the exercises at this stand, there are athletic sports to take place upon the adjoining field. Also, in the evening, there will be fire-works in and about this grove and plain. We will now listen to music by the Saranac band.

Upon motion of John Farr, Esq., a vote of thanks was tendered to the several speakers, and it was also voted that each speaker be requested to furnish the committee with a copy of his remarks, for future publication.

APPENDIX.

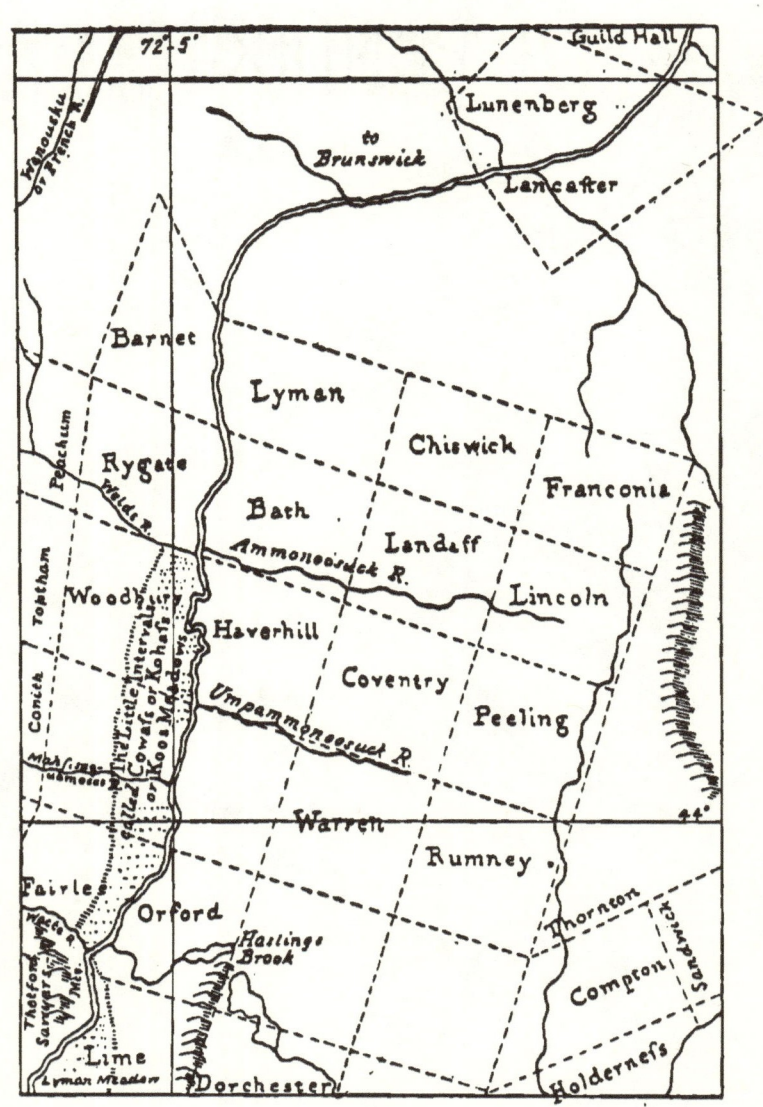

Copied from a map contained in an Atlas of
North America and the West Indies,
Engraved by Tho. Jeffery's,
        Geographer to His Majesty.
LONDON, 1768.

THE EARLY HISTORY AND GEOGRAPHY OF LITTLETON AND THE VICINITY.*

AN ADDRESS DELIVERED AT THE VESTRY OF THE CONGREGATIONAL CHURCH IN LITTLETON, DECEMBER 19, 1859, BY ADAMS MOORE, A.M., M.D.

A large portion of New Hampshire and Vermont was divided into townships by Benning Wentworth, who was governor of New Hampshire for a period of about 30 years. He went out of office in 1767. Nearly all the valley of Connecticut river, embracing two tiers of towns on each side, was granted by him to companies of men, consisting of about 60 members in each charter. In the short space of time between the years of 1760 and 1765, he granted some hundreds of townships in New Hampshire and Vermont, which was then regarded as a part of his colony, taking about $60 for each, or six shillings on each right, as fees for his private treasury.

This was done by the direction of the British government. When the British ministry decided to make the experiment of taxing the American Colonies to raise funds to meet the extraordinary expenditures of the king, George the Third, they directed the governors of the Colonies to make liberal grants of land to all citizens, who might apply for them. What Horace Greeley and the friends of a homestead law are now contending for, to give every man a farm out of the public domain, who will engage to cultivate it, was then done by the government, and is by no means a new idea.

---

*The map which accompanies this paper shows a township of Chiswick. It covers the present territory of Lisbon. That Chiswick is the one that was granted by mistake soon after the grant of Concord. Finding that the two grants would conflict, that of the first Chiswick was abandoned, and its proprietors were compensated by the grant of another tract by the same name—Chiswick—which was located on the river between Lyman and Lancaster, on the space which appears vacant on the map. As the second Chiswick—the predecessor of Apthorp—was granted in 1764, it would seem that the material for the original of this map was prepared several years before its publication.

The motive of the government, at that time, might have been really selfish. It might have been really a bribe to secure the good-will of the people. Governor Wentworth, accordingly, caused printed blank charters to be prepared, to be filled up with the names of from 60 to 70 individuals, to whom he gave a township of land.

These charters, in some respects, resembled a deed, with various conditions, or a lease, liable to be forfeited on failure to perform certain stipulations. The owners of these charters have always been regarded as corporations, although not declared by them to be so, allowed to hold meetings, have officers, raise money and keep records of their doings.

Governor Wentworth always reserved to himself, in each township, a tract of 500 acres, and located it in a specified corner of the town. If the town lay on the east side of the Connecticut river, the governor's lot was in the northwest or southwest corner; if on the west side of the river, it was in the northeast or southeast corner. These were very good locations for his excellency. In all the river towns he was sure of having his farm on the river, and his right often covered some of the finest meadow of the noble Connecticut. Some of them are now the most valuable farms in New Hampshire and Vermont. The one in Haverhill covered the ground of Woodsville. It was purchased by Col. Moses Little, who was the principal grantee of this town. It descended from him to his son, Moses, and remained in the family three-fourths of a century, and is now divided into three farms, besides the ground of the village.

The governor's right in Claremont is still entire. It was the homestead of the grandfather of James B. Sumner, descended to his son, David H. Sumner, and is very valuable. The right was not distinctly located in this town by the second charter, of which I shall hereafter speak, but was so by agreement, and is, much of it, still in a state of nature, covering the forest lands lying on the Connecticut river adjoining Dalton.

Certain *friends* of the governor were generally remembered, more or less of them, in all his charters. Among these, was one John Downing, Esq., of Newington, a little town adjoining Portsmouth. He was one of the governor's council, and, I suppose, the illustrious ancestor of Jack Downing, the politician. I had the misfortune to purchase his right in the town of Winlock, Vt., for a small sum, and got involved in a law suit with trespassers, which brought me to an intimate acquaintance with the Downing family, whose title I established. These charters commenced with the language of those times, when they spoke of any act of the King. It was as follows; "George the Third, by the Grace of God, of Great Britain, France and Ireland, King, Defender of the Faith, &c." Such phraseology has gone out of use in this republican country, and must have sometimes appeared absurd to British ears, when used in reference to such a creature as George the Third. To call such a man, Defender of the Faith, is as ridiculous as to call the kidnapper, defender of the rights of the negroes. But royalty, in its own dominions, must not be disrespectfully spoken of. A case, showing the extreme sensitiveness of British subjects, in regard to this matter of speaking disrespectfully of the *Sovereign*, occurred a few years ago. An uneducated citizen of this town was in Stanstead. The people were admiring the picture of Queen Victoria. One democratic Yankee, without due regard to polite language, looked at the portrait, and said : "She is a darned pretty looking creature." The subjects of royalty were shocked. The constable arrested the offender, marched him down to Montreal, and brought him before a magistrate, charging him with the use of the offensive language in reference to her sacred majesty. After due examination, the defendant disclaiming the use of the vulgar Yankee epithet, "darned," they paid him well and let him go as too raw a Jonathan to punish for vulgar language.

These townships were nominally six miles square, containing 23,000 acres, with an allowance of 1060 acres free, for highways and lands unimprovable by rocks, ponds, mountains and rivers. Many of them, in fact, very much exceeded these limits, by the courses and distances named in them, and the surveyor general allowed his deputies to make very large measure. The upper line of Dalton was, by the charter, but four miles long, and is actually four and a half.

There were certain provisions that were considered as privileges in those days, but have not been so considered by the subsequent inhabitants. One was, " that as soon as 50 families should be resident and settled in the town, they should have the privilege of holding two fairs each year." These fairs, as held in England and Ireland, in those times, and, I believe, to some extent now, are meetings at stated times and places for the purpose of traffic. I know of only one town in the state where they were ever established. That was Londonderry. The Scotch-Irish settlers of that town, from whom I claim my descent, regarded this provision as binding upon them, and, I think, it was enjoined in their charter as a duty. A fair used to be held a whole week in the month of October.

Many years ago, I attended one-half day. The trafficking was mainly in horses, too old, infirm, and vicious to be disposed of in any other way. Horse racing, betting, card and dice gambling, dancing and getting drunk, formed a large part of the performance, while auctioneering peddlers, and small shows of puppets and animals, were abundant. The whole matter was a great public nuisance, which I hope and trust has been entirely abolished.

Another provision in these charters, mentioned as a privilege, was, " that as soon as said town shall contain 50 families, a market may be opened and kept one or more days in a week, as may be thought most advantageous to the inhabitants." There were other things enjoined as duties. 1st. That every grantee or owner, shall plant and cultivate five acres of land, for every 50 acres of his share, and continue to improve and settle the same, within five years from the date of the charter, on penalty of the forfeiture of his share to the king, to be regranted to such person as will cultivate the same.

This was a very wise provision on the part of the governor at a time when men were talking politics very loudly, and denouncing the ministers of government. It would tend to insure the settlement of the towns, and to spread the population over the whole colony, instead of having them concentrated in only small parts, where they could the more readily unite in opposition to the measures of oppressive rulers.

Another provision was, that all white pine and other trees, suitable for masting the royal navy, be carefully preserved for that use, and none to be cut without the governor's permission, or special license. Another was:—Before a division of the town should be made, a tract of land, as near the centre of the town as practicable, should be laid out into house lots of one acre for each proprietor. This division was followed by the proprietors of Lancaster and Haverhill, but by no other town in this region, I think. Another provision was, that for the space of ten years from that date, every grantee was to pay to the governor, on the 25th of December, one ear of Indian corn, if demanded. A grand sight it must have been to see the citizens coming from all parts of the colony, each bearing an ear of corn, depositing it in the governor's granary, and wishing him a "merry Christmas."

The next was a more substantial provision: "Every proprietor, settler, or inhabitant shall yield and pay unto us, the governor, etc., yearly, and every year forever, one shilling for every one hundred acres he owns, and in that proportion for a less or greater quantity, which shall be paid in our council chamber in Portsmouth." This was called proclamation money. By this requisition, every town six miles square would pay annually to the governor about forty dollars. In the year 1760, Gen. Bailey made a survey of Connecticut river for the purpose of laying out the townships on each side of it. The original plan was, to lay them out six miles in a straight line up and down the river, on each side, and directly opposite each other.

In 1761 Haverhill was granted to Gen. Hazen *et al.;* from Haverhill, Mass., and Newbury, to Gen. Bailey *et al.*, from Newbury, Mass., on the opposite side of the river. These towns were long known as the Lower Cohos. (The Indian word *cohos*, or *cohas*, means crooked.) It was a name given to the lands lying on the Connecticut river, in this region, where the river crooks and forms the "Ox Bows" and other peninsulas. A similar crooked state exists at and above Lancaster. This was called the Upper Cohos. Colebrook has since sometimes been called the Cohos above the Upper Cohos.

The *h* has been dropped from the word, improperly, I think, as it leads strangers to a wrong pronunciation of it. I was once in company with a Boston gentleman who had a pocket map of New Hampshire for a guide. He inquired if we were in Kos county, very naturally supposing that C-o-o-s spelt Kos. If the *h* were retained, the true pronunciation would be plainly indicated.

Soon after, Haverhill, Bath, and Lyman were chartered on the east side of the Connecticut river, and, about the same time, the town of Guildhall on the west, and a town directly opposite on the east side of the Connecticut river, called Stonington. This place was called the Upper Cohos, and was regarded as a much more eligible location, on account of the extensive meadows, than the lands further down along the Fifteen-Miles falls, where we live. The lower corners of these towns on the river were fixed by the charters thirty miles in a straight line above the Ammonoosuc river's mouth, which is the upper point of the Lower Cohos.

The town of Lancaster was then chartered on the lower line of Stonington, its upper line running back seven miles, and its back line ten miles down, nearly parallel with the river. The lower line of Lancaster then was placed near the ground where Cushman's tavern, now in Dalton, stands, and its southeast corner near Round pond, in Whitefield. It covered about two thirds of Dalton, and covered very little good meadow land. Then there were two sets of grants, with a considerable tract as yet ungranted between them. It was not a very desirable portion of the country. It contained no meadow except what lay on Ammonoosuc river. In 1763 the township of Concord was granted, and planned so as to connect the two sets of grants, and cover some good meadows on the Ammonoosuc. To effect this purpose, the main body of the town was placed on the southeasterly line of Lyman, its southeasterly line running up to the southeasterly corner of Lancaster, then back at a very acute angle to near the mouth of the south branch, now in Lisbon, and then up to the northeast corner of Lyman. This long, narrow, triangular strip, ending in a sharp angle at the southeast corner of Lancaster, was called the Concord Gore—a term still used in Bethlehem. Between this Concord Gore and the Connecticut river was still a considerable piece of ungranted land.

On the 31st of January, 1764, the town of Landaff was granted, and on the same day a charter, named Chiswick, was given to James Avery of Connecticut, *et al.*, covering the present ground of Lisbon; but, about a month after, it was discovered that this charter was on land already granted to Concord proprietors. Avery and his associates therefore gave up the Concord land and took what lay between Concord Gore and the Connecticut river, and called this Chiswick. This is the origin of our town of Littleton. It was the last of these grants. Its want of extensive meadows, its rocky soil, and forests of pine gave it a very repulsive aspect.

Such was the appearance of all these towns, except those covering Cohos meadows. One of the first proprietors of Bath, it is said, came up to the mouth of the Ammonoosuc river, where he could find no meadows, but, instead, a large mountain, went back and reported that the whole town was not worth the charter fees of $60 due the governor.

I have already observed that Benning Wentworth retired from office in 1767. At that time the troubles between the colonies and the king were assuming a very formidable aspect. The governor had become old and feeble in health. He had also become quite wealthy. The regular salary, the fees taken for town charters, and the rights of land reserved for himself in each, had rolled up a great estate. He had no children to provide for, the cares of his office were burdensome and, in some respects, very annoying, and looked likely to become more so, and a prudent man must have been glad to transfer them to a younger and more vigorous person. He did so, and was succeeded by his nephew, John W. His fair consort was much younger than he. Tradition says that she was very fond of gay company, and did not much regard the nine o'clock bell in the evening, when abroad in agreeable society. His Excellency gently expostulated, requesting her to be a little more mindful of home at his hour of retirement. It is said she made light of the matter, replying only in smiles and jokes. After wasting much wholesome advice, with patient forbearance, the governor ruled that the door should be locked at a certain hour, at which time all sober people would be at home. The house stood near a large body of water, skirted with shady trees. At a late hour of the night Madam Wentworth came home and found the door locked. She rang, —no answer. Knocked,—no answer. She called for the servant to open it,—still no answer. She threatened, begged, and cried, but the door did not open. She, however, spied her lord peeping from the upper window watching the effect of his domestic remedy. In an apparent fit of distraction she ran down to the water and plunged in—something that was not herself—and disappeared. Her husband was horror-stricken, ran down stairs, opened the door, and hastened to save his beloved wife. While he was anxiously looking into the water, to see where she would rise and struggle, ready to plunge to the rescue, she slipped into the house and fastened him out. It then became his turn to sue for admission. The matter was finally settled by a promise on his part to interfere no more in her social pleasures, and Benning Wentworth, governor of New Hampshire as he was, after that time, himself, was under what I have sometimes heard called " petticoat government."

The country between the Connecticut river and Lake Champlain, being the whole of the present state of Vermont, was, for a considerable time, in dispute between the colony of New Hampshire and that of New York. The former claimed that their territory extended west to the lake; the latter, with equal firmness, claimed that theirs extended east to the river. The governors of each issued charters covering the same grounds. The present town of Waterford was chartered by B. Wentworth, and called Littleton.* The governor of New

---

* Dr. Moore was probably in error on this point. Littleton in Vermont was incorporated by act of the Vermont assembly.

York chartered it and called it Dunmore. I have seen both these names on old maps.

Governor Wentworth chartered the whole country west of the Green mountains, from the line of Massachusetts to Canada, and west to the lake, and to the east line of New York. Bennington was named by and for him, and was a place of some importance at the time of the Revolution. It gives name to an important battle, when Gen. Stark defeated the British, who were after some stores of provisions and ammunition lodged at that place. The battle was fought four miles beyond, and in the town of Hoosuc,—west of the state line.

The question of ownership was finally settled in England in favor of New York, before B. Wentworth went out of office. Extensive settlements had already been made by people from Connecticut, under the Wentworth charters. Being New Englanders, they sympathized with New Hampshire, from whom they took their land titles, and had the case been decided by the king in favor of New Hampshire, they would have gladly remained a part of that colony; but, rather than submit to New York, they set up a government of their own. The war with Great Britain coming on, favored them, and diverted the attention of New York to graver matters until the close.

After this, the New Yorkers renewed their claim to the lands, and flourished charters with the king's big seal. The Vermonters had lost all respect for kings, and cared but little for seals or law. Ethan Allen was the type of the race. They told the New Yorkers that they had charters from God Almighty, and would seal them with beech sticks well applied to the New Yorkers' backs if they did not keep away. A squatter sovereignty prevailed. New Hampshire did not really want Vermont. In a few years congress admitted them into the Union as an independent state, and in the courts the Benning Wentworth charters are treated as good and valid.

When John Wentworth came into office, he did so with a very popular reputation. The people regarded him as their friend—as he really was and had been. He had, as a private citizen of the kingdom, taken the side of the colonies against the odious stamp act, and had been active in procuring its repeal by the British parliament. By this act, the government required the people to pay a small tax for deeds of land, and for the paper on which a note to secure the payment of money was written; and all such papers must bear the king's stamp, otherwise they would be void and of no effect.

But when John Wentworth took the office of governor of New Hampshire, his position was changed. He was then the agent of the crown, sworn to execute and obey all the laws, right or wrong. What he could legally do to serve the interests of the people, he was eager to perform. He was the patron of Dartmouth College, which was founded by him in 1769. But the democratic opposition became too strong for him. His last official act was to dissolve the colonial legislature, and retire to the Isles of Shoals, whence he embarked, finally, for England. Some years after, somebody wrote him a letter of inquiry respecting a charter covering most of the town of Bethlehem, called "Lloyd Hills." It appears by the charter of Whitefield that that town was bounded on the southwest by a town with that name. Some person interested in land matters, and finding no record of it in the office of secretary of state, wrote to Gov. Wentworth, who, it appears, lived at a place in England called "Hammer-Smith." I have seen his answer, which, from sinister motives, was kept rather private, as it was a key to some land disputes, and, if seen, would operate against the parties holding it. It contained a plan of the town of Lloyd Hills—now Bethlehem. The Ammonoosuc river was laid down with great accuracy, the line between that town and this distinctly placed as crossing a certain bend in the river near Alderbrook mills, where the proprietors of this town have supposed it to be, but from which they have been crowded back this way about fifty rods. The survey purported to have been made in 1744, by Dudley Coleman, who had surveyed this town four years before.

The governor must have taken from this country a book of plans of all these townships, furnished him by the deputy surveyors of his time, which would unravel the snarls of many a lawsuit past, and, perhaps, to come.

When John Wentworth came into office, his predecessor had chartered all the best lands, but very little attention had been given to the provision in the charters for clearing and settling the towns.

One very important difference from the present location of the same, was that of the town of Lancaster, it then being several miles lower down the river. This was the location of it as granted by Benning Wentworth.

There was not a settler on Connecticut river above Haverhill and Newbury. As soon as the five years from the date of each charter expired, there was a rush made for a renewal, by the grantees, or for a new charter by a new set of land speculators, on the ground of a forfeiture for non-performance of conditions.

John W. was ready to grant their requests—more ready, perhaps, on account of liberal fees. Leonard Whiting, the grandfather of Geo. W. Whiting of Lisbon, was a man of substance and influence in those days, and he applied for and procured a charter for himself and others to cover the ground of Concord, leaving out the Gore and taking a small piece of Chiswick, and making a good shaped town, which is now called Lisbon, but they called it Gunthwaite. He took possession and proceeded to settle it.

David Page, one of the ancestral family of Gov. Page, was a proprietor of Lancaster. He explored the grant, and found that it did not cover the Cohos meadows to any great extent. Its upper line and upper corner on Connecticut river were a little above the great bend, where Col. White now lives, which was long known by the name of the Cat Bow. All the fine meadows above were in the town of Stonington. It is said that Mr. Page coveted these pine intervales. He probably, according to the notions of the times, supposed that the Stonington proprietors had forfeited them. He conceived the idea of covering them with the charter of Lancaster, without at all altering its language as to boundaries. Accordingly, he caused a survey of the town to be made, placing it about four miles further up the river, and covering most of the choice lands of Stonington. He then procured from Governor Wentworth a simple renewal of the charter of Lancaster. The Governor probably knew nothing of the change of location, nor the surveyor-general, as the survey was made by a deputy named Talford. Page and his associates took immediate possession, and proceeded to allot and settle the town. Immediately after this, the Messrs. Moses Little of Newbury and Newburyport, with Israel Morey of Orford, and Alexander Phelps of Connecticut, purchased of James Avery of Connecticut forty-two of the rights of Chiswick, which he had got from the original owners. There were about twenty more which could not be reached. Fifty-two was a sufficient majority.

Lancaster, by moving up the river on to Stonington, had vacated about 10,000 acres of land on each side of Johns river.

The Messrs. Little & Co. applied to one Col. John Hurd, who was one of Governor Wentworth's friends, to aid them in procuring a renewal of the charter of Chiswick. The owners suffered a forfeiture and surrender of it. A new charter was given to Messrs. Little & Co., covering the old ground of Chiswick, mainly, and the 10,000 acres abandoned by Lancaster. The new charter was named Apthorp, for George Apthorp, a London merchant, to whom was given a right of 400 acres, about which he never troubled himself to pay taxes, and it was bought in by Mr. Little.

Whether Col. Hurd worked for pay as an adviser of the governor, or not, does not very clearly appear, but as soon as the new charter of Apthorp was issued, the proprietors conveyed by quitclaim to him the 10,000 acres dropped by Lancaster for a mere nominal consideration. The outlines of the new town were run out by a deputy surveyor named Dudley Coleman, and the quantity certified by him to be 40,800 acres, and no more; but it really contained from 5,000 to 10,000 acres more. This charter was dated, January, 1770. The outlines were run in December, 1769, a month before. The marks made on the trees by the axe could be seen eighty years after, and, by cutting out the wood grown over them so grains could be counted in the chips, showed the exact age of the line.

A settlement of the town was begun in 1770 by a Mr. Caswell, who begun on the meadow, two miles below the village. His son, the first child born in the town, was named Apthorp, and now lives in Canada.

The Messrs. Little bought out Messrs. Morey and Phelps. Messrs. Dalton and Tracy, two gentlemen of Newburyport, purchased Col. Hurd's 10,000 acres lying on Johns river, and, also, 6,000 more of Messrs. Little, adjoining. This body of 16,000 acres was, by act of the legislature, incorporated into the town of Dalton, and the remainder of the old town of Apthorp was at the same time named Littleton. This was done in the year 1784, just after the close of the Revolutionary war.

In many of the towns, the second charters issued by John Wentworth caused great uneasiness and trouble, and, in some instances, lawsuits. The owners of the Benning Wentworth charters took the ground that they had not parted with nor lost their titles. That difficulty was prevented in this town by the previous purchase and surrender of the old Chiswick charter.

The proprietors of Lancaster, in the spirit of squatter sovereignty, which was ripe in those days, as well as these, had usurped the lands of Stonington. The Stoningtonites were not all disposed to submit passively to be rowed up Connecticut river in this summary manner, and threatened to come down upon the Lancastrians with the big gun of the law. The latter were alarmed, and addressed their prayers to the governor to confirm them in their present location, and to grant them an explanatory charter, as they called it. Their early records disappeared in their clerk's log cabin, which took fire and burned up one day. They, after the Revolution, prayed to the legislature, year after year, to relieve them from their embarrassing position; but it does not appear that they ever obtained any aid. The last heard of the matter was about 1790—more than twenty years after their location. The Stonington claim probably died of old age, as the Lancastrians and their grantees are now in the undisturbed possession of the Upper Cohos.

Some of the Stonington proprietors sold to a few individuals, who, with other persons, got the charter of Northumberland, with a provision that it was the successor of Stonington, and laid it on the upper line of Lancaster, thus acquiescing in the location of that town. By so doing, they crowded Woodbury up river, which started another quarrel. Woodbury was the original of Stratford. The matter of this dispute was referred to Governor Wentworth, as arbitrator between the parties, who decided that Northumberland should hold their position, but that Woodbury, as a compensation, should have their compliment on the river and large gore lying back of them, in addition, which makes their territory more than twice as large as that of any river town lying below them. Woodbury was crowded up on to Cockburn—the original of Columbia—and that to Colburn, which was the parent of Colebrook. As a compensation for going up river, they all got large additions to their easterly territory.

All the proprietors of Stonington were not proprietors in Northumberland, or agreeing to this new arrangement, and they were the persons who caused so much annoyance to the people of Lancaster. In all Benning Wentworth's charters there was a right for the first settled minister. The Rev. Mr. Willard, who was the first minister of Lancaster, had so much fear that the Stoningtonites would dispossess him of his farm, that he required a bond of indemnity of the town against such an event.

I have observed that John Wentworth founded Dartmouth College. He gave it a charter of the town of Landaff, regardless of the rights of the proprietors of the first charter. These men had a little more combativeness and distinctiveness than the Stoningtonites, and gave battle to the trustees of the college in good earnest. They contended that Governor Wentworth had no right to dispossess them of their lands and give them away to somebody else, for a breach of any condition named in their charters, without having that matter first ascertained by due process of law. In this view, they were sustained by the supreme court, and held their township. As a remuneration for the loss thus sustained by the college, the state gave them two large tracts of land, one on the upper line of Stewartstown, now called Clarksville, and the other lying east of it, on the line of Maine, in the valley of the Androscoggin river.

This Landaff decision upset the Gunthwaite charter, and that town retook the name of Concord, which it retained until June 14, 1824, when it was exchanged for Lisbon. Leonard Whiting and Jonas Minot, who had sold largely under the Gunthwaite charter, succeeded in buying in a good number of the Concord rights, and thus protected themselves against much loss. In fact, land in those days was of little value. As late as 1810, Samuel Minot of Bath sold 3,000 acres in the town of Whitefield for thirty dollars ($30).

I might spin out this account further, with reference to the doings of the inhabitants, or of the proprietors, in the matter of promoting its settlement and cultivation in an age scarce of provisions, destitute of roads, mills, and markets for their hard earned products; or state some of their many and hazardous chases of the deer, moose, and bears, on which they relied tor meat, in a great degree, for many years, and in which they sometimes became bewildered in the interminable forest, endangering, nearly, their lives; but I will drop the subject.

TABLE I.

Statement showing the Nativities of the Inhabitants of Littleton, N. H., according to the U. S. Census of 1880.

STATES.	Native. White	Native. Color'd	COUNTRIES.	Foreign Born.	RECAPITULATION.	
Arkansas,	1		Canada,	410	Native White,	2,432
California,	1		England,	33	Native Colored,	2
Connecticut,	5		France,	2		2,434
Illinois,	4		New Brunswick,	3	Foreign born,	502
Louisiana,	1		Nova Scotia,	6		
Maine,	74		Prussia,	4	Total Population,	2,936
Maryland,	1		Scotland,	6		
Massachusetts,	71		Spain,	1		
Mississippi,	6		Germany,	1		
Michigan,	4		Ireland,	36		
Minnesota,	1		Total,	502		
New Hampshire,	1841					
New Jersey,	1					
New York,	36					
North Carolina,	1	1				
Ohio,	1					
Pennsylvania,	5					
Rhode Island,	7					
Vermont,	370					
Virginia,	1	1				
Total,	2432	2				

TABLE II.

Productions of Agriculture in Littleton.

FROM CENSUS OF 1840.

Number of horses,	381
Number of cattle,	1,791
Number of sheep.	6,170
Cereal grain, bushels,	22,522
Potatoes, bushels,	38,203

FROM CENSUS OF 1880.

Acres of land tilled, including fallow and grass in rotation (whether pasture or meadow).	6,742
Permanent meadows, permanent pastures, orchards, vineyards,	11,205
Woodland and forest,	12,501
Other improved, including "old fields" not growing wood,	679
Farm values—of farms including land, fences, and buildings,	$609,750
Of farming implements and machinery,	$25,640
Of live stock,	$111,131
Fences—cost of building and repairing in 1879,	$5,360
Fertilizers—cost of amount purchased in 1879,	$1,222
Labor—amount paid for wages for farm labor during 1879, including value of board,	$22,670
Weeks hired labor in 1879 upon farm (and dairy), including housework,	$4,848
Productions—estimated value of all farm productions (sold, consumed, or on hand) for 1879,	$158,865
Grass lands—acres of acreage in 1879, mown,	6,307
" " " " not mown,	334
Products harvested in 1879:—	
Hay, tons of,	5,856
Clover seed, bushels of,	40
Grass seed, bushels of,	4
Horses of all ages on hand June 1, 1880.	499
Mules and asses of all ages on hand June 1, 1880,	—
Neat cattle and their products on hand June 1, 1880:—	
Working oxen,	264
Milch cows,	854
Other,	1,302
Movement, 1879, cattle of all ages:—	
Calves dropped,	787
Purchased,	525

Sold, living,	594
Slaughtered,	381
Died, strayed and stolen, and not recovered,	38
Milk sold or sent to butter and cheese factories in 1879, gallons of,	13,890
Butter made on the farm in 1879, lbs. of,	104,955
Cheese made on the farm in 1879, lbs. of,	4,405
Sheep on hand June 1, 1880,	3,088
Movement:—	
Lambs dropped,	1,588
Sheep and lambs:—	
Purchased,	1,413
Sold living,	1,502
Slaughtered,	1,215
Killed by dogs,	65
Died of disease,	166
Died of stress of weather,	1
Clip, spring, 1880, shorn and to be shorn:—	
Fleeces,	2,219
Weight, lbs.,	10,415
Swine on hand June 1, 1880,	489
Poultry on hand June 1, 1880, exclusive of spring hatching—barn-yard,	3,126
Other,	482
Eggs produced in 1879, dozens of,	21,792
Cereals:—	
Barley, 1879, acres,	20
" bushels,	481
Buck-wheat, 1879, acres,	77
" " bushels,	1,689
Indian corn, acres,	164
" bushels,	5,051
Oats, acres,	721
" bushels,	29,182
Rye, acres,	5
" bushels,	120
Wheat, acres,	170
" bushels,	3,356
Pulse:—	
Canada peas (dry), 1879, bushels of,	91
Beans (dry), 1879, bushels of,	455
Fiber—flax-straw, tons of,	2
Sugar:—	
Maple, 1879, lbs. of,	54,815
Molasses, 1879, gallons of,	248
Hops, acres,	18

Pounds,	275
Potatoes (Irish), 1879, acres,	243
Bushels,	33.676
Orchards, apple :—	
Acres,	151
Bearing trees,	6.706
Bushels,	751
Value (total) of orchard products of all kinds sold or consumed,	$1.985
Market gardens—value of produce sold in 1879,	$500
Bees, 1879—honey, lbs. of,	355
Wax, lbs. of,	33
Forest products :—	
Amount of wood cut in 1879, cords,	5.571
Value of all forest products, sold or consumed in 1879,	$18,265

Manufacturing Statistics.

The manufactures of the town of Littleton, according to the United States census of 1880, were as follows :—

Number of establishments,	33
Capital invested,	$258.450
Average number of male employes above 16 years of age,	238
Average number of female employes above 15 years of age,	73
Average number of children and youth employed,	1
Amount of wages paid,	$103.297
Cost of materials used,	$485,339
Value of product,	$786,196

ADDITIONS AND CORRECTIONS.

Page 6, for George H. Bellows read George S. Bellows; *p. 8*, for George L. Whittaker read George S. Whittaker; *p. 34*, for Hughbastis Neel read Hurbartus Neal: for comma in note after figure 10, substitute a period in punctuation; *p. 63*, for Alvah read Alba; *p. 86*, it should not be said of Col. Tilton that he is prominently identified with glove industries otherwise than that he is a large owner of real estate occupied by those industries; *p. 89*, for H. H. Kinnerson read A. H. Kenerson; for Calvin Cate read Calvin F. Cate; for Chamberlain read Chamberlin; *p. 91*, for Evarts G. Worcester read Evarts Worcester; *p. 98*, for John L. Harriman read James L. Harriman; *p. 123*, for Litska read Zeitska; the passage "Peter Bonney, the first representative from Littleton in the General Court," should not be read as meaning that the town had not been represented by its own residents before this period elected by the class of towns, with which the town was associated for purposes of representation; *p. 133*, for 1700 read 1770 in fourth line of the address on the Profession of Medicine; *p. 153*, for Newburyport read Newbury; *p. 154*, for Newburyport read Newbury; *p. 157*, for Nancy J. Eile read Nancy J. Gile; *p. 166*, in sketch of Geo. R. Bugbee for 1871, read 1881; *p. 169*, in the sixteenth line, a comma should be placed after the name Burns, and not after the name Winch; *p. 170*, add to list of practitioners abroad, who were of Littleton, the name of E. Carleton, M.D., New York City, son of Edward Carleton, Esq.; *p. 173*, for Abel Bugbee read Abel G. Bugbee; *p. 174*, for Robert Whittaker read Robert H. Whittaker; *p. 200*, line 6, for attention read attrition; last line but one, for location read vocation; *p. 202*, line one, for bound read bounded; *p. 210*, for Ezra Hall read Ezra Hale; *p. 238*, for —— Miner read Salmon G. Miner; *p.p, 240, 241*, for George H. Whittaker read George S. Whittaker; *p. 268*, for James B. Smalley read James H. Smalley; *p. 308*, for 1744 read 1774.

INDEX.

INDEX

INDEX.

A

Abbey, C. C., ... 156
   Solomon, ... 157
Abbott, G., ... 174
   G. F., ... 174
   Edwin, ... 265
   Isaac, ... 51, 234
Abenaquis, ... 33
Adams, John C., ...
Addresses, President's, . . 13
Additions and Corrections, . 318
   Centennial, Rankin, . 14
   Agriculture, Lyford, . 223
   Education, Dame, . . 205
   Geography of Littleton, Moore, 299
   Law, Aldrich, . . 126
   Littleton and the State, Batchellor, ... 32
   Littleton and Bethlehem, Sinclair, ... 72
   Littleton and Vermont, Eastman, ... 77
   Littleton Abroad, Page, . 199
   Littleton in War of the Rebellion, Farr, . . . 292
   Manufactures, Remich, . 232
   Medicine, Tuttle, . . 133
   Merchants, Bellows, . . 242
   Newspapers, Metcalf, . 102
   Pioneers, Jackson, . . 58
   Town and Railroads, Mitchell, 259
   Women of Littleton, Millen, 276
Agriculture, ... 223, 315
Ainsworth, Americus, . . 149
   Calvin, . . . 128, 149, 201
   Dr. Calvin, . . 147, 148, 151
   Edward, ... 148
   Laban, ... 148, 149
   Susannah, ... 149
   Sybil P., ... 149
Albee, C. L., ... 68
   Frank, ... 6
   Joseph, ... 9
Aldrich, Edgar, . . . 8, 126, 131
   G. H., ... 239, 240
Alexander, Anson, . . . 195
   Eldad, ... 171, 172
Allen, Mrs. Abijah, . . . 100
   Ethan, ... 307
Andrews, H. M., . . . 196
Applebee, Ellen M., . . . 281
   Nathan, ... 208
   Warren, ... 197
Apthorp, . . 6, 33, 36-45, 60, 65, 67
   George, ... 60, 310
Arnold, Abigail, . . . 121
   E. R., ... 156
   Jonathan, ... 121
Atkins, Hiram, ... 116

Atkinson, J. P., ... 198
Atwood, M. G., ... 120
   S. W., ... 174, 256
Avery, James, . . . 58, 59, 305, 310
   Ephraim, ... 62, 69

B

Bailey, Jacob, . . . 41, 62, 139, 303
   James, ... 39
   William, ... 107, 254
Balch, John W., . . . 248, 249, 253
   Sylvanus, . . . 100, 236, 253
Barker, Albert, ... 119
   Mary, ... 159
   T. A., ... 266
Barnes, G. S., ... 92, 194
Barney, J. W., ... 115
Barret, J. J., ... 214
   Mrs. J. J., ... 94
Bartlett, E. J., ... 143
   G. E., ... 35
Bass, Van N., ... 108-110
Batchellor, A. S., . 6, 7, 10, 32, 94, 105, 131
   Jennette C., ... 152
   Mrs., ... 94
Batchelder, G. F., . . . 248, 256
   Otis, . . . 99, 235, 248, 249, 256
   Mrs. Otis, ... 279
Bath, . . 38, 41, 48, 52, 53, 60, 67, 70
Baxter, Lewis, ... 268
Bean, J. W., ... 194
Beane, Samuel, ... 192
Beebe, George, ... 182, 194
   Minnie, ... 219
Bedel, Timothy, . . 38, 41, 44, 62, 65, 145
Bellows, G. S., . . . 6, 8, 239, 255
   H. A., . . 53, 92, 93, 99, 103, 127
   John A., ... 197
   Josiah, ... 249
   Major, ... 53
   W. H., ... 239, 255
   W. J., 5, 6, 8, 85, 93, 107, 113, 114, 128, 198, 214, 242, 253, 255, 262.
Bemis, Lieutenant, . . . 204
Benton, R. C., ... 210
Bethlehem, . . . 35, 48, 70, 72-76
Bickford, J. M., ... 106
   Joseph, ... 210
Bingham, A. W., ... 257
   Captain, ... 53
   G. A., 7, 9, 10, 55, 95, 99, 107, 131, 132, 214, 257.
   Mrs. G. A., ... 288
   Hannah, ... 60
   Harry, 5, 6, 8, 95, 99, 104, 107, 130-132, 214, 267, 276.
Bishop, H. D., ... 9
   R. M., ... 63
   Samuel, ... 63

Blanchard, Enoch, 172
Blodgett, Jeremiah, 266
Bolles, C. W., 130, 177
Bond, Aaron, 169
Bonney, B. W., 130, 201, 283
  Maria, 202
  Peter, 123, 130, 207, 210, 235, 283
Bowles, Frank, 8
  M. A., 240
Bowman, A. H., 7, 177
  C. C., 234
  E. M., 105
  John, 234
Brackett, Aaron, 99, 243, 246, 253
  C., 263
  C. W., 253
  Cephas, 9, 175, 246
  Major F. R. T., 53
  Sewell, 99, 235
  Susie, 210
  William, 99, 243-246, 250-254
  W. C., 243
  W. R., 268
Bray, Nicholas, 195
Brickett, Harry, 169, 182, 210
  Thomas, 137
Bridge, J. D., 119
Bronson, Mrs, 94
Brooks, 9
Brown, E. J., 166
Brownlow, J. S., 257
Bryant, G. N., 194
Buck, Horace, 99
Bugbee, Abel G., 173
  Frank, 169, 173
  G. R., 159, 165, 169, 173
  Lafayette, 169, 173
  Ralph, 97, 159, 165, 172, 173
  Ralph, Jr., 159, 172
Burkley, Elder, 193
Burleigh, C. M., 268
Burnham, F. J., 215
  H. B., 9, 239
Burns, William, 128, 149, 150, 152, 155, 165, 169, 171, 179, 180, 219.
Burton, Lorenzo, 265

C

Calhoun, Clementine, 210
  Isaac, 254
  James, 209
  Luella, 210
  Mary, 210
  Sarah, 210
Carding mill, 236
Cargill, Dr., 172
Carey, C. E., 114-116
Carleton, B. G., 169
  Dwight, 210
  Edmund, 51, 128
Carleton, E., M.D., 170
  Thomas, 241
Carpenter, Asa, 192
  E. L., 193
  E. I., 53, 91, 105, 153, 187
  Mrs. H. S., 279
Carriage factory, 237
Carroll, James, 87
Carter, A. B., 179
  Truman, 194, 197
  W. H., 137
Caswell, 9, 21, 40, 41, 44, 134

Caswell, Alba, 9
  Alice, 63
  Alvah, [Alba] 63
  Andrew, 60
  Apthorp, 61, 63, 311
  Charlotte, 62
  Daniel, 63
  Elizabeth, 63
  Erastus, 63
  Ezra, 60
  Jedediah, 63
  John, 63
  Nathan, 42, 60, 61, 62
  Nathan, Jr., 60-64
  Ozias, 60, 62, 64
Cate, Benjamin, 89
  Calvin F., 89
Cemetery corporation, 279
Census, 1880, 314
Chadwick, A. G., 103
Chair factory, 239
Chamberlain, Abiel, 141
  A. R., 169
  H. E., 89, 267, 268
  J. E., 89, 264
Chandler, W. H., 198, 239
Charlton, John M., 67
  Misses, 210
  Robert, 67, 209, 210, 219
  Walter, 210
Chase, C. P., 8
  C. M., 116
  D. F., 7
  John, 69
Cheney, E. H., 114, 120
Chiswick, 33, 35, 58-60, 68, 77, 299
Churchill, L. D., 108, 109
Churches, 187, 204
  Advent, 197
  Baptist, 195
  Calvinist, 195
  Congregational, 192
  Episcopal, 196
  Liberal Christian, 198
  Methodist, 193
  Romanist, 194
  Unitarian, 196, 198
  Universalist, 198
  Y. M. C. Association, 197
Church John, 268
Chutter, F. G., 198
Clark, A. W., 157, 171
  G. A., 158
  Israel J., 169
  John, 39
  Mary L., 119
  Morris, 262
Clay, Charles, 241
  Sherared, 241
Clement, William, 268
Cleveland, Elisha, 39
  John, 266
Clough, J. M., 266
  J. T., 266
Cobb, Misses, 210
Cobleigh's meadow, 53
Cobleigh, N. E., 122, 197, 201
  N. F., 192
  Ward, 226
Coburn, C. R., 7
  Joseph, 264
Cofran, Mrs. Frank, 219
Cohos, 303

Colby, Ethan,	86
John,	195
Cole, Lizzie C.,	197, 202
Mrs. R. M.,	282
Stephen,	172
Coleman, Dudley,	308, 310
Collins, L. E.,	8
Conant, Ellen H.,	155
Concord Gore,	35, 305
Cook, Quinton,	80
Corning, B. H.,	6, 264
Corrections and Additions,	318
Couillard, E.,	118
Cowing, C.,	194
Crane, W. A.,	7
Crosby, A. B.,	178
Dixi,	161
W. S.,	166
Cummings, E. G.,	176
E. K.,	170
H. A.,	265, 268
Curl, G. M.,	7, 11, 194, 198
Currier, John,	92, 194
Sargent,	68
Curtis, Ephraim,	237, 243, 250
R. H.,	236
Cushman, Clara M.,	282
Ebenezer,	236
Gustavus,	209
Horace,	9, 160
L. P.,	92, 194, 282
Lizzie,	219
Mary E.,	160
Parker,	209
T. T.,	163, 180
Cutter, L. F.,	121

D

Dalton,	35, 44, 47, 48
Dame, Dana P.,	5, 8, 205, 218
Danforth, Silvia,	120
Darling, C. B.,	158, 161
Dartmouth, (Jefferson),	41, 48, 312
Davis, J. L.,	268
Noah,	121
Lieutenant,	204
William,	111, 112
Day, Angle,	210
C. P.,	257
J. R.,	194
Dean, Edward,	148
Dennison, Avery,	68
Desire,	68
W. B.,	89
Dentistry,	175
Dewey Guards,	280
H. K.,	210, 280
Robert, Jr.,	268
Dimick, J. E.,	267, 268
Dinsmore, Freedom,	172
Diphtheria,	184
Doctors,	133–186
Dodge, J. A.,	264
Dow, A. F.,	255
L. T.,	238, 255
James,	255
J. E.,	127
Moses,	127
Moses A.,	120, 127, 201, 214
R. M.,	255
Downing, John,	301
Dresden,	39
Drew, A. E.,	196
Francis,	79
Dunbar, Dr.,	169
Dunklee, Peter,	265
Dysentery,	185

E

Eames, Jeremiah,	41, 42
Eastman, Azra,	9
Abiel,	17
Ebenezer,	85, 103, 255, 262
C. F.,	5, 10, 84, 86, 241, 257
Mrs. C. F.,	83
Cyrus,	6, 9, 53, 86, 99, 104, 214, 238, 257, 265
F. J.,	5, 8, 77, 85, 86, 99, 124, 214, 242, 263
Mrs. F. J.,	100
Francis A.,	103, 107, 109, 201
Mrs. E.,	100
Jonathan,	69, 233, 235
George, W.,	266
G. W.,	268
L. L.,	194
Mrs. L. A.,	104
Miss Mattie,	105, 255
Stephen A.,	103
Eaton, Charles,	254
G. C.,	268
E. Augusta,	167
H. A.,	8
Edson, Timothy,	100
F. A.,	236
S. A.,	235
Education,	205
English, F. H.,	8
Fred,	87, 254
Elie, Nancy J., [Gile]	157
Ely, G. W.,	248
Emery, Ira,	196
Erysipelas,	185
Estabrook, Miss F. T.,	115
Eudy, L. M.,	163, 171
William, F.,	163

F

Fairs,	302
Fairbanks, Drury,	91, 192
Farnham, Walter,	265, 268
Farr, A. B.,	202
C. A.,	255
Caroline,	168
Edwin L.,	169
Evarts W.,	90, 130, 203
George,	6, 7, 10, 11, 203, 214, 324, 292
H. H.,	8
Hannah B.,	210
John,	9, 93, 105, 129, 168, 173, 253, 255, 295
Mrs. John,	280
Lena A.,	179
Nelson C.,	253, 254, 256
Noah,	59, 235
Philander,	188
T. A.,	204
Felton, N. B.,	216
Ferguson, David,	268
Finnegan, J. P.,	195
Fisher, E. P.,	268
O. M.,	256
Fitch, Elijah,	47, 207, 208

Fitzgerald, Al,	239
Michael,	234
Flint, E.,	255
Foundry,	236
Forts, Gunthwaite,	61
Northumberland,	61
Foster, John L.,	130
Franconia Wares,	79
French, Annie,	219
Frye, J. S.,	89
Fuller, G. W.,	127
Furber, Geo. C.,	6, 8, 89, 119
Mrs. H. M.,	218
Miss M. E.,	218

G

Gaskell, Lieutenant,	204
Gates, Curtis,	89, 174, 235
Ezra,	89, 235
Horace,	235
Lucretia W.,	163
Geography of Littleton,	299
Genereaux, L. A.,	167
Gibbs, J. L.,	80, 82, 83, 175
S. C.,	80, 82
Gibson, W. F.,	219
Gile, Aaron,	238
F. W.,	107, 124, 248, 253
John,	197, 235, 236, 239
Nancy J.,	157
R. T.,	8, 11
Timothy,	235
Gilford, Elijah,	196
Glenwood Cemetery,	279
Glynville Library,	127
Goddard, E. M.,	146
Goodall, Mrs. Alpha,	100
David G.,	262
David,	48, 49, 69, 130, 192, 207, 219
David, Jr.,	69, 99
F. A.,	8
Ira,	69, 130, 262
Solomon,	69, 209
Goodenough, J. C.,	99
Goodrich, J. B.,	196
Goodwin, Charles,	9
C. M.,	35
Samuel,	203
S. G.,	266
Goold, M. L.,	85, 119, 253, 254
Goold, Luella,	281
P. R.,	113, 119
Goss, H. L.,	99
S. W.,	120
Granger, N. M. D.,	92, 194
Grant, Miles,	197
Grants, towns,	303
Graves, A. R.,	196
Green, C. H.,	90
Charles,	268
Daniel,	268
H. F.,	6, 99, 254
Lieutenant,	204
Greenleaf, Harvey,	266
Seth,	265, 268
Grist mills,	235
Groton, Conn.,	67, 68
Gunthwaite (Lisbon),	40. 60, 77

H

Hadley, Georgiana A.,	281
J. L.,	83, 264, 267
Hadley, William,	210
W. A.,	193
Hale, E. J. M.,	85, 88, 236, 263
Ezra,	210
James,	236, 237
J. W.,	236
Otis G.,	6, 127, 238
Stephen,	79
Hall, Daniel,	106
E. F.,	240
Ezra, [Hale]	210
E. L.,	174
Hardy, Mary Jane,	163
N. K.,	192
Harriman, James L.,	98, 160, 171
John L., [James L.]	98
J. A.,	268
M. F.,	6
Harrington, C. E.,	214
Hartshorn, Charles,	83, 238
Mrs. Charles,	280, 288
Hazeltine, A. A.,	176
Lieutenant,	204
Enoch,	87, 239
Frederick,	87, 239
Haskins, W. A.,	6, 90, 286
Hastings, Fatima,	157
Hat factory,	238
Hatch, Ansel,	209, 210
F. B.,	174
J. K.,	268
P. C.,	6, 89
Haynes, H. H.,	198
Hazen, Moses,	235, 303
Haverhill,	36, 38–40, 47, 52, 53, 59, 66–70, 127
Heath, B. F.,	7
Health, Boards of,	177
Herrin, John,	88, 236
Hewes, A. F.,	194
Heywood, William,	210
Highways,	46
Hinds, Elisha,	127
Hines, O. M.,	268
Hitchcock, Luke,	69
Hodge, Ida,	235
John,	235
Hodgman, Charles,	252
F. F.,	252
Francis,	174, 252
Holt, Daniel,	51
Hohman, E. C.,	198
Sullivan,	92, 194
Holmes, Ariel,	87
Mrs. Ariel,	94
J. C.,	268
Hollis,	58
Hopkinson,	41, 63, 65
Caleb,	64–66
David,	64, 65, 144
John,	64, 65
Jonathan,	63, 64, 144
Jonathan, Jr.,	64, 65
Hoskins, E. B.,	176
Hosmer, Jefferson,	236
Houghton, Elizabeth T.,	121
Howe, Susannah,	149
Hoyt, Geo. W.,	266
Hughes, Roxanna,	163
Hurd, Colonel John,	59, 310, 311
Hutchins, F. D.,	216

I

Ide, Joseph,	7
Invocation,	11

J

Jackson, Andrew,	94
James,	242
James R.,	6, 7, 10, 57, 94, 177, 214
Jennie M., [Mary J.]	281
Julia,	94
Mary J.,	94
William,	9, 117
William, Jr.,	94
James, Charles,	268
Jewett, Dr.,	172
Luther,	174
Johnson, H. A.,	6, 8
J. G.,	194
S. B.,	51
Jones, G. C.,	196
S. E.,	35
Judkins, Hiram,	268

K

Kelly, Dr.,	172
Kelsea, G. S.,	169
Kelsey, H. L.,	92, 194
Kenerson, A. H.,	8, 9, 217
Kenney, Mrs. E. O.,	94
Kent, Jacob,	138
J. G.,	196, 198
Kilburn, Addie,	119
B. W.,	10, 236, 239
Edward,	119, 237
Josiah,	9, 236, 244
Lieutenant,	204
King, Ben.,	80
J. E.,	194
Kingman, Si,	265
Kinne, Nathan,	99
Kinnerson, H. H., [A. H. Kenerson]	89
Kneeland, Ianthe C.,	161
Knight, Jonathan,	171
Knox, M. V. B.,	198

L

Ladd, John J.,	89, 215
Lancaster,	34-40, 48, 52, 53, 58, 64
Lane, G. F.,	8
Landaff,	38, 48, 63
Langdon, J. F.,	266, 268
Laplante, L. M.,	195
Larned, Abijah,	36, 37, 41
Larnard, Samuel, Jr.,	234, 242
Learned, G. L.,	36
Lawyers,	126-142
Leavitt, D. P.,	194
Leavens, Penuel,	236
Lee, Jesse,	191
Lottie,	219
Leonards,	69
Lewis, Asa,	191, 234, 235
Libbey, H. C.,	241
Lindsey, David,	69
Emma E.,	106
Susan T.,	110
Little, G. W.,	266, 268
George,	247, 251
Lou. M.,	102
Little, Col. Moses of Newbury,	6, 59, 153, 247, 300, 310
Moses of Newburyport,	6, 39
Moses Jr. of Newbury,	68, 181, 233, 300
Lloyd Hills,	308
Lord, John,	191
Lovejoy, G. E.,	8, 254
William,	195
Loveland, J. S.,	194
Lyford, F. H.,	8, 10, 196, 198, 223
Lyman, Eliphalet,	179
Lyman,	34, 35, 38, 40, 48, 68, 70
Lyon, J. E.,	264
J. W.,	268

M

Mac Donald, Julia A.,	116
Mann, E. B.,	268
E. F.,	267, 268
Jesse,	266
Solomon,	234, 235
Manufactories,	232, 317
Carriages,	237
Chairs,	239
Furniture,	240
Gloves,	236, 240, 241
Hats,	238
Iron,	236
Leather,	235
Lumber,	233, 241
Potash,	237, 243
Scythes,	238
Sash and blinds,	239
Starch,	238
Stereoscopic views,	239
Textile fabrics,	236
Tools,	239
Underwear,	240
Map,	295
Marble, D. P.,	121
Marsh, Sylvester,	269
Martin, William,	268
Mattocks, C. P.,	86
Henry,	86
McDole, Thomas,	172
McDuffee, John,	34
McGregor, G. W.,	167, 170, 177
McGregory, W. A.,	167
McIntire, Frank,	245
H. H.,	218
H. E.,	170
Warren,	5, 170, 209
McKeen, Dr.,	34
McLaughlin, G. A.,	194
Mead, Mrs. A. K.,	282
H. B.,	197
Merchants,	242
Merrill, John,	9, 256
J. W.,	237
Henry,	240, 256
Merrimack,	150
Meserve, Clara,	219
Hattie D.,	118
Metcalf, H. H.,	8, 102, 115, 116, 198
H. B.,	117
E. B.,	117
Laura P.,	117
Miles, Abner,	172
Millen, C. W.,	276
John,	207
Josie,	210

Millen, David,	9
C. E.,	5
C. W.,	124, 182, 197
Miller, Anderson,	89
A. G.,	218
Chas. R.,	172
Milliken, C. E.,	193, 219, 212
George,	235
Sylvanus,	235
Mills,	233
Minard, Burton,	196
Miner, Salmon G.,	238
Isaac,	9, 67
Robert,	240
Thomas,	67, 70, 190
William,	68
Minot, George,	263
Jonas,	313
Samuel,	313
Mitchell, J. M.,	5, 8, 129, 259
W. H.,	6, 7, 12, 94, 131, 177
Alden,	9, 53, 164
Moffett, Frank T.,	6, 164, 170, 171, 177, 247
Susan,	210
Moore, Adams,	5, 34, 42, 59, 148–152, 155, 156, 165, 169, 171, 180, 185
Anna M.,	154
Elizabeth,	281
Elizabeth A.,	154
Hannah,	278
Isabella M.,	154
Isaac,	136, 145
James W.,	154, 169
Maria L.,	154
William,	152, 268
W. A.,	154, 203
Morey, Israel,	6, 40, 41, 59, 60, 310
Morris, Sarah,	113
Morrison, C. L.,	266
J. B.,	198
M. F.,	172
Morse, Helen,	281
Joseph,	207
Robert,	264
J. W.,	69
Moulton, E. P.,	196
F. P.,	217
G. G.,	9
G. V.,	268
Luthera,	156
Mowry, William,	216

N

Nash, Samuel,	145
Nashua,	81
Neal, Hubartus,	34
Nelson, Robert,	90, 268
Newell, Dr.,	172
Newhall, Josiah,	191
New Ipswich,	149
Newspapers, Ammonoosuc Reporter,	104
Ammonoosuc Valley Argus,	118
Caledonian,	103
Granite State Whig,	103
Littleton Argus,	118
Littleton Gazette,	114
Littleton Journal,	119
People's Journal,	110
White Mountain Banner,	109
White Mountain Republic,	115
New York controversy,	306

Noiseaux, I. H.,	195, 198
Northumberland,	36, 40, 41, 61, 64
Northwood,	49
Norwich, Vt.,	58, 60
Nurse, John,	69, 207
Jonas,	69, 207
S. P.,	237

O

Orford,	40, 59, 60
Osgood, G. W.,	193, 198
Ouvrand, P. F.,	8, 256
Stephen,	256

P

Paddleford, G. K.,	174
Peter,	88
Page, B. F.,	168
David,	309
S. B.,	8, 131, 168, 199, 210
Palmer,	69
Brooks,	265, 268
Joseph,	208
Parker, E. B.,	115
Albert,	174
Ezra B.,	204
Ezra,	204
Charles,	210, 241
H. M.,	89
Ira,	6, 236, 240, 241
James,	236
N. K.,	169
Nelson,	240
Silas,	236
T. L.	9
Parks, Isabel,	219
Patterson, Daniel,	267
Patrons of Husbandry,	230
Peabody, Misses,	210
Richard,	209
R. W.,	9
Peavey, J. S.,	118
Peck, Isaac,	198
Petticoat government,	306
Pharmacy,	173
Phelps,	6
Alexander,	310
Fred.,	169
Pierce, Samuel,	63
Pingree,	69
E. M.,	122, 197, 203
G. E.,	123, 204
Joseph,	122
Place, Mary,	156
Plaistow,	137
Pollard, M. C.,	35
Postmaster, First,	69, 127
Potash,	237
Powers, Keziah,	67
Peter,	33, 34, 58, 138
Presby, J. W.,	197
Programme,	7
Prouty, Emily L.,	116

Q

Quimby, A. H.,	91, 268
Alden,	7, 204
Daniel,	237
Lieutenant,	237
S. E.,	194

R

Railroads, - 52, 259
   Ammonoosuc Valley, - 262
   Atlantic & St. Lawrence, 262, 268
   Boston, Concord & Montreal, 261
   Boston & Ontario, - 261
   Connecticut River & Montreal, 264
   Mount Washington, - 269
   Portland & Connecticut River, 264
   Portland & Ogdensburg, - 271
   White Mountains, - 262, 269
   White Mountains (N H.) Railroad, - 263
Rand, C. W., 107, 129, 177, 198, 214, 267
   Mrs. C. W., - 198, 288
   E. D., - 129
   Hamlin, - 234
Ranlet, N. W., - 237, 243
Rankin, Elizabeth, - 197, 202
   Andrew, - 191, 197, 207
   David, - 50, 53, 234, 235
   James, 46, 48, 48, 68, 71, 190, 234, 235
   James, Jr., - 193
   J. E., - 7, 14
   Melinda, - 209, 212, 284
   Samuel, - 207
Ready, John, - 239
Redington, G. B., 9, 88, 238, 248, 249, 267
   H. C., - 238, 240, 248, 250
Reed, B. T., - 263
Remich, D. C., - 6, 8, 94, 131, 232
Representatives, classed, - 36, 38
   List of, - 47
Revolutionary War, - 42, 64
Richardson, David, - 236
   G. W., - 6, 206
   Luther, - 62, 65
   M. H., - 8
   Nathaniel, - 53, 99
   Rennie, - 204
   W. A., - 83, 99
Roble or Roby, Joseph, - 236, 243
Robins, Douglas, - 207, 208
   Joseph, - 208
   J. E., - 8, 187, 197
   Joseph, Jr., - 183
   Thomas, - 268
   W. F., - 6, 174, 257
Robinson, Mrs. A. L., - 94
   B. F., - 8, 119, 217
   F. A., - 6, 177
Rogers, G. O., - 176
   Robert, - 58
Rollins, W. M., - 268
Ross, Carrie, - 219
   H. P., - 266, 268
   J. S., - 169, 170
   Smith, - 209
Rounsevel, R. D., - 253
Rowell, Clinton, - 131
   Dennison, - 124
   H. W., - 88, 110, 124
   J. H., - 7
   L. W., - 114
   Richard, - 172
Ruland, G. W., - 194
Russ, J. S., - 265, 268
Russell, L. A., - 80, 237
   Rev. Mr., - 193

S

Sabine, E. R., - 192
Sabine, S. A., - 174, 175, 176
Sanborn, Benjah, - 172
   D. P., - 239
   H. E., - 268
   J. R., - 265, 268
   L. D., - 198
Sanders, Marshall, - 90, 203
Sanger, Ezra, - 160
   T. E., - 97, 160, 169
Sargent, John, - 177, 209
   Levi, - 262
Sash and blind factory, - 239
Sawyer, S. C., - 176
Saw mills, - 233
Scarlatina, - 184
Schools, - 205-222
School District, Union, - 213
Scott, C. W., - 158
   G. R. W., - 121
   M. L., - 158
   Nathan, - 158
   N. H., - 169
Scythe factory, - 238
Simpson, C. H., - 268
   Henry, - 268
   John F., - 7
Sinclair, Asa, - 265, 268
   C. A., - 235
   J. G., - 7, 72, 104
Smalley, J. H., - 268
   Small-pox, - 146, 164, 182
Smillie, Dr., - 169
   John, - 89, 177, 256
Smith, B. H., - 195
   C. C., - 87, 177, 198, 256
   H. B., - 87, 99, 256
   Miss M. A., - 124
   N. G., - 89
   W. M., - 176
Southworth, H. H., - 254
Spotted fever, - 183
Stanley, Abner, - 147, 150
Starch factory, - 238
Stark, John, - 33, 65
Steamboats, - 260, 261
Steere, Russell, - 233
Stevens, E. C., - 6, 131, 177
   J. M., - 268
   Truman, - 9, 80, 88, 252, 255
   Mrs. Truman, - 100
   W. H., - 89
Stinchfield, J. P., - 194
Stocker, G. K., - 6, 87
Stoddard, - 171
Stonington, - 35, 310, 311
Stowell, W. A., - 268
Streeter, Geo., - 210
Sumner, J. B., - 169, 300
   D. H., - 300
Sutherland, David, - 48, 147

T

Taft, Dennison, - 82
   Richard, - 81-83
Tannery, - 235
Tarbell, C. D., - 254
Taxation, - 43, 44
Taylor, Miss A. B., - 112
   Charles, - 254
   W. M., - 177
Temple, Jonas, - 209
Thayer, D. E., - 87
   Mrs. D. E., - 100

Thayer, Mrs. E.,	280
Frank,	6, 80
H. L.,	6, 80, 107, 175, 255
Major,	53
Thompson, C. E.,	170
M. S.,	170
Tifft, Phebe J.,	159
Tilton, F. A.,	255
Frank,	85
Franklin,	214, 255
G. H.,	8
Henry L.,	6, 86, 99, 214, 253
Mrs. H. L.,	288
J. F.,	255
Joseph,	84
Tool factory,	239
Towle, G. S.,	103
Town Organization,	42, 44
Towne, Francis,	169, 171
L. B.,	35
Tracy,	6
Trudell, F. X.	195
Tuttle, A. M.,	156, 169
Alice L.,	156
C. M.,	8, 95, 96, 97, 107, 132, 156, 164, 169, 171, 176, 177, 180
Mrs., C. M.,	100
Horatio,	156
Lizzie A.	156
Betsey Thomas,	156
Mary S.,	156
Jennie H.,	156
John,	156
Socrates,	156

V

Vermont Controversy,	39–42
Votes for Governor, etc.,	49–52

W

Wallace, C. J.,	236
Dennis,	117, 255
Walton, Mrs. E. M.,	123, 210, 283
Wardwell, J. M.,	268
Warner, E. M.,	130
Waterman, G. C.,	198
Watson, H. P.,	169, 198
H. L.,	98, 161, 162, 168–171, 174, 177, 178
I. A.,	165, 171, 178
P. B.,	178
Webster, Nathaniel,	68, 190
Weeks, Alonzo,	87, 107, 240, 257
Mrs. Alonzo,	100
Weller, Asa,	237
F. G.,	237, 239
Mrs. F. G.,	198
W. W.,	90
Mrs. W. W.,	157
Wentworth, Gov.,	35, 58, 60
Wesson, Ephraim,	39
West, Henry,	169
Wheeler, Gilman,	207
Dr.,	169
I. C.,	113
Wheeler, Peggy,	66
Sarah,	65, 66
Silas,	207
T. B.,	147
Tillotson,	243
Whitcher, D. S.,	129
Whipple, Joseph,	41
Rufus,	235
Whitcomb, Moses,	169
White, Horace,	169
Mary,	138
Nicholas,	137
Noah,	138
Prescott,	238
R. P.,	254, 256
Samuel,	136, 147
Whiting, G. W.,	309
Leonard,	309, 313
Solomon,	9
W. H.,	256
Whittaker, G. S.,	8, 240
R. H.,	7, 174, 256
Wigglu, Richard,	205
Silas,	194
Wilder, Chas. C.,	107
Wilkins, Daniel,	210
Willard, John,	179
Rev. Mr.,	312
Willey, Miss G. P.,	158
Williams, G. W.,	176
James,	48, 68, 69, 190, 191, 207
Joseph,	91, 111
J. P.,	193
Peleg,	21, 41, 45, 46, 64–47
Providence,	66, 234
Willoughby, Ebenezer,	35
Winch, Albert,	160, 169
Winslow, J. A.,	129
Wilson, Adams,	161
A. B.,	98, 161
Mrs. L. M.,	209
Wise, Daniel,	209
Withington, William,	192
Witherell, James H.,	7
Woods, A. S.,	130, 262
Woodbury,	312
Woodward, Dr. C.,	170
Woolson, E. S.,	107
Mrs. E. S.,	247
Worcester, Evarts,	91, 155, 192
E. C.,	153, 156, 182
Isaac R.,	91, 155, 192
Leonard,	155
Noah,	155
Worthington, Sarah N.,	159
Wright, F. B.,	177

Y

Young, Elbridge,	7
John,	39, 44, 68
M. F.,	8, 176
Samuel,	62
Youngs,	41

www.ingramcontent.com/pod-product-compliance
Lightning Source LLC
Chambersburg PA
CBHW030009240426
43672CB00007B/883